Unruly Tongue

Unruly Tongue

Identity and Voice in American Women's Writing, 1850–1930

Martha J. Cutter

University Press of Mississippi/Jackson

http://www.upress.state.ms.us

Copyright © 1999 by University Press of Mississippi
All rights reserved
Manufactured in the United States of America

02 01 00 99   4 3 2 1

Library of Congress Cataloging-in-Publication Data

Cutter, Martha J.
Unruly tongue : identity and voice in American women's writing,
1850–1930 / Martha J. Cutter.
p.   cm.
Includes bibliographical references and index.
ISBN 1-57806-085-0 (alk. paper)
1. American fiction — Women authors — History and criticism.
2. Feminism and literature — United States — History — 19th century.
3. Feminism and literature — United States — History — 20th century.
4. American fiction — 19th century — History and criticism.
5. American fiction — 20th century — History and criticism.
6. Domestic fiction, American — History and criticism.   7. Women and
literature — United States.   8. Women — United States — Language.
9. Group identity in literature.   10. Ethnic groups in literature.
11. Authorship — Sex differences.   I. Title.
PS374.F45C87   1999
813´.4099287 — dc21
98-36109
CIP

British Library Cataloging-in-Publication Data available

Contents

Acknowledgments

This book would not have been possible without the generous support of students, friends, and colleagues. Since this manuscript has emerged out of my teaching experiences, I must begin by thanking my students, particularly those in my seminars on American women's writing at Swarthmore College and the graduate students who took my classes at Kent State University. I heartily thank Barton Levi St. Armand for introducing me to the fiction of Mary Wilkins Freeman and for his enthusiastic praise of my early work. Thanks also to Ellen Rooney, whose astute commentary has sharpened my thinking. I also owe an enormous debt to the English department faculty and staff at Kent State University, who have supported my research in numerous ways, not the least of which include my voracious xeroxing requests; in this regard I would especially like to thank Ruby Riley and Liz Siciliano. I am also indebted to the helpful staff of Kent State University's library, especially those working in circulation, who expedited my numerous requests. This book would certainly not have been finished without the Division of Research and Graduate Studies at Kent State University, which granted me a research leave in the spring of 1996 and additional financial support to hire editorial assistance, pay permission fees, and create an index. In particular, I owe the Kent State University Research Council an enormous debt of gratitude for their generous support of this work.

Numerous individuals have contributed to this work in both specific and general ways. I thank Ray Craig, Ronald Corthell, and Fredric Schwarzbach for guidance concerning the University Research Council. I am grateful to the following individuals for feedback on individual chapters or the idea of the manuscript as a whole: José Aranda, Lisa Logan, Paula Kot, Eric Purchase, Elon Fischer, Maggie Anderson, Kathe Davis, Patricia Dunmire, Margaret Shaw, Zee Edgell, and Karen Boyle. I also thank my research assistants, Shawn St. Jean, Penny Tinker, and Chris Roman. I thank Seetha A-Srinivasan, of the University of Mississippi Press, for having faith in the manuscript and for her excellent editorial support. Lewis Fried consoled me over numerous cups of coffee, and Claire Culleton gave me invaluable professional and personal support. A very special thanks to the members of my research group, Lisa Brawley, Debby Rosenthal, and Carolyn Sorisio, who offered much needed criticism of the manuscript, and to Peter Schmidt, who gave me extensive feedback on my introduction. Finally, I thank the numerous critics of American women's writing who have provided the foundational thinking in my field, only some of whom I can mention in this book.

For permission to reprint the first part of chapter 3 I thank *American Literature*. The second section of chapter 4 originally appeared as "Losing the Battle but Winning the War: Resistance to Patriarchal Discourse in Kate Chopin's Short Fiction" in *Legacy* 11 (1994): 17–36, copyright 1994, Pennsylvania University Press, and is reproduced (in an altered form) by permission of the Pennsylvania State University Press. A section of chapter 5 appears in a very different form in *American Literary Realism*. I also thank the New York Public Library for permission to use Tom Fleming's lithograph, and Simon and Schuster for permission to use Miguel Covarrubias's "Blues Singer."

This book is dedicated to my parents, Eve and Philip Cutter, who have had faith in me through the long years of academic endeavor; their support has meant far more than I can ever express. It is also dedicated to my English teacher, Timothy C. Averill, at Manchester Junior-Senior High School in Massachusetts, who first encouraged me to take myself seriously as a scholar of literature; having become a teacher myself, I know now that the work of inspiring young minds is the challenge of a lifetime. Mistakes, of course, are my own, but I hope this book does participate in the spirit of dialogue in which it was engendered.

Introduction

In Mary Wilkins Freeman's short story "A Church Mouse" (1891), Hetty Fifield, a domestic servant, cannot find a job. Is she a bad worker, mean, unskilled, or unreliable? No. Rather, Hetty has a reputation for "sharp, sarcastic sayings" (416) that make people wince. She is also known for "always taking her own way, and never heeding the voice of authority" (416). Hetty has a mind of her own and a voice of her own. In fact, her unruly tongue becomes a symbol for an unruly identity that challenges not only her place within nineteenth-century stereotypes of femininity but the theoretical structure of patriarchal authority in the world she inhabits. No wonder, then, that, as Freeman comments wryly, "people did not want a tongue like that in their homes" (416).

In the early and middle nineteenth century, many American women writers were hesitant to sanction a "tongue like that" in the "house" of literature, or even in the heads of their female characters. Influenced by the cult of domesticity, they often endorsed heroines who were domestic, pious, pure, submissive, and — as this work documents — silent, or else confined within a historically limited conception of women's speech. But in the last two decades of this century, African American and Anglo American women authors begin to emphasize female characters who articulate a self-defined identity and voice. Most important, these late-nineteenth-century writers approach the problem of women's voice from both a historical and a theoretical standpoint. Although they are aware of specific practices of language that silence women (such as historical stereotypes of femininity), they are most concerned with the larger, transhistorical structures of identity and voice undergirding these historical practices. These writers begin to articulate a theory of how language has functioned under patriarchy to silence women, and they also seek to reformulate this theory. While early writers often focus on language practices, then, turn-of-the-century writers are most interested in the processes of identity construction and voice these practices reveal.

These turn-of-the-century writers often find that in the world they inhabit, language itself is gendered as masculine and as "belonging" to speakers who are male and white. This is the theory of language they find existing not only in a specific time period, however, but throughout time, the theory of language they seek to revise. Language, as Charlotte Perkins Gilman says, is "androcentric," relegating women to the place of prepositions: "[Woman] has held always the place of a preposition in relation to man. She has been considered above him or below him, before him, behind him, beside him, a wholly relative existence — 'Sydney's sister,' 'Pembroke's mother' — but never by any chance Sydney or Pembroke herself" (*Man-Made World* 20). Women are prepositions in language — elements defined through their linguistic relation to a male. But they are not, as Gilman indicates in another passage, subjects — individuals posed of authentic identity and voice: "Even in the naming of other animals we have taken the male as the race type, and put on a special termination to indicate 'his female,' as in lion, lioness; leopard, leopardess; while all our human scheme of things rests on the same tacit assumption; man being held the human type; woman a sort of accompaniment and subordinate assistant, merely essential to the making of people" (20). Language itself initiates a process whereby some individuals are granted voice and identity (or, to use a more modern term, subjectivity), while others are defined as silent and "subordinate" objects. Many Anglo American and African American women writers from the turn of the century share Gilman's approach to the problem of women's voice. To use terms from Margaret Homans's book on British writers, *Bearing the Word*, these American writers realize that "language is not a neutral medium but rather that its very construction is based on presuppositions about gender that devalue women: the speaking or writing subject is constitutively masculine while the silent object is feminine" (xii). For the turn-of-the-century writers I discuss, women's silencing can only be overturned by an engagement with language that revises the theory undergirding its fundamental power structures.

These writers often revise male-centered theories of language through the deployment of a voice that is specifically feminine (and often maternal). However, a feminine voice is sometimes validated over (and at the expense of) a male voice. For example, in Gilman's utopian novel *Herland* (1915), the women speak a language in which motherhood is the primary concept around which meaning is centered. Gilman claims voice for her fictional heroines by revising male-centered theories of language that structure meaning around male concepts of identity, or even around the male body. But where does this leave the men who visit Herland? What voice can they claim in a world where motherhood is the "transcendental signifier," the most important concept around which culture and language is organized? Gilman's maternal language finally seems more like an inversion of the old theory of language rather than the creation of a new one.

Like many late-nineteenth-century writers, Gilman is aware of this paradox, and some of her later short stories move beyond such inversions. But I use *Herland* as an example of the new approach to women's voice that first emerges in the late nineteenth century, an approach I call "theoretical" because it is most interested in how theories of language (rather than specific cultural practices) create women's silence. After formulating a feminine voice that enfranchises women, these writers attempt to move into a realm of voice where both men and women can become speakers and subjects. Their use of what we would call essentialism is meant to be strategic and temporary, then—a way of reconfiguring the theory of language that patriarchy has endorsed. Although this attempt to revise patriarchal theories of language is not always successful, I argue that it facilitates the creation of twentieth-century fictional artists and heroines whose voices work from within the boundaries of masculine and racist discourses to undermine them.

It is important to clarify what it means to claim that late-nineteenth-century writers seek a "feminine" theoretical voice. Some of these writers seek a "maternal" or "feminine" discourse that seems to reside outside of patriarchal language. Kate Chopin's heroine Edna Pontellier, for example, dreams of a voice of the ocean/mother (*mère/mer*) that transcends the chatter of women trapped within patriarchal discourse. But the central project of many late-nineteenth-century texts is unearthing a feminine voice that can work from *within* the parameters of patriarchal and racist discourses to undermine them. Chopin's later texts investigate covert feminine languages that traverse and destabilize the boundaries of patriarchal language. A writer such as Anna Julia Cooper examines the possibility of a musical, feminine, racially mixed voice that situates itself within existing discourses of race and gender. Therefore, although this book sometimes uses the work of French feminist theorists, it does not imply that late-nineteenth-century authors seek a purely female and radically experimental form of "body writing" (a "*parler femme*" or an "*écriture feminine*") that exists somewhere outside patriarchal language. Many of these writers seem aware, as Paula Treichler argues, that "to assume a formal dichotomy... between 'patriarchal discourse' and 'women's discourse' is false" ("Wall Behind" 324). Treichler describes language as a vast geographical terrain that different people and groups inhabit and "work" over in many different ways; language is thus "inhabited" by both patriarchy and women. But when some women writers "work" this terrain, they do so for radical purposes—purposes that change the way language has been "worked" over in the past by men.

Many late-nineteenth-century writers put language to different uses, but they are also aware that using language "differently" involves changing not only how language has been used in the past but also the way this usage of language contains a theory of identity and voice that must also be reworked. The theory underlying this vast geographical terrain must be unearthed, articulated, and regendered. Of course, the line between "theory" and "practice" is not always distinct. But I am interested in the fact that these writers do envision themselves as working primarily on the principles underlying language's usage rather than on specific, historical concepts or practices of women's voice. In this book, then, the terms "feminine voice" and "feminine, theoretical voice" refer to a concept of language employed by many turn-of-the-century writers; this concept attempts to revise the theory that language is inherently masculine, patriarchal, or white through the deployment of another theory of language. I use the term "women's language," or "women's voice," on the other hand, in a more general sense to refer to a variety of textual and narrative strategies that women writers use to explore their often conflictual relationship to language. All the writers discussed, then, are concerned with the problem of women's voice, but not all of them seek a "feminine voice."

As I have already suggested, the search for "feminine" voice is problematic, and many of these writers ultimately reject structuring their new theories of language around such an idea. Instead, many of them finally seek a voice that is metalinguistic—that works from within the bounds of patriarchal discourse to undermine it. Like Mary Jacobus, many of them describe women's language in terms of a traversal of patriarchal boundaries: "When we speak . . . of the need for a special language for women, what then do we mean? Not, surely, a refusal of language itself. . . . Rather, a process that is played out within language, across boundaries. . . . *Difference* is redefined. . . . *Difference,* in fact, becomes a traversal of the boundaries . . . but a traversal that exposes these boundaries for what they are—the product of phallocentric discourse and women's relation to patriarchal culture" (51–52). Anglo American and African American writers from the late nineteenth and early twentieth centuries undercut patriarchal categories of women's identity, thereby calling these categories into question. But the language marshaled by these writers also calls into question patriarchal theories of women's voice, traversing their boundaries to indicate that these theories are the products of male-centered and racist ways of thinking rather than of language itself.

The transformation to a more theoretical understanding of women's voice has not been examined but is crucial to an understanding of the development of American women's writing.[1] This book focuses on the period between 1850 and 1930 in order to delineate three phases in this movement. The first group of authors (Fanny Fern, Louisa May Alcott, and Harriet Wilson) are concerned with an understanding of historical practices that have limited women's voice; although their texts may indicate an awareness that language is patriarchal, their protagonists employ a "domestic voice" that ultimately does not challenge this idea. The second group of authors (Mary Wilkins Freeman, Anna Julia Cooper, Kate Chopin, Charlotte Perkins Gilman, and Frances Harper) foreground women's placement within a theory of language that assumes the speaker to be masculine (and for Cooper and Harper, white); to escape this theory of language they depict women searching for a "feminine" or "maternal" voice that might exist in the fissures of patriarchal discourse and culture, or even outside of them. The protagonists of the last group of writers (Willa Cather and Jessie Fauset) reject the notion that there might be a "feminine voice" outside of patriarchal culture; they create a metalinguistic, ethnic voice that exercises power not through its refusal of patriarchal language but through a deliberate disclosure of the limitations of patriarchal and racial discourses. All of these writers are therefore concerned with the problem of voice. However, over time there is a movement from a domestic/historical voice (1850–1880), to a feminine (or maternal)/theoretical voice (1880–1915), to a metalinguistic/ethnic voice (1915–1930).

Although these writers' texts move toward a more theoretical examination of voice, I do not claim that these stages are always separate and discrete. For example, a mid-nineteenth-century writer such as Louisa May Alcott explores the possibilities of a radical maternal voice but finally concludes that empowerment for women must work from within historical images of femininity. And late-nineteenth-century writers like Freeman, Cooper, Chopin, and Gilman may begin by seeking to displace patriarchal discourse through the deployment of a feminine voice of the mother but conclude by creating a metalinguistic voice that attempts to break down the boundaries between masculine and feminine discourses. And then there is the deliberate dissonance of a writer such as Frances Harper, who recoups certain elements of the cult of domesticity—such as its emphasis on the home—while rejecting its submissive practice of "women's speech." Furthermore, the early works of twentieth-century writers such as Cather and Fauset sometimes demonstrate an inability to overturn the concept of a domestic voice, and some of their later works return to more conservative concepts of women's speech. In short, writing from this time period does not reflect a linear movement from submissive silence to empowered voice, or from a practice of voice to a theory. However, I am arguing that American women's writing in the later part of this time period generally endorses forms of voice that are more destabilizing and theoretical than those used by earlier writers. And I am also insisting that these forms of voice are more destabilizing precisely because they are more theoretical; they attempt to change the theory and process of identity formation and voice underlying language.

This book presents an argument about the development of this new, more unruly, and more theoretical approach to the problem of women's voice. I have selected several writers from each time period, writers of fiction or expository prose whose works closely examine the problem of women's voice. My investigation of turn-of-the-century writers (1880–1915) is most detailed because I believe that in this time period women writers' ideas about language undergo the most profound change. My analysis of writers from the earlier time period (1850–1880) provides a starting point for this investigation but is not meant to be definitive. Similarly, the chapter on Cather and Fauset (1915–1930) does not provide a thorough investigation of modernist women writers' relationship to language but instead offers some brief thoughts about how two writers from the next generation modify and overturn the concept of a maternal, feminine voice. Finally, although many African American and Anglo American women writers from this time period are congruent with my argument, not all are.[2] This book is not, then, an exhaustive investigation of the problem of women's voice from 1850 to 1930; rather it opens up debate about American women writers' preoccupation with language and highlights the profound changes foregrounded in many turn-of-the-century texts.

I discuss works by African American and Anglo American writers because (as explained in more detail later) there is some degree of continuity in their treatment of the problem of women's voice. Many of the questions about language and identity these writers ask originate in specific stereotypes of women's identity and voice that influence both African American and Anglo American women. Ann duCille comments that "however powerful its prescriptions, 'true womanhood' was not an uncontested ideology, and the fiction of white women writers was one site of contestation. The challenge to patriarchal authority written between the lines of some of these women's novels was part of what made the form attractive to early African American writers" (*Coupling Convention* 6). The cult of domesticity was a common cultural matrix for both African American and Anglo American writers, and though these two groups of writers did not have the same relationship to it, for both it functioned as a space where patriarchal concepts of women's identity and voice could be investigated, and sometimes overturned.

This study also focuses on these writers' thematization of their relationship to language, rather than on their invention of radical styles. These writers' stylistic experimentation often remains limited, but what is radical is their re-creation of their relationship to language. For instance, Gilman's *Herland* never presents a concrete example of how the Herlanders' maternal and communal language of the "ants and bees in their hives" might sound, or even of what it might look like on the page. And Cooper's *A Voice from the South*, while arguing for a rich mix of voices from all different spheres and races, is written in prose that is classical, intellectual, and dense, but not radically experimental or heterogeneous. In both texts, the radical language remains an abstraction rather than being actualized or presented. But the theoretical insight behind this abstraction (that language has been centered around masculine constructs and can be recentered around feminine ones) is crucial to the formulation of a new relationship to language. This is also one of the reasons that I have chosen to examine fiction and expository prose. I wanted to hear what these writers had to say about the subject of a radical language, and I could hear their ideas most clearly in texts where — oddly enough — the language itself was not the focus. I was interested in the theory behind the language, and this theory was made most manifest in works of fiction and prose rather than in more language-centered forms (such as poetry).

Although I am primarily interested in the movement toward a theoretical treatment of women's relationship to language, this shift cannot be understood without some consideration of cultural changes in stereotypes of women's identity and voice. This book therefore begins by discussing stereotypes of women's identity and language prevalent between 1850 and 1930. Historians such as Barbara Welter, Nancy Cott, and Caroll Smith-Rosenberg have demonstrated that from 1780 to 1860 Americans were preoccupied with the feminine virtues of purity, piety, submissiveness, and domesticity — a constellation of attributes known as the domestic saint, or True Woman. As Cott explains, the ministers, preachers, doctors, and other writers endorsing the cult of domesticity assumed "that women would be happy insofar as they served others and made them happy" (*Bonds* 71). According to this rhetoric, women were "passive, submissive responders" since, as Welter argues, "submission was perhaps the most feminine virtue expected of women" (*Bonds* 158). What has gone almost unnoticed is that this image also contained a concept of women's voice. For example, advice manuals such as William Alcott's *The Young Wife, Or Duties of Woman in the Marriage Relation* (1837) tell women that even when in the right, "It is better to forbear. Think twice before you speak once . . . 'the tongue is a fire — a world of iniquity' " (211). Women's voices were to parallel the attributes of the cult of domesticity itself: to be passive, submissive, domestic, and self-denying.

Beginning in the 1880s, however, another image of women became available, as Robert Riegel explains: "The expanding activities of women were so obvious by the late nineteenth century that people came to discuss something labeled the New Woman. By this term was meant a woman who was better educated and trained than the women of the past; willing and able to earn her living . . . and hence under less pressure to marry; holding independent views on all sorts of subjects, including national and international affairs; and who, above all, was less dependent on men, both economically and intellectually" (240). The most crucial feature of New Womanhood was its recognition of woman's right to an autonomous selfhood and voice. I use historical materials such as speeches, essays, cartoons, photographs, and drawings to illustrate the slow emergence of woman's "unruly member," her unruly tongue. These materials also demonstrate that the New Woman represented a more contradictory set of ideas about women's identity and voice than the True Woman, and this allowed women writers to manipulate the later image for subversive purposes. The years from 1850 to 1930 therefore reflected a great deal of cultural change, as the New Woman gradually displaced the True Woman, and the domestic voice was replaced by one that was more concerned with the theoretical basis of women's silencing.

The literary component of this book begins when the stereotype of the domestic saint and the domestic voice have begun to crumble: the 1850s and 1860s. In texts such as *Ruth Hall* and *Little Women*, Fern and Alcott are critical of the silence of the domestic saint, and they depict women writers who seem to move into the realm of public action and voice. Yet, in the end, the writing of these female characters supports and embellishes the domestic realm; domestic voices empower the family, not the individual woman. Women who exhibit an unruly tongue are punished and silenced, even in more radical texts such as Alcott's sensational stories, "A Marble Woman," "A Whisper in the Dark," and *Behind a Mask*. Unlike Fern and Alcott, who portray writers, Harriet Wilson does not allow Frado, the African American heroine of *Our Nig*, to become a writer within the text. In a trickster-like series of camouflages Wilson grants herself an identity as writer, but Frado remains a good—that is, voiceless—domestic saint. Although these writers sometimes consider women's relationship to language from a theoretical standpoint, they do not usually attempt to create a new theory of language.

Writing from the turn of the century does not abandon a historical consideration of women's voice. In the texts of Freeman, Cooper, Chopin, Gilman, and Harper, the New Woman and the True Woman are often in conflict with each other—both across generations and within individual characters—and a domestic, historical voice and a theoretical, feminine one often compete. Yet later texts such as Freeman's "The Revolt of 'Mother,'" Cooper's *A Voice from the South*, Chopin's "Elizabeth Stock's One Story," Gilman's *Herland*, and Harper's *Iola Leroy* begin to investigate and undermine those theories of language and identity that engender women's silencing. These writers conceive of, and sometimes create, a new theory of language that allows both men and women to become speaking subjects. Cooper and Harper also recuperate voices that are distinctly African American and female in order to undo a racist configuration of the speaking subject as white and male. For all these writers, a recurrent focus is the attempt to change the theoretical ways that patriarchal language has constrained the voice of the feminine "other."

These turn-of-the-century writers therefore provide a connection between a historical understanding of women's relationship to language and a more theoretical one, and between a domestic and a modern vision of women's identity. Although twentieth-century authors such as Willa Cather and Jessie Fauset sometimes seem explicitly hostile to the concerns of their nineteenth-century predecessors, they still implicitly use these authors' treatment of women's struggle for voice. Indeed, like earlier writers, Cather's short stories and Fauset's *There Is Confusion* depict women artists destroyed by domesticity. Yet Cather's *The Song of the Lark* and Fauset's *Plum Bun* break with the image of the domestic saint by finding an unruly voice that can articulate women's sexuality and desire. However, these writers are less interested in the possibility of an exclusively feminine or maternal voice and more concerned with a metalinguistic interrogation of discourses of gender and race. Cather's and Fauset's characters also empower themselves by drawing on an ethnic voice. Cather's heroine Thea finds a metaphor for her voice in the Native American Cliff Dwellers' pottery and in Mexican American art forms, while Fauset's heroines Angela and Joanna find expression through African American folk art. But the voices of these characters are also "ethnic" in a more general sense, since, as Werner Sollors has noted (27), ethnicity is associated with boundaries. In Fauset's and Cather's texts, a "marginal" or ethnic voice is brought to the center to disrupt its power structures. In so doing, these writers create a new discursive formulation that I call a metalinguistic, ethnic voice.

However, I do not mean to imply that both these writers have a social or discursive agenda that entails the liberation of an ethnic voice in anything but a metaphorical sense. Cather empowers her white, female heroine through an ethnic voice, but fundamental inequalities of language and power between "Americans" and ethnic individuals remain intact. The African American writers discussed in this study employ an ethnic discourse more overtly than their white contemporaries, and they also marshal it in a more subversive way. Even so, writers such as Fauset or Harper sometimes introduce new inequalities, enfranchising their upper-middle-class female characters through a silencing of (for example) a character from a different class background. Is it possible to move "beyond the binary" (to use Jacques Derrida's term) — to find a voice that undoes certain inequalities (man over woman, for example) without creating others, such as white over black, upper class over blue collar, or intellectual over folk? My study concludes with this question.

This work as a whole suggests that although African American writers have a different relationship to images of women's voice and identity designed for, and by, a white audience, they share some cultural and linguistic concerns about the problem of women's voice. African American women writers did not adhere to images such as the True Woman and the New Woman but rather both undermined and adapted them to what Carla Peterson would call their "local place." These writers' portrayal of women's relationship to language also has parallels with Anglo American writers. Both Anglo American and African American women writers describe language as patriarchal. Gilman calls it "androcentric," while Anna Julia Cooper argues that African American women have been dominated by a phallic and colonizing patriarchal law that renders them "voiceless" and "mute" (*Voice from the South* i–ii). In both groups of writers, there is an important shift in the late nineteenth century; Cooper and Harper configure women's language as not only a historical problem but also a transhistorical, theoretical one with multiple roots in social ways of thinking and knowing. Mae Henderson argues that African American women speak from a complex social, historical, and cultural position; they must therefore "speak in tongues" — speak "in a plurality of voices as well as a multiplicity of discourses" (147, 149). In *A Voice from the South*, Cooper speaks in tongues, calling up the multiple discourses of race, gender, and class that have constructed her, speaking both against, and through, these discourses. In *Iola Leroy*, Harper creates a hybridized text that seeks to overturn the many racial, gendered, and narrative frames that have constrained African American women's voice. And like Freeman, Chopin, and Gilman, Harper and Cooper sometimes deploy a feminine, maternal voice they hope will dismantle male-centered theories of language and subjectivity.

The Anglo American authors discussed in this study sometimes consider the dilemmas of racialized women. Writers such as Chopin (in, for example, "La Belle Zoraïde" or "Désirée's Baby") and Cather (in *The Song of the Lark*) demonstrate an awareness that not all individuals in society experience the same struggle for language. But late-nineteenth- and early-twentieth-century Anglo American writers overwhelmingly show white, female characters struggling for voice. Furthermore, very few Anglo American writers consider their own race — the way their whiteness is constructed through the erasure of "race." To their credit, however, a number of these writers structure such issues into their texts. Chopin, Gilman, and Cather, for example, do not ignore the questions race raises in a portrayal of "women's" relationship to language. But neither do they fully engage these questions.

Late-nineteenth-century texts written by Anglo American and African American women, then, cannot be conjoined solely on the basis of their consideration of race. However, they can be conjoined on the basis of their consideration of the problem of women's voice, for within these texts there is an understanding of how theories of language grant men the right to be articulate subjects, while portraying women and "others" as silent objects. Yet within these works there is also an awareness of the availability of alternative language systems, and female characters struggle to find a theoretical space in which the speaking or writing subject is not defined as male and white. Julia Kristeva has argued for a movement away from a static and fixed concept of language (*langue*) toward a focus on language as "a heterogeneous signifying process" (*Desire in Language* 27) — as a process that works differently in different situations for different speakers. These late-nineteenth- and early-twentieth-century Anglo American and African American writers search out the heterogeneous, alternative processes of language that do exist in culture and that undermine male-centered and racist languages and ways of thinking.

This book builds on the foundational work of prior critics in the field of American women's writing but expands it to a larger time period, while also presenting an approach that considers interconnected historical, linguistic, and racial issues. One of the most significant shifts in this time period is the movement toward a more theoretical approach to women's voice, and it is the purpose of this book to analyze how this shift occurred and the ways it manifested itself in literary and cultural texts.[3] Yet if the unruly tongue of late-nineteenth-century writing is such a radical departure, why do later writers seem to abandon it? As I have already indicated, authors such as Cather and Fauset are uninterested in voices that are specifically feminine or maternal, and the same might be said of a number of other writers such as Edith Wharton, Zora Neale Hurston, Djuna Barnes, Ellen Glasgow, and Ann Petry. However, I would argue that although these writers abandon the concept of a "feminine" voice, they do not abandon the central insight behind this concept: that voice has been gendered as inherently masculine in the past, and that women writers must refuse this gendering of language. This does not always involve finding a "feminine" voice, but it does involve rejecting the dominant theory of voice that has silenced women in favor of a new, more heterogeneous process of language.

Like twentieth-century writers, many nineteenth-century authors do not finally endorse a voice that is specifically, or essentialistically, "feminine." To return to my opening metaphor, Hetty Fifield never does find a "house" she (and her unruly tongue) can live in but instead inhabits the town's church, taking on the traditionally "masculine" role of sexton. Freeman implies that the unruly tongue of such characters does not always place them within a "feminine" ideology of voice and language but sometimes overturns these ideologies, and in the process creates an entirely new idea of "voice." Hetty's tongue is finally radical, then, not because it insists on being "feminine" but because it refuses to accept that women must be contained within theories of language and identity that deny them subjectivity and voice. Foreshadowing the strategies of many early-twentieth-century writers, Hetty finds a way of thinking about language that allows her not to inhabit a "feminine" space but rather to create a new space of identity and voice that she can claim as her own.

Unruly Tongue

The Problem of Voice in
American Culture, 1850–1930

As argued in the introduction, the transition from the "True Woman" to the "New Woman" created profound changes in women's identity and voice. Literature both reflects and shapes this transition, but the focus of this chapter will be how this shift was manifested in cultural and historical texts. Advice manuals and other cultural materials illustrate that the cult of domesticity interconnected women's identity and a subservient language, encouraging women to be silent in the face of male authority. Yet, as my discussion of speeches at the 1893 World's Congress of Representative Women demonstrates, by the late nineteenth century both African American and Anglo American women were contesting these ideas and embracing a more radical concept of women's voice. As the New Woman's unruly tongue became a force of social instability, newspapers, cartoons, poems, and drawings were marshaled both to endorse and to critique this image. Such cultural materials demonstrate that the New Woman's voice was feared not only because it reflected a different use of language but also because it reflected a more theoretical approach to women's social and linguistic empowerment. In the early twentieth century, woman's "unruly member," her unruly tongue, was set loose, and American culture would never again be the same.

Although a number of critics have recently discussed the cult of domesticity, few consider this subject in terms of women's conception of voice. Rather, they examine whether this set of ideas was a rhetoric rather than a reality, arguing that most women exercised power both in the realm of the home and in the public sphere. Nina Baym, for example, believes that women who wrote history from

1790 to 1860 "thought of themselves as part of the nonofficial public sphere and intended to make themselves influential in forming public opinion" (*American Women Writers* 6). Karol Kelley questions Barbara Welter's findings about the cult of domesticity, asking if Welter's "picture of antebellum female life [could] be accepted as 'true,' as historically accurate, or was she really dealing with the customary rhetoric of this time period?" (170).

But can rhetoric (discourse) and reality (the way people actually behaved and acted) be separated? We can only know "reality" through rhetoric. Karol Kelley admits that the "data that could give a true description of how the great majority of people lived and acted [during the nineteenth century] are simply missing" (170). The cult of domesticity was a powerful idea shaping both rhetoric and reality. Advice manuals from the 1820s onward hammered its four cardinal virtues (purity, piety, submissiveness, and domesticity) into women's heads. The books were written by men and women, by ministers and laypeople. They were reprinted again and again. They are often inscribed with loving dedications: "To my dear sister," "To my friend Emily," or "to my loving daughter." These books were read, given as gifts, and swapped back and forth between friends, sisters, mothers, and daughters. Women may not have consciously emulated the cult of domesticity, but given this tidal wave of rhetoric it certainly influenced their formation of identities.

The identity promoted by the cult of domesticity was not, of course, completely homogeneous. Barbara Bardes and Suzanne Gossett argue that in the early to mid-nineteenth century, some women writers' female characters use the Declaration of Independence to assert their own equality with men and their right to participation in the public realm (1–2). Yet, cultural documents from this time period often efface the possibility of feminine independence in the public realm by confining women to a separate and unequal sphere within the home. According to manuals such as E. H. Chapin's *Duties of Young Women* (1848), woman does not aspire to "social equality" (10), since she "has been created for a different sphere, or rather hemisphere, than man" (12). Several of the anonymous contributors to Cotesworth Pinckney's anthology/gift-book, *The Lady's Token* (1848), argue that "the scepter of empire is not the scepter that best befits the hand of woman. . . . Home, sweet home, is her theater of action, her pedestal of beauty, and throne of power" (48–49). But it was not only anonymous writers for gift books and male authors who advocated a separate and unequal sphere for women, as the writings of Maria McIntosh and Lydia Sigourney demonstrate. McIntosh's *Woman in America: Her Work and Her Reward* (1850) argues that "the unqualified assertion of equality between the sexes, would be contradicted alike by sacred and profane history. There is a political inequality, ordained in Paradise, when God said to the woman, 'He shall rule over thee,' and which has ever existed, in every tribe and nation" (22). Women are secondary to men and deserve not equality in the public realm but a more limited sphere of power in the home. Sigourney's argument is more subtle but makes a similar point. In her *Letters to Mothers* (1838) she advocates women's right to be fully educated yet focuses on maintaining men's and women's separate spheres. Especially in educating sons, Sigourney argues that mothers must "ever keep in view the different spheres of action allotted to the sexes" (126); she adds that "the mother, who in the infancy of her children, puts in the arms of the girl a doll, and patiently endures the noise from the hammer of the boy-baby" exhibits great wisdom (172). Sigourney uses the same patriotic rhetoric as the writers cited by Bardes and Gossett, but she puts it to different purposes, saying that "a long period allotted to study, a thorough implantation of domestic tastes, and a vigilant guardianship over simplicity of character are desirable for the daughters of the republick" (171). Daughters of the republic are not to declare their independence; they are to be given dolls and inculcated in domestic values appropriate to their separate spheres.

Many of these texts thus promote a concept of identity that exercises a secondary power from within the limited realm of the home. They also encourage women to define themselves through others (men and children). In *The Sphere and Duties of Woman* (1848), George W. Burnap states that after a woman has chosen a husband she "has now something to live for. . . . What more can she want?" (100). In *The Young Lady's Companion* (1838), Margaret Coxe is willing to allow women a bit more leeway; she understands they might enjoy such accomplishments as painting, piano playing, and writing, and she sanctions them — as long as they serve others and do not interfere with the wife's domesticity (180, 182). That this service to others is not required by men is made clear by two poems in Cotesworth Pinckney's *The Lady's Token*. The boy's poem is called "I Love to Live," while the girl's poem is called "I Live to Love" (8–9). Here women's lives are defined through their love for others and spurred by relational, internal, and selfless goals. Men's lives, on the other hand, are defined through autonomous, external goals such as the search for fame, career, gold, or a wife.

Historical documents from this time period therefore demonstrate the way feminine agency was co-opted by the rhetoric of domesticity. Did these ideas influence African American women? Certainly most of this writing was directed toward white women, and African American women may have been defined precisely through their "lack" of the key virtues of purity, piety, submissiveness, and domesticity (Carby, *Reconstructing Womanhood* 33). Furthermore, the material conditions of both enslaved and free African American women often made it impossible for them to adhere to these attributes (Riley 76). Yet, as Hazel Carby points out, an ideology can have force even when it does not correspond to historical realities (*Reconstructing Womanhood* 24). Both Carby and Ann duCille argue that African American women were influenced by the cult of domesticity. Carby demonstrates that African American women "addressed, used, transformed, and, on occasion, subverted the dominant ideological codes" (*Reconstructing Womanhood* 20–21) of True Womanhood, while duCille contends that African American writers worked from within this image to challenge patriarchal authority (*Coupling Convention* 6). Furthermore, as Evelyn Brooks Higginbotham's research has documented, many working-class African American women aspired to the moral ideals of True Womanhood. Therefore, although these advice manuals were not directed at African American women, confronting this ideology was nonetheless crucial in their struggles for identity. Indeed, as I show in the next chapter, it is primarily through a manipulation of the cult of domesticity that Harriet Wilson constructs a voice for her female character Frado.

Carby argues that to gain a public voice as orators or published writers, African American women had to confront the dominant domestic ideologies and literary conventions of womanhood (*Reconstructing Womanhood* 6). Anglo American women also had to confront this ideology to find voice. Women may have looked to these manuals for advice on conversation, verbal control, and writing practices, but these books only provided a voice paralleling the cult of domesticity. Women were to speak relationally and domestically. And whenever possible, they were to erase their own voices by being silent in the face of male authority.

Women's discourse was to be oriented to the home; as Chapin puts it, a woman's voice "interweaves with a never-resting shuttle the bonds of domestic sympathy" (86). Chapin's imagery connects women's domestic tasks (weaving and sewing) with her discourse. Woman's voice is also linked to her subservience; these books repeatedly advise women to use deferential language. Burnap comments that "there is no dagger so sharp as the tongue of an insolent, disobedient daughter" (57). (One must wonder why the tongue of an insolent, disobedient son would not be equally sharp.) He encourages women to gain control over their tempers, as well as their tongues (84–85). An essay in Pinckney's gift book called "Directions for the Ladies" tells women even more explicitly to "avoid contradicting" their husbands and giving them advice; moreover, they are instructed that "when a man gives wrong counsel, never make him feel that he has done so, but lead him by degrees to what is rational, with mildness and gentleness" (120). Chapin's section on conversation urges women to avoid speaking in a manner that is gossipy, contemptuous, overly witty, sarcastic, humorous, angry, or contradictory (90), while *The Young Lady's Friend* (1836) urges women to use only sparingly the rhetorical skills of ridicule, exaggeration, wit, and irony (375–82). What remains for women? What is the point of speaking if one is not allowed to complain, make quips, use irony, or express anger? These authors do not address this question, but the answer seems patently clear: women's language does not express her identity but rather functions as an extension of the male psyche. William Alcott, too, sees women's voice as supporting male identity, so even when a wife disagrees with her husband she should not contradict him: "Whether the husband concedes or not, she must. If she insists too long or strenuously for what she deems to be true or right in small matters, she does it at the expense of her own comfort or peace" (32). He implies that verbal disputes may be seen as a challenge to male authority — a risk he does not advise.

As Bardes and Gossett point out, "vocal women are powerful women" and, therefore, "like the larger society, authors repeatedly attempt to limit and control this power" (12). Threaded throughout these advice manuals is a fear of women's unruly and (potentially) disruptive tongues. Sigourney encourages women to learn simplicity of language (175), while *The Young Lady's Book* counsels that "a mild answer turneth away wrath" (3). William Alcott also emphasizes plainness of speech (108) and expresses fearfulness about women who gossip or scold too much (205). Although he counsels that a woman "should say just what she thinks," he does not mean to imply that she "should say *all* that she thinks" (109). As Coxe puts it, "the unruly member, the tongue" must be "so far bridled as not to be led, by the secret workings of corruption, to give vent to pride, anger, or other unruly feelings, in language" (38). The unruly female tongue must be constrained if it is to support male authority, patriarchy itself.

Control of language is also linked to control of female sexuality: to speak out is to be immodest, sexual, unruly. William Thayer's *Life at the Fireside* (1857) explicitly connects an aggressive voice and women's purity: "I cannot respect the virtue of a female who contends on the public rostrum for 'Women's Rights,' claiming equality of the two sexes in respect to the immunities and callings of life. It is such a breach of modesty, that I cannot suppress the suspicions of moral obliquity that rise in my heart" (348). He even goes so far as to call Joan of Arc immodest: "We wonder to see her mounted on a fiery steed, leading the armies of France to victory. . . . We cannot admire her character" (347). Thayer somehow manages to connect Joan of Arc's entrance in the public realm, her being "mounted on a fiery stead," her public voice, and her "immodesty" (347). To be in the public sphere is to demand an unruly — potentially sexual, and certainly not submissive — voice. Yet even private speech can be connected with lack of chastity. *The Young Lady's Friend* (1837) urges women when conversing with friends to keep a firm hold on the "unruly member" (373) — presumably the tongue.

Of course, the safest feminine virtue is silence. Chapin and numerous others quote the biblical maxim that women should possess "a meek and quiet spirit" (102). Coxe believes "little can be expected of a woman who does not know how to be silent" (40) and argues that "silence is the best ornament of the female sex" (132). She also tells the story of a young woman whose fiancé overhears her contradicting her mother. The fiancé reacts swiftly: "Shocked and astounded by the alarming discovery which he had made so unexpectedly, the gentleman . . . wrote a kind and feeling letter to her who had thus deceived him so grossly, relinquishing her hand forever" (206). What is this shocking discovery? Simply that his fiancé has a tongue—and an unruly one at that. To give vent to this voice is dangerous, as Coxe and numerous other writers show.

Woman's speech, then, like her identity, should be self-denying, domestic, subservient, and (at its best) silent. Many of the writers thus implicitly connect feminine subjectivity and voice. William Alcott and Caroline Howard Gilman, however, make this link explicit. Gilman's *Recollections of a Housekeeper by Mrs. Clarissa Packard* (1834) provides an illustration of how silence and a domestic identity were intertwined in the lives of women. Gilman's heroine Packard is a smart and educated woman who narrates with a good deal of wit and verve, but she still adheres to the idea of women's subservience and silence. Packard states, for example, that the wife should reverence her husband and his wishes (123). As a child of eight she reads Shakespeare and Pope (6), but as an adult she loses interest in literature (75) and asserts that women should give up all but domestic accomplishments. She quotes in full a letter from a friend schooled in intellectual knowledge, emphasizing her friend's remark that "I would have given up all my French, German, and every accomplishment, in exchange for the knowledge which would make me a good housekeeper" (115). Housekeeping is woman's proper study, her proper language. Packard describes her early blunders in housekeeping as being comparable to those of "the lawyer who blunders in his maiden *speech*" (14, my emphasis); she herself abjures any but a domestic discourse. Packard also emphasizes her silent submissiveness. At one point, she grows jealous of her husband's legal books because they consume his attention, yet says nothing. Finally, her husband learns of the problem from a young boy, but while the boy reports his observations, Packard sits silently sewing "as if [her] life hung on [her] needle" (57). The needle, not the tongue, is her instrument of salvation. Packard's subservient domesticity eventually allows her to overcome—albeit passively—this situation of neglect. From this example we can clearly see that, for Caroline Gilman and her heroine, linguistic "power" is exercised through the constrained practice of women's speech promoted by the cult of domesticity.

William Alcott also explicitly links a domestic identity and a subservient vision of women's linguistic "power." Women's secondary status in the creation myth allows Alcott to assert an unequal identity for women that he connects to a submissive voice. He states that "there is a species of submission to the husband sometimes required of the wife" since "the man is not created for the woman . . . but the woman for the man" (27). So in marriage a woman must "merge her own name in that of her husband," which implies a sort of "concession" or "submission" to male authority (29)—a connection between language and social practice that later writers (such as Charlotte Perkins Gilman in "Lost Women") will directly challenge. Alcott also encourages women to stay in the domestic realm to avoid a "flippant tongue" (84). The domestic realm enforces a simplified, domestic discourse, and the simplified discourse supports the domestic realm. And silence is always the best defense of a True Woman: the silence of her own voice when it has been stripped of all individuality, of its unruly and disruptive tongue.

Of course, many of these writers are women, some of whom write multiple tracts. How is this possible, given these injunctions against women's voice? Mid-nineteenth-century writers such as Sigourney, Coxe, and Caroline Gilman (in the genre of the advice manual) and Fanny Fern, Louisa May Alcott, and Harriet Wilson (in the genre of the novel) find voice by situating their writing within a domestic context and by containing (for the most part) their female characters' aggressive voices. This allowed them to expand women's power while not breaking in any fundamental way from the domestic ideology. Later nineteenth-century writers, however, begin looking for the underlying causes of women's silencing; in so doing they paved the way for the New Woman's more unruly tongue. Yet the process was a cautious one, as the 1893 World's Congress of Representative Women demonstrates.

From May 12 to 23 of 1893, under the auspices of the Woman's Branch of the World's Congress Auxiliary, the World's Congress of Representative Women met in Chicago, Illinois. Papers on every conceivable topic of interest to a nineteenth-century woman were delivered by participants from the United States, England, Scotland, Germany, France, Bohemia, Canada, Sweden, Denmark, Finland, New South Wales, and elsewhere. Susan B. Anthony, Elizabeth Cady Stanton, and Frances Harper participated in discussions of women's rights and political future; Fannie Barrier Williams, Anna Julia Cooper, Fannie Jackson Coppin, and Hallie Q. Brown analyzed the intellectual progress of African American women; Mrs. William E. Burke gave a paper on the Women's National Indian Association; and Hanna K. Korany discussed the position of women in Syria. Just a few of the diverse subjects approached during the ten-day symposium were "Cooperative Housekeeping," "Woman's Place in Hebrew Thought," "The Polish Woman in Literature," and "Woman's Dress from the Standpoint of Sociology."

Historians such as Glenda Riley argue that during the Progressive Era (1890–1917) thousands of women become active participants in reform efforts and broadened their areas of employment, yet it would "gradually become apparent that the characterization of the American woman as passive, dependent, and domestic would continue" (153–54). However, historians such as Caroll Smith-Rosenberg believe this era saw profound changes in women's behavior, attitudes, and beliefs, resulting in real political power for women (245). It is my argument that the World's Congress of Representative Woman demonstrates that a shift occurred in African American and Anglo American women's identity in the last decades of the nineteenth century, when women began to insist that they were not defined through their relationship to men and to patriarchal discourse. But in both literary and political texts the break is often incomplete, creating both political and artistic dissonance. For example, subservient domesticity may reassert itself at the end of a novel depicting a heroine's gradual growth as an artist, or a rhetoric of feminine passivity may pervade a speech on women's political enfranchisement. In the late nineteenth century, then, there were still numerous unresolved questions about what a "representative woman" was and about how her identity would be constituted.

Moreover, the World's Congress was fraught with racial and ethnic tensions that threatened to undermine the notion that African American and Anglo American women shared commonalties. The Congress was assembled as part of the Columbian Exposition in Chicago, an event that through its refusal to include African Americans and other racial groups embodied the "definitive failure of the hopes of emancipation and reconstruction" (Carby, *Reconstructing Womanhood* 5). Only six African American women were present at the World's Congress of Representative Women, and their demands for an involvement in its preparations were rejected. Furthermore, while African American women like Frances Harper and Anna Julia Cooper were speaking as part of the women's platform of the Congress, Ida B. Wells was circulating pamphlets protesting the exclusion of African Americans from the Chicago Exposition itself. Thus, as Carby explains, "to appear as a black woman on the platform of the Congress of Representative Women was to be placed in a highly contradictory position, at once part of and excluded from the dominant discourse of white women's politics" (*Reconstructing Womanhood* 6). Yet it is important to look in detail at this event in 1893 because, although fraught with racial tension, it nonetheless depicts the enmeshment of Anglo American and African American women's concerns about voice.

Some historians claim that True Womanhood had disappeared by the 1890s, but the World's Congress does not substantiate this argument. For example, Florence Collins Porter's address "The Power of Womanliness in Dealing with Stern Problems" (391–94) harps back to the utter selflessness and complete morality of the True Woman. The older image is also present in texts such as J. Ellen Foster's "Woman as a Political Leader," which argues that women's first priority should be to the home: "none dispute woman's preeminence in the home, and a true woman desires most of all to be faithful there — to prepare the food, to make the garments, and to minister in the nursery to little children" (443). True Women do not desire public, political power but only the gentle influence they can exercise from within the domestic realm.

Yet the majority of speakers argue that women can be more than an influence — they can enter the public sphere outside the home as activists and leaders. Ellen Henrotin, vice president of the Woman's Branch of the World's Congress Auxiliary, argues that women "must bestir themselves to be good citizens of the city, the state, and the nation; to enter into the paths of commerce and finance; to supervise and educate the young; to create new trades and professions for women" (12). Henrotin believes that women's lack of involvement in public affairs stands in the way of their own progress and of the world's progress. In "The Civil and Social Evolution of Woman," Elizabeth Cady Stanton also argues that women must achieve equality with men: "Women are to do whatever they find to do with all their might. They are to be properly trained for business, profession, or art" (329). Becoming part of the public sphere is also a goal for African American women. Anna Julia Cooper, for example, applauds the increase in educated and professional African American women entering fields such as teaching, medicine, and law ("Discussion" 714).

Specific talks on suffrage, communal housekeeping, and dress reform also manifest this urge to transform women from Domestic Saints to New Women. In a later speech, Stanton argues that suffrage means "equal place in the trades and professions; equal honor and credit in the world of work" ("Ethics of Suffrage" 485). Beyond political rights, "New Womanist" reforms are also advanced in Mary Coleman Stuckert's address on cooperative housekeeping, which explains the plan for a building with a communal laundry, dining room, and kitchen staffed by skilled cooks (626). This reorganization and professionalization of housework would free women from the domestic realm and is the cornerstone of a number of Gilman's later short stories. Sociologist Ellen Hayes discusses another "New Womanist" idea — dress reform — linking it to women's liberation: "In [the dress reform] movement woman breaks with the traditions of the past, and declares herself not content with the status assigned her by primitive man. Around the world she is beginning to want education, and a less humiliating position in the church and state. She is beginning to grope for her share, as half of the human race. She is beginning to want a pocket" (360). For Hayes, pockets symbolize the movement from object to subject, from being a possession to being a possessor: "The absence of pockets betrays the fact that woman not only is not accustomed to possess goods and chattels, but has been herself goods and chattels" (360). Writers like Hayes see the transhistorical roots of women's oppression in theories of subjectivity that have granted men power while denying women's right to identity. Therefore, although some women who attended the Congress still seemed preoccupied with True Womanhood, a far larger group advocated new mechanisms for women to achieve power, autonomy, and a self-defined identity.

Writers such as Julia Ward Howe and Frances Harper took another route, attempting to formulate a synthesis between the True Woman and the New Woman. As a good domestic saint would, Julia Ward Howe argues that women's higher moral nature shapes men (317), but she also advocates the political enfranchisement of women (320). If women have "the moral initiative," as Howe claims, why then do they also need political power, the vote? A True Woman would say that women's moral initiative is itself the most persuasive power women can have. With its odd mix of political and domestic feminism, Howe's essay exhibits the dissonance of conflicting belief systems. More skillful is Frances Harper's blending of domestic and political feminism in "Woman's Political Future" (433–38). Harper argues that society stands "on the threshold of woman's era, and woman's work is grandly constructive" (433–34). She details women's increasing presence in society, literature, the church, and politics, arguing that women have exerted a great moral influence over all these institutions. Yet Harper then backs away from this crucial principle of the cult of domesticity — women's inherent ability for moral uplift — saying: "I am not sure that women are naturally so much better than men that they will clear the stream by the virtue of their womanhood; it is not through sex but through character that the best influence of women upon the life of the nation must be exerted" (435). Harper, then, utilizes some of the rhetoric of the True Woman, but she also combines it with the notion of a morality not tied to women's gender or limited to the domestic realm. As she will do in *Iola Leroy*, she creates a liminal space between the True Woman and the New Woman where both images can be remade.

In the late nineteenth century, African American writers like Harper are cognizant of the limitations of the cult of domesticity; yet, labeled for so long by society as "breeders" or "Jezebels," they may still wish to claim some of its rhetoric of high morality. Perhaps for this reason, several speakers are careful to show that African American women are "ladies." Fannie Williams's "The Intellectual Progress of the Colored Women of the United States" emphasizes that African American women are inherently moral. According to Williams, after slavery's abolition African American women's "native gentleness, good cheer, and hopefulness made them susceptible to those teachings that make for intelligence and righteousness" (697–98). She believes that since the days of slavery African American women have uplifted themselves and the men of the race and that "out of this social purification and moral uplift have come a chivalric sentiment and regard from the young men of the race that give to the young women a new sense of protection" (703). This veneration of African American women parallels the pedestal upon which white women were placed in the cult of domesticity and demonstrates the way some African American women deliberately situated their concerns within Anglo American ideas of womanhood.

Williams also emphasizes, over and over again, that African American women are not different from Anglo American women. They are moral, involved in social reforms, and in search of freedom: "Liberty to be all that we can be, without artificial hindrances, is a thing no less precious to us than to women generally" (709). She stresses that, like Anglo American women, African American women are finding voice: "To-day [African American women] feel strong enough to ask but one thing, and that is the same opportunity for the acquisition of all kinds of knowledge that may be accorded to other women. This granted, in the next generation these progressive women will be found successfully occupying every field where the highest intelligence is admissible. In less than another generation,

American literature, American art, and American music will be enriched by productions having new and peculiar features of interest and excellence" (700). This extraordinary passage shows where Williams's true focus lies — not in the "inherent gentleness" of African American women but rather in a more aggressive New Woman agenda that breaks from past oppression to gain employment and voice. Williams also explicitly states that African American women's voices must be part of American art: "American literature needs for its greatest variety and its deeper soundings that which will be written into it out of the hearts of these self-emancipating women" (700). Williams enmeshes her concerns with those of Anglo American women, insisting on a presence within — not outside — the dominant tradition of "American" literature. She also interrogates ideologies by speaking through them.

Although African American women initially may have been included in the World's Congress of Representative Women as part of a discourse of exoticism, these speeches demonstrate a deliberate positioning of African American women's concerns within Anglo American discourses of womanhood, as well as a deliberate transformation of these same discourses. Anna Julia Cooper, for example, emphasizes that African American women, like Anglo American women, are seeking political liberation. But, as she will also do in *A Voice from the South,* Cooper points to the ways African American women have experienced a double enslavement of their voices: "The white woman could at least plead her own emancipation; the black woman, doubly enslaved, could but suffer and struggle and be silent. I speak for the colored women of the South, because it is there that the millions of blacks in this country have watered the soil with blood and tears" (712). Cooper depicts an evolution from the women of the past, who were silent, to the women of the present — women who speak the history of the race, who understand how discourses of race and gender have functioned transhistorically to disempower them. Several other speakers also emphasize that African American women are achieving self-expression. Hallie Q. Brown describes numerous women who have entered the fields of journalism and literature and in so doing transformed these fields (726). Williams, Cooper, and Quinn therefore break from the silencing of African American women in the past, as well as from the limited discourse of women under the cult of domesticity, through assertion of a voice that refuses to curtail its scope or sphere.

Anglo American women like Josephine Bates and Annie Nathan Meyer also connect the silence of women in the past with their construction as objects, and contrast this with women's present vocality and agency. In a session devoted to women's place in art and literature, Bates argues that women have been spoken of rather than speaking themselves: "At the feet of literature has sat through the ages its lowly handmaiden, woman. Rarely in the past has her untutored thought found hardihood for utterance, but in her life she lived the dreams her dumb lips might not speak. In every country and in every age man has symboled his highest in her image" (153). Women's silence is part and parcel of a system of patriarchal representation that labels them as passive objects rather than active creators. In explicating this theoretical approach to women's linguistic oppression, however, Bates begins to break from it: "With the deathless voice of the seer woman speaks to-day, calling all to the heights on which her gaze is set" (153). Women are breaking "the silence of the centuries" (153) — their transhistorical linguistic oppression. Annie Nathan Meyer also argues that women are breaking the silence of the past: "Well, woman is still in her first age. She is slowly awakening from a long sleep, and is just beginning to look about her and see the world around. She is still brooding thereon. I am sure the time is not far distant when she shall translate life into forms of perfect truth and poetry" (144). Meyer asserts the New Woman's right to experience the world and to translate these experiences out of patriarchal discourse and into a more perfect form of language.

According to Smith-Rosenberg, New Women "defended the new ways in an old language" (264). Of course, there was a danger in this strategy: "Women's assumption of men's symbolic constructs involve women in a fundamental act of alienation" (265–66). However, Smith-Rosenberg's argument does not accurately characterize the New Women at the World's Congress. These women understand how old forms of language have oppressed them, but they also translate this "old language" into something more liberating. While understanding the way language has functioned transhistorically to silence them, they still reject the notion that language itself is *inherently* patriarchal, or inherently alien to their subjectivity. Many of these women agree with Elizabeth Cady Stanton's statement that "woman must be brought to a common denominator with man" (329), and they use language to achieve this enfranchisement. At the turn into the twentieth century, then, both Anglo American and African American women asserted a fundamental association between women's equality and the forms of language used to inscribe this equality. They began to understand the theoretical connection between patriarchal discourse and women's social and personal subjugation — and in understanding this connection they initiated the first steps towards severing it. But it was not until the beginning of the twentieth century, when the New Woman emerged fully onto the scene of American culture, that the domestic voice was finally laid to rest.

Monstrous. Titanic. Hideous. Revolting. Rebellious. Screeching. Shrieking. Shrill. Extraneous. Odd. Queer. Mannish. Sexless. Oversexed. Undersexed. Indecent. Abnormal. Disobedient. Self-Centered. Self-Assertive. Self-Defined. Immoderate. Excessive. Wild. These are just a few of the diverse terms used to describe the New Woman, who came into being in England in the 1890s, crossed the Atlantic Ocean with a gigantic stride, and by 1900 began inspiring trepidation and exhilaration wherever she went. In the United States, the New Woman was thoroughly interrogated well into the late 1920s. Underlying many of these debates was a fear of her unruly subjectivity, sexuality, and voice. As a cultural stereotype the New Woman was liberating precisely because the ideology was more contradictory. It is true, as Ellen Todd argues, that " 'new womanhood' can be shown to reproduce or challenge dominant ideologies depending on when, how, by whom, and in whose interest the term is used and to what ends" (xxviii). Yet since no clearly defined set of virtues characterized this image, women could pick those attributes that supported a self-defined voice and identity, and New Womanhood was deployed in literary and political texts in a more open and liberating manner than True Womanhood. When the furor over the New Woman subsided, it became apparent that women had used the new image to claim personal, political, linguistic, sexual, and social freedom. The domestic realm and the domestic discourse would never again have the same sanctity as women's "natural" destiny. The chains had been broken; the cage had been sprung.

The startling transition from the True Woman to the New Woman was caused in part by changing economic conditions. Margaret Wilson credits the phenomenal upsurge in urbanization and industrialization between 1870 and 1920 with "the permanent enlarging of the accepted sphere of activity for women and the change in the image of feminine propriety" (3). Between 1870 and 1920 the number of women in the workforce increased by 63 percent, and more women left the domestic realm for at least a portion of their lives (M. Wilson 6). Wages for women also increased in the 1880s, making women's self-support more economically feasible (Smith-Rosenberg 33).

Despite the rapid pace of this social change, the New Woman did not become the subject of controversy until three popular British novelists brought her to the public's attention. George Egerton's *Keynotes* (1893), Sarah Grand's *The Heavenly Twins* (1893), and Grant Allen's *The Woman Who Did* (1895) all depicted independent, self-supporting, sexually active women. Grand and another journalist, "Ouida" (Mary Louise de la Ramée), focalized the controversy by christening the New Woman and debating her merits in the 1894 issue of the *North American Review*. American writers swiftly became part of this debate, which lasted almost half a century. A symposium on the New Woman in the American journal *Current History,* for example, demonstrates that as late as 1927 her merits were still being argued. Some authors deride the New Woman as an abnormal creature who violates both biblical and social protocols about men and women's separate spheres (McMenamin 31, 30) and blame a variety of social evils on her (Ludovici 22–24). But others vigorously defend her. Charlotte Perkins Gilman finds a new respect for women's opinions and preferences ("Woman's Achievements" 9), Leta Hollingsworth argues that women are no longer victims of their "cumbersome reproductive system" (15), and Joseph Collins asserts that women are throwing off their subservience to men and asserting their sexual nature (36). As Smith-Rosenberg explains, such arguments about the New Woman interrogated the very foundations of society. Through the New Woman, Americans argued "about the naturalness of gender and the legitimacy of the bourgeois social order. They agreed upon only one point: the New Woman challenged existing gender relations and the distribution of power" (246). That the New Woman was able to hold the attention of the public so long is testimony to her challenging of not only a specific conception of women's "place" but also the entire theoretical structure that sustained male authority.

A number of studies also suggest that New Womanhood transcended racial and class distinctions. Mary Thomas argues that by the 1890s, "middle-class white and black women experienced a dramatic expansion of opportunities that took their domestic concerns and values into the public arena. Working-class women also experienced a greater autonomy in their lives as employees and participants in the new commercialized leisure of modern urban life" (2). Ellen Todd's research suggests that "new womanhood crossed class, ethnic, and gender boundaries" (3). And Nancy Cott believes that by the early twentieth century, women of all races were participating in activities outside of the domestic realm and also finding their voices (*Grounding of Modern Feminism* 7). In fiction, African American writers such as Zora Neale Hurston, Nella Larsen, and Jessie Fauset portray women who seek sexual and economic autonomy. African American women may have had a more equivocal relationship with New Womanhood than Anglo American women, but they still utilized its positive aspects.

The New Woman image was enabling for both African American and Anglo American women because the discourse surrounding it was never stable, as a brief survey of pictorial and textual images demonstrates. On the one hand, the New Woman was seen as a Gibson Girl — an athletic, attractive young woman. Collections of drawings such as Howard Chandler Christy's *The American Girl* (1906) portray women in a variety of settings but still focus on her domestic nature: "the hand that swings the tennis racquet is the hand that rocks the cradle" (38). Of course, marriage and motherhood is this woman's rightful destiny. As Martha Patterson argues, the imagery surrounding the Gibson Girl implied that she produced children, not social or political change (74). Christy's drawings also emphasize that women are defined through others. In many a male companion sits behind or above the American Girl, looking down at her ("At the Theater," "The Dance," "Gathering Arbutus," "On The Beach," "Canoe Mates," "Mistletoe," etc.; see fig. 1).* Women are thus doubly reinscribed as the object of the gaze, constructed by both the viewer's and the male companion's focus. Christy's collection also objectifies the American girl by continually focusing on her external beauty — her clothes,

*All illustrations appear at the end of this chapter.

her hair, her costumes. The figure of the New Woman, then, is coopted and rendered less threatening by such imaging.

Of course, the Gibson Girl was a racialized norm. Ethnic and immigrant women were often excluded from its confines, as an essay such as Gertrude Lynch's "Racial and Ideal Types of Beauty" (in a 1904 *Cosmopolitan*) makes clear. Lynch sees no beauty in "primitive" types nor in Native American, Chinese, or Japanese women; the most distinctly beautiful women are English, French, and Greek (228, 231). And while saying that the "American" type of beauty is "the world's type" (233), she makes clear that this type has classical and European roots. The beauty of the Gibson Girl is produced by her caucasian heritage, not by racial or ethnic diversity. As Martha Banta expresses it, "the American Girl could only be as fine as she looked, and looking fine meant looking like the WASP Princess" (104). Yet the popular press realized that this image might be used to attract readers from outside this racialized norm, and sometimes held out the promise of the American Girl to "all pretty young women who might 'pass' socially, economically, or racially for the true type" (Banta 105).

Furthermore, the imagistic power of the Gibson Girl was occasionally coopted by African American periodicals such as the *Voice of the Negro* and the *Colored American Magazine*. John Adams's "Rough Sketches: A Study of the Features of the New Negro Woman" (1904), for example, depicts a series of African American women as Gibson Girls. As Patterson argues, this use of iconography "undermine[s] the Gibson Girl's assurances of white racial supremacy by broadening the availability of 'womanhood' currency. The Gibson Girl trappings may be freely appropriated and transformed in order to argue for Gibson Girl privileges while challenging Gibson Girl ideology" (82). Yet how radical is John Adams's challenge? Adams describes the New Negro Woman as "a college president's daughter," not a college president, "home-trained" in the realm of domesticity rather than educated in the rough-and-tumble world of commerce outside the home (323). At heart she is a "true woman . . . the same as her white or red or olive sisters" (326). This woman is pure, noble, and passive—defendable but not a defender (325). Although she may have the voice of the New Woman, she does not use it to break with a historically constrained vision of women's speech and women's sphere, as the caption under one of Adams's drawings makes clear: "a sweet singer, a writer—mostly given to essays, a lover of good books, and a home-making girl, is Gussie" (326; see fig. 2). Adams challenges racial aspects of the Gibson Girl image but not its confining construction of gender norms.

The beautiful Gibson Girl was therefore one pictorial image of the New Woman held out to both African American and Anglo American women, but a far more pervasive and destabilizing image of her was the "mannish" woman. *Punch* cartoons from 1891 and 1894 show mannish New Women leaving their husbands ("Ibsen in Brixton," 2 May 1891) or refusing to thank men for their aid ("Metropolitan Railway Types," 10 Jan. 1891: 18). *Punch* also seems to fear that these women will take over the world, as the 24 February 1894 cartoon "What It Will Soon Come To" portrays. In this drawing, a large woman towers over a diminutive man, saying, "Pray let me carry your bag, Mr. Smithereen!" (90; see fig. 3). The cartoon implies that the New Woman is reversing gender roles, blasting men's power to "smithereens." Such satirizing of the New Woman was not limited to British journals, however. "The New Navy, about 1900 A.D.," a *Life* magazine cartoon from 1896, features a brigade of tough, mannish New Women amassed defensively as if to attack the viewer (16 April 1896: 310–11). Another *Life* cartoon from 1895, called "In a Twentieth Century Club," shows mannish New Women lounging in bloomers, eyeing a ballet-skirted male who cavorts on stage (13 June 1895: 395). Once again, gender roles are reversed by the mannish New Woman and balances of power are blasted to smithereens.

Magazines also directly caricatured ethnic or racial individuals who dared to attempt to be New Women. For example, a 1909 *Life* cartoon by Orson Lowell called "Election Day" shows a series of African American, immigrant, and working-class women lined up to vote, greatly outnumbering the "real" New Women who look on in chagrin (see fig. 4). The "real" New Women are stylish and dignified, waiting their turn peacefully; the African American women, on the other hand, look like "primitives" and "mammies," and the working-class women are disheveled and disorderly. Another cartoon, "When the Cook Votes" (*Life* 23 Sept. 1909) shows a working-class woman exiting the balloting place with a foolish grin on her gap-toothed mouth; the derogatory and racist implication here, as with Lowell's cartoon, is that New Womanhood represents a threat because it offers rights not only to women who might be able to handle this power but also to those who clearly cannot. These cartoons fearfully assert that balances of power not only between men and women but also between rich and poor, upper-class and working-class, nonethnic and ethnic, will be blasted to smithereens by New Womanhood.

There are some neutral pictorial images of the New Woman. The frontispiece from *Current History*'s 1927 symposium features a drawing titled "The New Woman Emerging Out Of the Past" (see fig. 5). In this drawing, the New Woman's knee-length skirt and high heels suggest a certain femininity and fashion-consciousness. Yet the arms folded across her chest suggest self-control, and she meets the viewer's gaze with a clear, intelligent, no-nonsense look. It is rare to find such neutrality, however; as a pictorial image the New Woman resides in extremes—as an innocent and beautiful Gibson Girl, a shrieking feminist, a mannish virago, an oversexed flapper, an undersexed spinster, but rarely an average or typical woman. Smith-Rosenberg sees the New Woman as a perennially liminal figure (257), and these pictorial images reflect both her liminal status as well as the way the press fixed on her as a fearful extreme that could lead to society's downfall.

Yet liminality, as Victor Turner has argued, is a space where social constructions are not; it therefore offers the possibility of revision. The New Woman was feared precisely because her emerging subjectivity, sexuality, and voice threatened to remake the theoretical grounds of patriarchy. The New Woman's lack of fixity suggests a world turned topsy-turvy, a world in which anything was likely to happen. But beyond her liminal, unstable nature, the New Woman's demand for an autonomous subjectivity also inspired fear. New Women were often preoccupied with self-development rather than self-sacrifice, and they made autonomous decisions about their careers and personal lives. Some writers tried to insist that women's natural destiny was still marriage (Jeune 273), self-sacrifice, and serving others (Abbott 154), but the majority seemed to agree with Mona Caird that the New Woman was ridding herself of all vestiges of the master and slave relationship that had previously existed between men and women (122). New Women insisted on independent identities that threatened patriarchal power. Perhaps because of this, the New Woman was associated not only with social downfall and evil (Ardis 2) but also with occult phenomena such as vampirism (Senf 34) and even with disasters such as the sinking of the *Titanic* (Larabee 7).

Most threatening of all, however, was the New Woman's emerging sexuality. As Gail Cunningham argues, sex was the factor that made the New Woman "a symbol of all that was most challenging and dangerous in advanced thinking" (35). During the late nineteenth and early twentieth centuries birth control methods were increasingly effective, available, and accepted. Or as a 25 September 1915 article in the *New Republic* puts it: "A large minority of husbands and wives already know how not to have too many children and it is only a question of a decade or two when the rest will know" ("The Age of Birth Control" 196). In and of itself, birth control did not inspire fear. After all, the concept of "voluntary motherhood" (or limiting reproduction through abstinence) preceded New Womanhood. But the New Woman used birth control to promote her sexual freedom, and this was a radical change. As Linda Gordon explains, "Birth control now meant reproductive self-determination along with unlimited sexual indulgence. This new definition . . . understood sexual activity and reproduction as two separately justified human activities" (190). It is no wonder, then, that the Reverend Hugh McMenamin would make jibes against the notion of companionate marriage with its necessary "instruction in the use of contraceptives" (32). As practiced by the New Woman, birth control represented a self-defined feminine sexuality. And the fear was that once women had tasted sexual freedom, they would be unrestrained. As the journalist May Jeune warns, "women, like their Mother Eve, will not be content with a little knowledge, but will probe as deeply as possible and will eat the fruit of the tree of knowledge to their fill" (275).

The sexual liberation of the New Woman was most often portrayed in Anglo American women, but some texts do suggest that African American women might partake of this freedom. Harlem Renaissance writers such as Nella Larsen and Jessie Fauset show New Woman seeking sexual freedom. Pictorial images from this time period support the concept of a sexuality that is self-defined, overt, but also contained. For example, Langston Hughes's poem "Nude Young Dancer" appears in Alain Locke's *The New Negro* (1925) above a drawing by the illustrator Miguel Covarrubias called "Blues Singer." In Hughes's poem the dancer is a free spirit, a "dark brown girl of the swaying hips" who sleeps under a tree, dances at midnight, takes the moon as her lover, and offers her lips to a "mad faun" (227). This poem borders on the primitivizing of African American women common during the Harlem Renaissance, but Covarrubias's accompanying drawing presents a rather different image (see fig. 6). Here the woman is not a dancer but a blues singer, someone who molds and shapes songs. The drawing portrays her as stylish and attractive, with a short haircut and revealing dress that align her with the modern New Woman. Though seductive, the blues singer seems self-contained; her arms frame and embrace her own hips, and she is angled away from the viewer, as if to protect herself from a direct gaze. As an image, she suggests the sexual freedom of the New Woman, yet also a desire that will only be shared if, and when, she chooses.

Drawings, novels, and articles from this time period thus suggest that both Anglo American and African American New Women manifested a degree of sexual self-definition that broke from prior images of women's identity. However, the New Woman's sexual freedom extended beyond actual behavior, for she insisted on a sexual candor that was very different from the True Woman's voice. Carol Senf explains that "when it came to sex the New Woman was more frank and open than her predecessors. She felt free to initiate sexual relationships, to explore alternatives to marriage and motherhood, and to discuss sexual matters such as contraception and venereal disease" (35). Women also wrote openly about such subjects in popular novels and magazines. Early twentieth-century critics of New Womanhood were quick to notice that women's unruly sexual behavior connected to their language. McMenamin states that "The 'New Woman' has no sense of shame and she endeavors to save her self respect by putting a halo on her wickedness. She attempts to hide her sordidness under fine phrases — 'Art for art's sake,' 'To the pure all things are pure' " (31–32). McMenamin links the New Woman's sexuality to a decadent discourse.

Although the majority of early-twentieth-century authors acknowledged such radical differences of the New Woman's voice, reactions to these differences varied. Writers such as Rhoda Broughton and Ruth Hall defended this voice, while a variety of cartoonists and essayists attacked it bitterly. Broughton's 1920 *Ladies Home Journal* essay called "Girls Past and Present" claims that women of her generation (mid to late Victorian) "were more modest both in our raiment and in our speech." But Broughton praises this change in women's discourse and behavior: "On how immensely superior a footing of freedom and agreeability does the relation between man and woman now stand. There is practically no bar any longer placed between the sexes, either in the matter of sharing each other's interests, occupations and amusements, or in that of discussing any and every topic" (38). Personal and linguistic freedom are clearly linked by Broughton. A poem in the *New York Truth* by Ruth Hall called "The Fin de Siècle Duel" also links the New Woman's verbal candor with her willingness to fight for social and educational equality:

> You fight for a place in business;
> > You fight for a chance to speak;
> You fight for the right to study
> > With men their Latin and Greek.
>
> (23 March 1895: 3)

For Broughton and Hall, New Womanhood means a positive liberalization of women's voice and identity.

But the New Woman's passion for self-expression was not always commended. An 1894 poem in *Punch* ridicules the New Woman's refusal to be quiet:

> There is a New Woman, and what do you think
> She lives upon nothing but Foolscap and Ink!
> But though Foolscap and Ink are the whole of her diet,
> This nagging New Woman can never be quiet!
>
> (26 May 1894: 252)

This poem is somewhat playful, but its author's dislike for the New Woman's "nagging" tongue is clear. Another *Punch* poem, "A Valentine: To an Advanced Woman," is more biting, unfavorably contrasting the voice of the New Woman with that of the True Woman:

> Once we numbered 'mid your charms,
> > Soft low voice and tender yes;
> Now you wave a Maenad's arms,
> > On the platform shrieking high.
>
> (16 Feb. 1889: 81)

New Women are here depicted as "shrieking" harpies who continually contend for "selfish" political and social rights. George B. Luks's column in the *New York Truth* "The Mannish Girl" (21 Jan. 1893) also berates the New Woman's "selfishness" and connects it to her outspokenness. Luks acknowledges the New Woman's verbal and social freedom (7) but then punishes it by consigning such women to "eternal spinsterhood or the divorce court" (3). These unfavorable contrasts and harsh tone have one goal: the return of women's speech to its safe locus within the home, as a support for male identity.

Underlying many of these attacks on the New Woman's voice is a fear that her unruly language might challenge the theoretical underpinnings of patriarchal society. Caroline Ticknor's 1901 *Atlantic Monthly* essay, "The Steel-Engraving Lady and the Gibson Girl," explicitly connects women's new voice with such a challenge. Here the New Woman tells her predecessor: "When a man approaches, we do not tremble and drop our eyelids, or gaze adoringly while he lays down the law. We meet him on a ground of perfect fellowship, and converse freely on every topic. . . . Whether he *likes* it or not makes little difference; *he* is no longer the one whose pleasure is to be consulted" (106). This essay links "conversing freely on every topic" with a self-defined, nondeferential female identity. Women are no longer defined through men who have the power to "lay down the law" (the authority of patriarchy), and their language no longer supports the desires of the male. Ticknor fears the changing identity and voice of the New Woman and is clearly aware of its potential for radical social destabilization.

It is no wonder, then, that the New Woman's unruly tongue becomes a synecdoche for an unruly identity. This symbolism is manifested in Tom Fleming's 1915 poster "The Home or Street Corner for Woman? Vote No on Woman Suffrage" (see fig. 7). Fleming contrasts a True Woman kissing her child with a shrieking militant suffragette. As Ellen Todd explains, the suffragette with her "teeth bared, eyes rolled upward in satanic agony, and hair in Medusa-like disarray (a reference to her rejection of childbearing)" (27) fearfully symbolizes what New Womanhood promotes. Fleming asks, "Which do you prefer?" and his answer is obvious: the True Woman's closed mouth and silence is vastly preferable to the New Woman's shrieking and shrill voice. Fleming's poster presents in a startlingly graphic way the binary oppositions that have been used to structure patriarchy, as well as fear of the social instability that might result if these oppositions are overturned. The woman in the circle on the left is silent, passive, and safely located in the home; she clearly defines herself through others (her child). The woman in the circle on the right is outspoken, active, roaming the streets; she defines herself through "selfish" desires for political rights, desires that threaten to unleash social chaos. The poster thus articulates an understanding that the New Woman's unruly tongue threatens not only men's power in a particular historical moment but the foundational principles of patriarchy as a whole.

The theoretical threat to masculine control that the New Woman's unruly tongue represents is also recognized in carnivalesque cartoons from *Punch* that portray the effects of a world turned topsy-turvy by her assertion of voice, and in repeated attempts by other writers and illustrators simply to shut her up. In the full-size *Punch* cartoon "Hymen, Fin De Siècle" (2 May 1891), for example, a group of jeering, open-mouthed women laugh at Hymen, the god of marriage, as he attempts to sell them his ribbons and bows. The point of this cartoon seems to be that the New Woman scorns men and marriage, but it also demonstrates a fear of gender-role reversal caused by women's unruly tongue; the male figure is powerless and silent, the object of the gaze, while the females are vocal, jeering, and aggressive. Clearly, *Punch* has tired of the New Woman's tongue and would like her to just shut up, as a cartoon titled "Parting Shot" makes particularly graphic. Here a well-dressed, independent-looking woman says to her husband, "And now, my dear, having given you a bit of my mind, I'm off to the dentist to have my tooth stopped." Her husband's response summarizes *Punch*'s reaction as a whole: "Excellent, dear. And while he's about it, ask him to stop your tongue also!" (24 Mar. 1894: 135). The New Woman's unruly tongue must be "stopped" before it destroys patriarchy.

American periodicals exhibited a similar desire to silence the New Woman. William Lee Howard tries to curtail outspoken women by categorizing them as perverts: "The female possessed of masculine ideas of independence, the virago who would sit in the public highways and lift up her pseudo-virile voice, proclaiming her sole right to decide questions of war or religion, or the value of celibacy and the curse of woman's impurity, and that disgusting antisocial being, the female sexual pervert, are simply different degrees of the same class — degenerates" (280). The article contains the threat of the New Woman by implying that women who lift up their voices are abnormal perverts. Another strategy of containment — or even denial — of the New Woman's voice is reflected in an anonymous 1927 *Harper's Monthly* essay called "Feminism and Jane Smith." This article reflects a nostalgic desire for a return to a past when women fulfilled their rightful, limited place as objects in men's constructions of their identity. The writer argues that because men are naturally the "superior" (8) sex, women should defer linguistically: "To Jane Smith, who has accepted Nature's discriminations against her, comes now the necessity of accepting the logical sequel. . . . She will put it to herself that the interests of order and efficiency are best served by [the man] having the final word" (8). The essay affirms Jane Smith's subservient voice, but — more insidiously — it also silences the voice of the New Woman. Because the New Woman is childless and independent, she is unqualified "to speak about the rights and needs of the average woman" (3). Jane Smith, the "average woman," accepts her own subservience and linguistic inferiority (10), and the essay as a whole asks its readers to reject the voice of New Womanhood as atypical, unnecessary, and unnatural.

"Feminism and Jane Smith" attempts to return to the domestic image, which insisted on a secondary status for women and a male-defined theory of identity. But of course, by the early twentieth century, many women had rejected the view that they should define themselves primarily through men. New Womanhood was liberating because it postulated an intellectual, social, and verbal equality between men and women. It was also enabling because it presented women with numerous ways of creating their identity, their "place" within language and society. Cott argues that this flexibility finally destroyed the cult of domesticity: "As girls and women swarmed on to terrain culturally understood as male — the street, factory, store, office, even the barbershop — the domestic definition of women became obsolescent" (*Ground-*

ing of Modern Feminism 7). Some authors did try to deny this development and return women to a domestic identity, but the image of New Womanhood simply allowed too many avenues of escape. The New Woman broke with the domestic realm by asserting a self-defined identity and a right to sexual freedom. Yet what made New Womanhood most radical was its refusal of a scheme in which the speaking subject was inherently male and its insistence that women should seek an enfranchised voice in all the broad terrains of the new world they traversed.

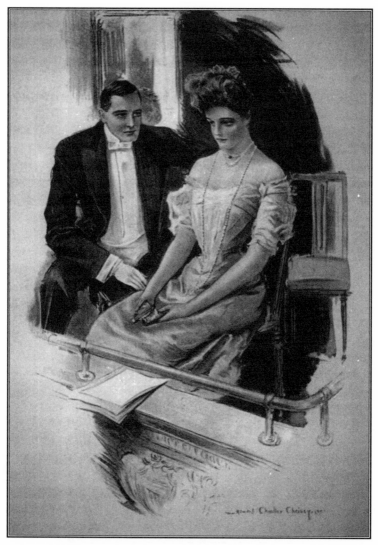

1. "At the Theatre," from Howard Chandler Christy, *The American Girl* (New York: Moffat and Yard, 1906).

2. John H. Adams, Jr., "Rough Sketches: A Study of the Features of the New Negro Woman," in *Voice of the Negro* Aug. 1904: 323–26.

3. "What it Will Soon Come to," in *Punch* Feb. 24, 1894: 90.

4. Orson Lowell, "Election Day," in *Life* Sept. 23, 1909: 410–11.

5. "The New Woman Emerging Out of the Past," frontispiece in *Current History* (symposium on "The New Woman") 27 (Oct. 1927).

6. Miguel Covarrubias, "Blues Singer," from *The New Negro*,
ed. Alain Locke (New York: Albert and Charles Boni, 1925), 227.
Reprinted by permission, Simon and Schuster.

7. Tom Fleming, "The Home or Street Corner for Woman? Vote No on Woman Suffrage," 1915. Reprinted by permission, from Rare Books and Manuscripts Division, New York Public Library, Astor, Lenox and Tilden Foundations.

American Women's Fiction, 1850–1880:

Domestic Discourses in the Writings of Fanny Fern, Louisa May Alcott, and Harriet Wilson

In Fanny Fern's novel *Ruth Hall*, the heroine's young, articulate, and witty daughter Nettie expresses her desire to become an author. Her mother's response embodies that of many women characters from 1850 to 1880; Ruth says, "God forbid . . . no happy woman ever writes" (175). In fiction from this time period, women write out of dire financial need, they write when they cannot sell hair tonics, they write to feed and clothe their children, but they do not write out of a need for self-expression. Writing is safely confined within the literal or figurative realm of the home, part and parcel of a domestic identity and voice. This is not to deny that a domestic voice can, and often does, become the basis for a female character's empowerment. But over and over again, Fern, Alcott, and Wilson show the constraints of working from within this paradigm.

Furthermore, when an unruly woman's voice seems to challenge the roots of patriarchal linguistic empowerment, it is quickly censored. Alcott's "A Whisper in the Dark" (1863), for example, articulates the theoretical problem of patriarchal discourse and even approaches the concept of a maternal speech that could undermine this discourse. But in the end this radical idea is discarded, and Alcott's character and her voice are safely reinscribed within a domestic realm. So the belief that "no happy woman ever writes" remains intact. For to write and be happy with writing as a method of self-expression is to move beyond the limited vision of women's identity embodied by the cult of domesticity and to envision one's speech as a destabilizing instrument of change—something these writers cannot do.

Empowered Domesticity: The Limited Victory of Fanny Fern's *Ruth Hall*

Who is the "real" Fanny Fern? Is she the lachrymose teller of conventional tales, dismissed for so many years as the "grandmother of all sob sisters," a "sentimental nonentity"? Or is she the subversive radical described in recent years by feminist critics?[1] In her most famous novel, *Ruth Hall* (1855), does Fern create a traditional "woman's tale" or a critique of this genre demonstrating the value of women's self-assertion? Most important, in *Ruth Hall* does Fern adhere to the ideology of True Womanhood, granting her title character only limited self-expression, or does she show a female character challenging this ideology as she grows into verbal power?

It is necessary, first, to consider both the similarities and the differences between the author and her fictional character.[2] Fern and her character Ruth Hall are both writers, but they have different motivations. While Fern was frank in urging women to write for self-expression, Ruth writes only to earn money for her children. While Fern urged women to pursue careers as writers in order to find "a way *out of* the home" (Wood 24), Ruth uses the money from her writing to build a better home. So while the "real" Fanny Fern may be closer to the portrait recently painted by feminist critics, the central character created in Fern's novel *Ruth Hall* is neither completely a rebel nor a conformist. Ruth Hall grows into self-awareness and voice, enacting a revision of women's roles and women's sphere, yet Fern continually places limits on Ruth's achievements. More specifically, Fern depicts her character working from *within* the paradigm of the True Woman to gain empowerment. The result is that Ruth finds an empowered domestic saint's voice that finally cannot challenge the binary oppositions of the patriarchal world she inhabits, oppositions that limit and constrain her identity and voice.

That a writer as radical as Fern depicts a heroine working from within the confines of the cult of domesticity testifies to the continuing force of this image at mid-century, for the text demonstrates a substantial investment in this ideology. Although Nancy Walker has argued that only a small part of *Ruth Hall* shows the heroine in a traditional domestic setting (45), over two-thirds of the novel is devoted to Ruth's domestic life. The novel has a tripartite structure: chapters 1–30 show the formation of a domestic saint, chapters 31–61 show the trials and tribulations of a domestic saint, and chapters 62–90 show Ruth's escape from these trials through the creation of her alter-ego/pseudonym "Floy." Ruth does not decide to write until chapter 56, and she does not sell her articles to a newspaper until chapter 62. Therefore, a large part of the novel depicts the formation of Ruth's identity as domestic saint, and although Fern criticizes this paradigm, she also gives Ruth all its attributes. Ruth has the frailty and purity of the True Woman; she is "delicately organized" (67) and "stamped with a holier beauty" (48). In the early parts of the novel Ruth is frequently described as saintly, pure, and passive (67). Like a good domestic saint, Ruth is pious, finding "many an answer" in the Bible (123). Ruth's piety is also linked to her domesticity. She first learns to pray by her child's cradle: "the weight her slender shoulders could not bear, she rolled at the foot of the cross; and, with the baptism of holy tears, mother and child were consecrated" (29).

Ruth also exhibits the relational subjectivity characteristic of the domestic saint. At school Ruth and the other young girls learn to devalue their education and value their ability to attract a mate (15). For Ruth, "history, astronomy, mathematics, the languages, were all pastimes now" because she has a new goal: "There was something worth living for—something to look forward to. She had a motive—an aim; she should *some* day make somebody's heart glad,—somebody's hearthstone bright; somebody should be proud of her; and oh, how she *could* love that somebody!" (16). As Susan Harris has pointed out, Fern often uses ironic language when describing the search for romantic love and a home, and these passages are certainly not meant to be taken entirely seriously. Fern criticizes historical socialization practices that urge young girls to define themselves only in terms of others, yet part of her criticism involves an acknowledgment of the difficulty of breaking this early cultural indoctrination. In this time period, society offered most Anglo American women no alternative way to formulate their identity. It is no wonder, then, that even at the end of the novel Ruth still longs for a home (193) and dreams of a reunion with her dead husband and child in which "the family circle is complete" (198). This utopian vision of a happy family reunion haunts the imaginations of other seemingly independent female characters. Even Alcott's wicked Jean Muir (in *Behind a Mask*) longs for a home of her own, and Harriet Wilson's Frado concludes *Our Nig* searching for a home for herself and her child. For these writers, women's relational identity has deep roots in historical practices of female socialization and schooling, and it cannot easily be discarded.

When Ruth has a home of her own, she rapidly (and apparently with no difficulty) learns to take care of it. Ruth even turns domesticity into an art, beautifying unconsciously everything her fingers touch (28) and collecting and artfully arranging wildflowers (34). As Harris argues, Fern calls up the codes of the domestic saint (children, flowers, religion, and so forth) to locate Ruth within the cultural matrix of her time period (115). Fern also calls upon other codes of domesticity such as motherhood, submission, and selflessness. Ruth is a "pattern mother" (46) to whom childbearing and child rearing seem almost innate—effortless and so much an expected course of events that the birth of Ruth's second and third children are not even mentioned. Selflessness is also an integral part of her character. For example, when told that her own life may be put in danger by her husband's illness her only comment is: "My *husband* has the *first* claim" (53). Ruth is willing to sacrifice herself for her husband, and later she will be willing to sacrifice herself for her children, even going without food. Ruth takes no actions indicating that her self is important in its own right. Fern criticizes these ideas, yet also demonstrates just how ingrained they are; after such an indoctrination, Ruth can never really stop being a domestic saint.

Chapters 62 through 90 therefore chart the growth of an empowered domestic saint, of "Floy," the professional (but still domestic) businesswoman that Ruth becomes. Two female characters enable Ruth's movement away from silent submission. Through the death of the perfect wife, Mrs. Leon, in an insane asylum, and the financial independence of the not-so-perfect wife, Mrs. Skiddy, Ruth learns that active, autonomous women survive, while submissive, dependent women are destroyed. Ruth becomes a writer and eventually achieves financial and personal autonomy. Her autonomy is demonstrated by the fact that she is uninterested in a marriage proposal she receives from a wealthy southerner named Victor Le Pont (153). However, the mail that same day also brings Ruth two offers from publishing houses. She finds contemplation of these business proposals much more stimulating than the proposal of Victor Le Pont, whose name symbolizes that he is a "bridge" into a world of secure marital bliss, a world Ruth rejects.

Through her writing Ruth achieves a degree of personal autonomy, and she feels no need to remarry. This personal autonomy is supported by Ruth's hard-won financial autonomy, which the last third of the novel charts. Ruth becomes a wise businesswoman, able to assess her own worth and to judge the sincerity of financial propositions. When Mr. Tibbetts, a publisher, threatens to put out a cheap edition of Ruth's book without her permission, she demonstrates a solid knowledge of business law and a refusal to be intimidated: "Mr. Tibbetts, you have mistaken your auditor. I am not to be frightened, or threatened, or *insulted* . . . think you my publishers will tamely fold their arms, and see *their* rights infringed? No sir, you have mistaken both them and me" (157). Ruth is rewarded for her business acumen: in a strong contrast with earlier domestic novels, which usually end with the heroine's marriage to an honest swain, at the end of Fern's novel Ruth receives one hundred shares of stock in the Bank of Seton.

Yet there are limits to Ruth's empowerment, as Fern makes clear. Financially, although Ruth does not rely on a husband, she does rely on a male — the publisher John Walter. Until Walter intervenes, Ruth earns a pittance writing eight articles a week. Furthermore, although Ruth has become a good businesswoman, she does not realize her worth until Walter points it out to her: "Why, you poor, dear little genius! what you write for those two papers is worth, to the proprietors, ten times what they pay you" (146). Walter's condescension is clear, and he takes control of Ruth's business matters, silencing critics like Mr. Lescom (148) and not allowing her "good womanly heart" (151) to interfere with making money. Although Ruth is perfectly capable of making her own financial decisions, she begins to rely on Walter's advice (162–63).

Through Walter, Fern shows that without the protection of influential male publishers, female writers may never achieve financial stability. No doubt this is a reflection of the publishing marketplace Fern knew, but Walter also intervenes in Ruth's life in more personal ways. It is with the aid of Walter that Ruth retrieves her daughter Katy from her in-laws, with the aid of Walter that Ruth becomes a bank-holder, with the aid of Walter that Ruth sets out to find a new abode. Walter's intentions are honorable, but a bit overbearing: "Well, I am glad to find you so comfortably housed after the fire; but the sooner I take *all of you under my charge, the better*, I think. What do you say to starting for ———— to-morrow?" (208, my emphasis). Walter to the rescue, once again. Fern also limits Ruth's autonomy by demonstrating that although she does not plan to remarry, Ruth still defines herself in terms of her relationship to others — to her (dead) husband and her children. The novel ends, for instance, in a scene that suggests Ruth has not abandoned her vision of herself as a domestic saint. Although she is now a widowed domestic saint, her heart remains true to her husband, Harry, and with a "mute appeal" (211) she asks Walter to bury her by Harry's side.

Fern also demonstrates that although Ruth is a successful writer, she is still constrained by the cult of domesticity. Her efforts to earn money are all on the behalf of her children: "She had not the slightest idea, till long after, what an incredible amount of labor she accomplished, or how her *mother's heart* was goading her on" (174). Fern uses italics to emphasis that Ruth writes not out of a desire to vent her pent-up consciousness, not out of revenge on others, nor even out of a simple desire to be heard, but out of her *mother's heart*. Ruth's book does not feed her own ambition but rather causes her to recall how it fed and sheltered her children: "Yes, there was the book. She could recall the circumstances under which each separate article was written. Little shoeless feet were covered with the proceeds of this; a little medicine, or a warmer shawl was bought with that. . . . Some virtues — many faults — the book had — but God speed it, for little Katy's sake!" (175). From these passages, it is clear that Ruth still fits the ideology of the True Woman; her writing is not a form of self-indulgence or self-expression but an extension of her domesticity, an extension of her commitment to her family. In short, the subject that writes is still defined through others. It is a subject that seems to lack an awareness that it might have needs of its own, and an unruly tongue.

Susan Harris (126) and Nancy Walker (50) both argue that Ruth grows out of silence and into voice. However, Ruth's attitude toward writing hints at profound ambivalences in her relationship with language. Fern traces Ruth's ambivalences to cultural factors, presenting a picture that corresponds to actuality: although women dominated the production of novels during the 1850s and 1860s, many males were threatened by women's presence in the hallowed halls of literature. Male critics, reviewers, and writers reacted defensively to the perceived female threat by claiming either that women could not write (despite the fact that they were obviously doing so), that they could not write well, or that they should not write—that writing was a violation of their nature and their "proper" spheres. In "A Gentle Hint to Writing Women" (1850), George Henry Lewes asks: "Does it never occur to [women writers] that they are doing [men] a serious injury, and that we need 'protection'? Woman's proper sphere of activity is elsewhere. Are there no husbands, lovers, brothers, friends to condole and console? Are there no stockings to darn, no purses to make, no braces to embroider?" (189). Despite the enormous popularity of women writers, Lewes still sees women's "proper" sphere as the home where they "protect" (that is, support) male subjectivity.

In *Ruth Hall*, "female literature seems to be all the rage" (206), yet men control the means whereby women's writing receives an audience—the journals and publishing houses. Ruth hopes that her brother Hyacinth, an editor, will help her career; as she explains, "if *he* could not employ her *himself*, he would be brotherly enough to point out to her some one of the many avenues so accessible to a man of extensive newspaperial and literary acquaintance" (115). Four times in this sentence Fern emphasizes the masculine gender of Hyacinth and other newspaper editors; she italicizes the pronouns "he" and "himself" and also stresses that the avenues of publication are open to *brothers* and *men*, but presumably not to unaided women. Later in the novel one of Hyacinth's fellow writers, Mr. Gates, hopes that Ruth does not need to write for her daily bread because "it's hard enough, as I know, for a *man* to be jostled and snubbed round in printing-offices" (159). Italics again emphasize gender, implying that although *men* may have some difficulty attaining success as writers, women have more. No wonder that when Ruth first decides to become a writer, she finds herself desperately struggling to understand an unfamiliar masculine discourse whose "free-and-easy tone fell upon her ear so painfully" (122). She does not know the language of the world she wishes to enter: "Ruth wandered about the business streets, looking into office-entries, reading signs, and trying to gather from their 'know-nothing' hieroglyphics, some light to illumine her darkened pathway" (122). Ruth wanders in a world whose semiotics she cannot decipher, whose semiotics seem to exclude female readers.

Ruth eventually learns to decode the signs, to speak and write in this masculine discursive realm, but such gendered assumptions about women's potential are made repeatedly by individuals in *Ruth Hall*. Even an individual sympathetic to women's writing such as Gates insists several times that he "fathers" texts for Hyacinth (158, 159). The extreme end of this sexist spectrum is presented in a letter to Ruth from another author, William Stearns. Stearns confesses that "it is my opinion, that the *female* mind is incapable of producing anything which may be strictly termed *literature*" (166). Stearns faults Ruth's writing for being "unmitigated trash," for violating "all established rules of composition," and for being "as lawless and erratic as a comet" (166). Such characterization of women's writing as stylistically erratic and empty of content appear in other nineteenth-century texts (such as

Chopin's "Elizabeth Stock's One Story") and reflect the idea that women are bio-logically or intellectually incapable of producing great — that is, masculine — lit-erature. Stearns's letter also reflects a historical view held by some people during this time period. Many nineteenth-century physicians felt that women's brains were not suited for intellectual stimulation. Therefore if women read or wrote too much, insanity would result. Such essentialistic medical theories are part of a spectrum of views that ranges from Stearns's position (women cannot write), to Gates's posi-tion (women have more difficulty writing), to Walter's position (women need pro-tection if they are to write).

Ruth must struggle to find her voice as a writer in this paradoxical, but over-whelmingly sexist, context. Ruth is also hampered by her indoctrination into the silence and self-suppression of the cult of domesticity. In the first sixty chapters of the novel, other voices continually construct Ruth. For instance, Ruth is defined by Hyacinth's statement that she is " 'very plain' " and " 'awkward' " (13). Ruth is talked about by her publisher (77), by her husband's former friends (80–81), by the boardinghouse men (73), and by servants (83). But Ruth's own speech is rarely quoted directly. Her identity is created by the voices that surround her, some of which are not even identified. For example, chapter 2 is written entirely in an in-direct discourse, and an anonymous voice remarks that "It was so odd in Ruth to have no one but the family at the wedding. It was just one of her queer freaks! . . . What the use of her looking handsomer than she ever did before, when there was nobody there to see her?" (17). Ruth rarely speaks for herself because she has been taught, as Fern comments ironically, to keep "her wise little mouth shut," and to be "deaf, dumb, and blind" (23). Like a good domestic saint, she knows si-lence is her best ornament.

Fern also depicts a deadly pattern in which generation after generation of women are encouraged to suppress their voices. Ruth's mother never chastised Ruth's rude and tyrannous father for his behavior towards guests but would only "whisper gently in his ear" (14). Fern implies that Ruth's mother was hounded to death by her husband's suppression of her voice and that while married Ruth follows this pattern, learning to "curb the spirit and bridle the tongue" when she is angry (23). And while at her grandparents' home, Ruth's daughter Katy is taught that " 'little girls must be seen and not heard' " (129). Such silencing and self-suppression have physical and psychological costs, as Fern makes clear: "Ah! could we lay bare the secret history of many a wife's heart, what martyrs would be found, over whose *uncomplaining lips* the grave sets its unbroken seal of *silence*" (23, my emphasis). Ruth's mother, Ruth, and Katy are taught a deadly pattern in which their voices and selves are suppressed right into the grave.

But Ruth does not remain silent until her death; rather, she is propelled into the world of business, where she must find her own voice. Ruth's movement out of silence is apparent in the middle section of the novel, when she tries to prevent her in-laws from causing her husband's death: " 'No, no,' whispered Ruth . . . 'you will kill him' " (56). Ruth's voice is reminiscent of her mother's powerless whispers to her father, but later it becomes more emphatic. When Ruth's father demands that she give up her children, her response, although quiet, is firm: "I can *never* part with my children,' replied Ruth, in a voice which, though low, was perfectly clear and distinct" (68). Finally, in the last third of the novel, Ruth moves from this low voice to the emphatic voice of "Floy." When her brother refuses to help her begin her career as a writer, Ruth takes a giant step into language, pronouncing herself to be an "I" capable of creating and controlling her own voice and destiny: "I *can* do it, I *feel* it, I *will* do it" (116). At first Ruth's voice is timid; when she asks her publisher for a raise, she pulls her gloves on and off and then "finally mustered courage to clothe her thought in words" (131). However, in a second interview that day she is a much more active speaker, and later in the novel, she holds her own in a verbal duel with the editor Mr. Tibbetts (157) and with her in-laws (185).

As several critics have argued, then, Ruth's voice does develop. Yet few critics have noticed the constraints Fern places on this voice. For example, Ruth's writing enacts the traditional True Woman's function of inculcating morality and piety. A dying woman tells Floy that "before I go, I would send you this token of my love, for all the sweet and soul-strengthening words you have unconsciously sent to my sick chamber" (136–37). A male reader comments that "I am a better son, a better brother, a better husband, and a better father, than I was before I commenced reading your articles. May God bless you for the words you have spoken" (183). Ruth's writings are also interwoven with her domesticity and her motherhood: "One minute she might be seen sitting, pen in hand . . . then writing an article for Mr. Walter, then scribbling a business letter to her publishers, stopping occasionally to administer a sedative to Nettie, in the shape of a timely quotation from Mother Goose, or to heal a fracture in a doll's leg or arm. Now she was washing a little soiled face, or smoothing little rumpled ringlets, replacing a missing shoe-string or pinafore button, then wading through the streets . . . with parcels and letters to the post-office" (173–74). Writers discussed later in this study often depict a conflict between domesticity and a career as a writer or artist; for example, female characters depicted in texts such as Gilman's "The Yellow Wall-Paper" (1892) and "Making a Change" (1911) seem to be offered an inevitable choice between motherhood or a profession. For Ruth, however, career and domesticity are not contradictory. Under better circumstances Ruth might agree with the poetess in Mrs. A. D. T. Whitney's novel, *The Other Girls,* who comments that "the best and brightest things I've ever thought have come into my head over the ironing-board or the bread-making" (434). Ruth's writing is configured as an enhancement of her role as a domestic saint rather than a search for an autonomous voice.

Perhaps Ruth feels no conflict between writing and domesticity because her career is initiated on the behalf of her children rather than for her own self-expression: "And still 'Floy' scribbled on, thinking only of bread for her children" (133). Even in her triumphant verbal duel with Mr. Tibbetts, Ruth is still thinking of her children: "I have two little ones dependent on my exertions, and *their* future, as well as my own, to look to" (156). This sentence's syntax shields Ruth's assertion of a future for herself within her assertion of a future for her children; the language of domesticity is privileged, and Ruth's orientation toward others is emphasized over her orientation towards self. Certainly, as Joyce Warren has pointed out, Ruth's writing gives her financial independence (131), but Ruth desires financial independence not for herself but for her children. Her career is actually configured in such a way that it perpetuates part of the patriarchal structure—the subordination of feminine identity to the needs of others, in this case, her children.

Fern also limits the radicalness of Ruth's voice by suggesting that it is the voice of a True Woman forced to write rather than one of self-assertion. Again and again, Fern emphasizes that Ruth has no ambition to write a book (136), that she has no ambition to be an artist (182), that she writes only out of necessity. Ruth's attitude toward female speakers also shows that she still defines herself as a True Woman. She does not believe that women should enter the realm of spoken, public discourse. She states that it is a "violence to...womanly nature" for a female to engage in "a public contention for her rights" (172). Ruth also claims to be horrified by the thought of ever becoming an actress, a preacher, or a lecturer, professions that all entail the use of spoken, public discourse. Ruth's comments about women lecturers also imply that she sees an indelicacy in these practices: "not long since I heard the eloquent Miss Lucy Stone one evening, when it really did appear to me that those Bloomers of hers had a mission! Still, I never could put them on" (173). Ruth cannot "put on" the public verbal presence of a feminist like Lucy Stone, and she rather looks down on women who can. She is as skeptical of these women's unruly tongues as are some of the cartoonists for *Punch*. Her own tongue is safely contained in a domestic discourse that empowers her without challenging the theoretical roots of women's psychological and linguistic oppression.

Ruth is also uneasy with the idea that women might write for reasons other than economic self-support. When Nettie asks, "when I get to be a woman shall I write books, mamma?" Ruth responds (as previously noted), "God forbid...no happy woman ever writes. From Harry's grave sprang 'Floy'" (175). Ruth reasons that women only write out of dire financial need, and she hopes Nettie will never experience such suffering. Ruth cannot imagine that a female—even her smart, precocious, extremely verbal daughter Nettie—might write for self-expression. Even in private moments with her daughter, Ruth cannot conceive of women's writing as a subversive act of rebellion, or as an act of self-expression, or as an act of ambition or artistry. Women's writing is simply a way of supporting others, not an assertion of a self-defined identity or voice. Through Nettie, Fern does look forward to a time when women are no longer bound by patriarchal limits to self-expression, but for Ruth such a future has not arrived.

Both Ruth Hall's and Fanny Fern's achievements in this novel are formidable. Ruth cunningly expands the domestic sphere so that it allows for a certain degree of empowerment and voice, and Fern brilliantly manipulates the codes of domesticity that confine Ruth. Yet part of Fern's critique of the cult of domesticity involves acknowledging the difficulty of breaking this historical indoctrination. Fern herself broke from this mold into the idea of writing as self-expression, as an empowerment that helps women escape the domestic realm and the notion that they are principally defined through others. But she does not grant her character quite so much freedom. In the end, Ruth finds a domestic, historical voice that does not challenge the theoretical structures that engender women's silence. Therefore, Ruth is still contained by the voices around her. Finally Mr. Walter's voice, not Ruth's, closes the novel. "Accept the omen, dear Ruth," says Walter upon hearing a bird's trill, "Life has much of harmony yet in store for you" (211). Mr. Walter has the last word, and his voice, though kind and hopeful, will not be the final one that limits and defines Ruth's subjectivity.

"When Shall I Be Liberated?": Louisa May Alcott and the Masterplot of Patriarchal Submission

Like *Ruth Hall*, Louisa May Alcott's writing can also be seen as a limited endorsement of the cult of domesticity. As Fern does, Alcott both invokes and critiques the image of the True Woman, showing that while it facilitates women's empowerment, such empowerment is attained only at the cost of great self-suppression. Perhaps it is this double movement of both invoking and critiquing this image that leads critics such as Elaine Showalter to argue that Alcott has a submissive, traditional voice as well as a radical, subversive one (Introduction ix). But in fact there is more continuity between Alcott's radical and submissive voices than Showalter acknowledges. *Little Women* and many of Alcott's pseudonymous thrillers depict a violent suppression of women's self and voice in the silence and selflessness of the cult of domesticity. Radical women's voices are present in Alcott's fiction, but they never function successfully to undermine patriarchal discourse.

The question "When shall I be liberated?" (asked by a female character in Alcott's "A Whisper in the Dark") is thus a recurring but unresolved issue in Alcott's work. Much of Alcott's fiction depicts a generational pattern in which a repressive, older father-figure silences the outspoken voice of both mothers and daughters, and with it their true selves. This is the "masterplot" of Alcott's fiction, the story she plays out in both her traditional fictions and her more lurid stories. The choices in this conflict are bleak: either submit to patriarchal dictates about women's voice and identity or defy them and receive your punishment—actual or metaphorical death. At times Alcott's characters see the theoretical structures oppressing them, but their immersion in the image of the True Woman leaves them powerless to change these structures.

As argued in the previous section of this chapter, although Fern shares both similarities and differences with her fictional character, she does not grant her character as much freedom as she grants herself. Alcott, on the other hand, often uses female characters to explore the way vocal, resistant women like herself are controlled by authoritative male discourse. This does not mean that Alcott's characters are mere parallels of the author, but rather that in Alcott's case, as in Fern's, there is a degree of psychological closeness between author and character. Specifically, many of Alcott's characters play out an important drama of her own life—the drama of the silencing of a radically rebellious feminine voice. As many critics have noted, one of the most important aspects of Alcott's early life was her relationship with her father. Bronson Alcott took over the training of his willful and sometimes violent daughter when she was only two. He notes in his journal that his daughter already demonstrated the "wild exuberance of a powerful nature" (Bedell 66). Bronson Alcott set out to break his daughter's rebellious spirit, using fear, guilt, physical punishment, and verbal harassment to create at least an external picture of subservience. The following extract from his journal records his methods:

> I told [Louisa] she must stop crying and sit in the chair or I should punish her—hurt her—for she "must mind *father*." "No! No!" she exclaimed with more decided vehemence than before. I said, "Father must *spank* Louisa if she does not do as he says. Will she?" "No! No! Sit with mother," she reiterated. I *spanked* her. She cried the louder. I then told her she must sit on her little chair by the side of the mother, and be still, or I should punish her more. She was unwilling to give up her purpose, and set up crying again. I repeated the punishment, and did not attain peace and quiet for her, 'till I had repeated it again. (Bedell 80–81)

Clearly, Bronson Alcott is disturbed by his daughter's rebellious actions but also by her refusal to "be still," to be "quiet."

Literally and figuratively, this passage shows Bronson Alcott's young daughter attempting to defy the Law of the Father. As Jane Gallop explains, "the Name-of-the-Father . . . is a powerful Lacanian term, actually a Lacanian displacement of what Freud bequeathed him/us, the Oedipal Father, absolute primal Father" (47). The young Louisa refuses to concede to the authority of her father's presence as law-giver and ultimate arbitrator of behavior. But she also refuses the authority of the Father's voice. For as Gallop argues, "Lacan's Name-of-the-Father operates explicitly in the register of language. The Name-of-the-Father: the patronym, patriarchal law, patrilineal identity, language as our inscription into patriarchy" (71). Louisa Alcott defies the Law of the Father by refusing to conform to her father's wish that she be silent, not willfully and verbally aggressive. The battle is played out over and within language, and Bronson Alcott is not satisfied until his daughter's aggressive voice, which challenges his law, has been silenced.

Later Bronson Alcott forced his daughter to internalize the Law of the Father. According to Veronica Bassil, Louisa Alcott eventually "learned to place the virtues of patience, love, and self-denial above the desire for self-actualization" (190). She also learned to value silent submission over self-expression, saying "If I can control my temper, I am respectful, gentle, and everyone sees it. . . . Everyone loves me and I am happy" (Bassil 190). As argued later, in Alcott's fiction "temper" is a signifier for an aggressive women's voice that attempts to resist patriarchal authority. Alcott learned to suppress this resistant voice in a facade of domesticity, and over and over again she shows her female characters learning the same lesson.

The feminine self that is most acceptable to patriarchal authority is, of course, one defined only through home and family. This identity is articulated most clearly by Mr. March in Alcott's *Little Women* (1868–69), and each of the March daughters ultimately conforms to this paradigm, repressing any deviant desire for self-expression or independence. Mr. March's power is reinforced at the novel's beginning, middle, and end; Alcott thus makes clear that the matriarchal world of Marmee is only a momentary way station on the road to patriarchal submission. In the first chapter, for example, Mr. March's letter to the girls emphasizes that they should conquer their unruly selves: "remember all I said . . . be loving children . . . do [your] duty faithfully, fight [your] bosom energies bravely, and conquer [yourselves] so beautifully that when I come back to [you] I may be fonder and prouder than ever of my little women" (16). If the girls heed the father, they will be transformed into that magical entity, a good "little woman." Indeed, at the end of the first book of *Little Women*, the father finds that his prophecy has been fulfilled: each girl has worked hard to become a dutiful daughter. In the novel as a whole, Mr. March is the standard-bearer, the arbitrator, the authority: "To outsiders the five energetic women seemed to rule the house . . . but the quiet man sitting among his books was still the head of the family, the household conscience, anchor and comforter" (294). Mr. March's function in the novel is therefore to represent the subtle but nonetheless insistent forces of male authority that inculcate True Womanhood.

The father's presence is indeed necessary to guide each woman into feminine submission. Mrs. March, for instance, seems to be a perfect True Woman; she believes that "to be loved and chosen by a good man is the best and sweetest thing which can happen to a woman" (123). Yet Mrs. March's embodiment of the role of domestic saint is not effortless. Specifically, Mrs. March has learned to repress her unruly tongue. As she tells Jo: "I am angry nearly every day of my life, Jo; but I have learned not to show it; and I still hope to learn not to feel it, though it may take me another forty years" (101). Mr. March (whom Mrs. March always refers to as "father") enforces and polices the mother's silence, as Jo notes: "I used to see father sometimes put his finger on his lips, and look at you with a very kind, but sober face; and you always folded your lips tight, or went away" (103). Mr. March gives his wife lessons in women's linguistic subservience, but Mrs. March's folded lips represent the remainder of the unacceptable emotions that refuse to die. Women's angry speech does not fit with patriarchal definitions of femininity, and so it must be contained and controlled, although it never can be erased completely.

Mrs. March therefore presents her daughters with a living model of domesticity and of a subservient woman's voice. In the early chapters of the novel, the girls toy with alternative ways of defining themselves, yet each is safely guided past this dangerous shoal of self-assertion. Meg, who is described as "a womanly little woman" (477), still must be taught, first by her father and mother, and then by her husband, to be properly self-sacrificing and self-effacing. Amy must learn to be less vain and self-centered before she can be a good domestic saint (275). Beth needs no guidance for she is already the "angel in the house" (295), "the household saint" (508); she is so selfless that even on her deathbed her "feeble fingers were never idle" (509). Beth's function is to act as a living lesson to her sisters in the values of domesticity and selflessness. When Beth is sick, Meg learns to put away her mercenary goals and concentrate on "love, protection, peace and health" (226). Amy learns the value of selflessness and believes that now "no service would be hard or irksome" (226). Inspired by Beth's example, Jo tries "to give up her own hopes, plans and desires, and live cheerfully for others" (534).

More than any other character in the book, Jo struggles against the cult of femininity's limitations. At a young age, Jo dislikes the constraints imposed by her gender: "I can't get over my disappointment in not being a boy...I can only stay at home and knit like a poky old woman" (10). Through her mother's and father's teachings and through Beth's actions, Jo learns the value of selflessness, piety, and duty. Despite all this, Jo finds it hard to be truly selfless until she meets Professor Bhaer, who schools Jo in the virtues of feminine submission. No wonder Mr. March sees Bhaer as a "kindred spirit" (554); this man — literally old enough to be his daughter's father — continues the father's role of guiding Jo into being a proper and true "little woman." Finally it is Bhaer who teaches Jo that "woman's special mission is supposed to be drying tears and bearing burdens" (589), that "families are the most beautiful things in all the world" (595), that her dreams of success as a writer are "selfish, lonely and cold" (601). Jo devotes herself to creating a "boy's paradise" at Plumfield, to nurturing the male gender, forgoing her own plans and dreams.[3]

The novel as a whole therefore depicts each woman's movement into a highly constrained vision of a domestic identity and her loss of any subversive, potentially nonsubmissive characteristics. As a parallel theme, the novel also depicts each woman's loss of an expressive and self-determined artistic voice. Alcott indicates that patriarchal forces tolerate women's art only to the extent that it embellishes or contributes to domesticity. Mrs. March is "a born singer" and Meg has a voice "like a flute" (19), yet they use this talent only to improve their homes. Beth's piano playing is her form of artistic self-expression, and for the silent Beth the piano is "the *voice* of a beloved friend" (77, my emphasis). But Beth never recognizes her talent, never contemplates the possibility of an artistic career, and dies before her "voice" can develop. Amy explores the possibility of pursuing a career as an artist, only to conclude that her "talent isn't genius, and no amount of energy can make it so" (498). But does Amy truly lack talent? Or has she merely internalized social views that deride women as artists? Her family continually trivializes her work; her sculptures are "mud pies" and "*little* clay models of birds, fruit and faces" (196, emphasis added), and her nickname is "*Little* Raphael" (53, emphasis added). As Mary Kelley argues, "Women of inferior self- and social regard could not presume to leave their lowly sphere for the higher spheres of men. . . . Their all but literal denial that they were artists was a confession that they truly were unable to envision themselves as emperors [of culture]" (219). Amy is the youngest and freest of the four daughters, but she has also internalized social standards that see men, not women, as the lords of artistic creation.

Jo, too, seeks artistic expression, but like Amy she has internalized the idea that the creation of high art is not within women's realm. Her family is amused by her "precious little book" (98), and even Jo refers to her writing as "my little book" (95). The implication seems to be that "little" women can only produce "little" books, and even when Jo is older she is quick to dismiss her writing as "rubbish" (426). Fortunately, Professor Bhaer saves Jo from writing such "rubbish," rescuing her as he would "put out his hand to save a baby from a puddle" (437). As Anne Murphy points out, this image trivializes Jo's art all the more, for the baby is Jo, and the mud puddle is her writing (583). Jo comes to see her stories as unfeminine and immoral, "trash" that "will soon be worse than trash" if she continues writing them (438). Her response is to burn the stories.

Jo's mature, nonsensational writing is also censured. She receives such contradictory advice on her one novel, her "first born" (335), that she is bewildered. Jo herself laughs at her "poor little book," although she does "believe in it still" (336). The ambivalence of this statement is compounded by Jo's comments that she is no "genius, like Keats" and that she had no deep theory to expound in the novel but only wrote it "for pleasure and money" (336). Moreover, in the next chapter, Jo's mangled "first born" (335), her aborted text, is contrasted with Meg's production of not one but two perfect "real" children. So while Jo wrestles unsuccessfully with her intellectual child, Meg enjoys "the deepest and tenderest [experience] of a woman's life" (351). Jo's mature writing is thus trivialized by her family and herself, as well as by the implied contrasts of the narrative. No wonder then, that after her marriage to Bhaer, Jo no longer writes. The text structures the conflict between women's writing and their roles as mothers in such a way that it cannot be neutralized or transformed: Jo (like many of Alcott's female writers/artists) can produce either mangled "child-texts" or beautiful infants—but not both. Like the title character of Alcott's "Psyche's Art" (1868), Jo hopes that someday her domestic experiences will become the source of a "better" art (*Little Women* 601). But will that day ever come? Alcott herself seems unsure.

In theory, art in *Little Women* offers an escape from domesticity. When Meg complains that "men have to work, and women to marry for money. It's a dreadfully unjust world," Amy's response is "Jo and I are going to make fortunes for you all; just wait ten years, and see if we don't" (196). However, this radical suggestion—that art could rescue women from a life of dependent domesticity, from the structure of patriarchal society—is quickly silenced. Each female artist figure is reinscribed in the realm of domesticity.

The text also stifles women's spoken voices, as the portrayal of Jo makes clearest. While young, Jo has "a decided mouth" (11) and a "quick tongue" (51); she also likes "good, strong words, that mean something" (48). But Jo eventually learns to imitate her mother's repression of speech. When Jo expresses herself forthrightly to her aunt, she receives "a timely lesson in the art of holding her tongue" (368); her outspokenness causes her to lose a chance to go to Europe. Jo understands this lesson all to clearly, saying: "Oh, my tongue, my abominable tongue! why can't I learn to keep quiet?" (381). Jo's temper also contradicts the verbal subservience required by the cult of femininity, and she must learn to control it by manifesting the facade of the True Woman. When Jo sees Fred Vaughn cheat at croquet, she puts her mother's technique of temper control into practice: "Jo opened her lips to say something rude; but checked herself. . . . She came back, looking cool and quiet" (136). After much struggle, Jo finally learns to suppress her temper altogether: "Poor Jo tried desperately to be good, but her bosom enemy was always ready to flame up and defeat her; and it took years of patient effort to subdue it" (94). Once again the unruly feminine tongue is suppressed.

This suppression has consequences, however. By the end of the book Jo is "thin as a shadow" (602), and the maternal, completely domestic woman she becomes is very far from the wild, ambitious girl she once was. What has been lost in this transformation is Jo's voice, the voice of the outspoken, angry, unacceptable female. As Anne Murphy puts it, little womanhood is built "upon an imprisoning set of values, and Jo's silence can be seen as voluntary incarceration in the only role she knows—the self-denying goodness of Marmee" (583). In a pattern that will repeat itself in fictions such as *Behind a Mask* and "The Marble Woman," Jo plays the role of the True Woman so long and so well that she finally becomes the role.

Like Fern, Alcott also indicates that this pattern recurs, generation after generation. Both Mrs. March and her daughters learn to silence their unruly tongues and deviant desires. In the third generation, Meg's twin children show how gendered child-rearing practices result in boys becoming dominant and knowledgeable while girls become subservient and silent. The male child is taught to read while the female learns to be domestic: "At three Daisy demanded a 'needler,' and actually made a bag with four stitches in it; she likewise set up housekeeping in the side-board and managed a microscopic cooking-stove . . . Demi learned his letters with his grandfather, who invented a new mode of teaching the alphabet by forming the letters with his arms and legs" (566). Literally, the Law of the Father is seen replicating itself in this passage, for Daisy is being schooled into silent subservience, Demi into linguistic and personal authority. Mr. March's odd method for teaching the alphabet also has the comic effect of Demi believing that letters themselves are masculine, for when asked to name a letter, Demi exclaims, "I knows *him* . . . It's a We, Dranpa, it's a We" (572, my emphasis). A "We" indeed it may be: Demi, "Dranpa," and Demi's father are the masculine "we" who control language. While Demi learns the masculine nature of language, Daisy becomes another Beth, an "angel" adored by everyone because of her selflessness and "feminine devotion" (568).

Through Daisy and Demi, Alcott demonstrates how a patriarchal society grants men active, empowered voices while transforming women into silent, entirely domestic, passive creatures. This scene demonstrates an understanding of the theoretical roots of women's silencing, but it also implies an inability to change this subjugation. Characters such as Marmee, Jo, Beth, Meg, Amy, and finally Daisy are presented with no other option for voice than the linguistic practices offered by the cult of domesticity. *Little Women* indicates that women can only achieve happiness by adhering to patriarchal norms. In so doing, they become a shadow of their former selves, a whisper of their former voices. But the alternatives, as the next section demonstrates, are far more deadly.

The sensational stories discussed in this chapter fall into two patterns. In the first pattern women submit to patriarchal authority; like the female characters of *Little Women,* they lose a piece of their selves and their voices, but they survive. The second pattern shows women with powerful voices who are punished harshly — often with death — for their defiance of the Law of the Father.[4] These women resist submission to the cult of domesticity, but the overall pattern of the fictions presents no viable alternative theory of voice.

A recurring motif in the first group of stories depicts women living out the unreasonable demands of patriarchal authority and silencing themselves to be dutiful daughters. In "Ariel, A Legend of the Lighthouse" (1865), for instance, a young girl named (significantly) Ariel *March* falls in love with a poet named Southesk. At first, Ariel's father approves of the match because the husband can take over the father's protective role. However, when Mr. March realizes that Southesk is the son of a man who was his enemy, he flees with Ariel to enact vengeance. Later,

March relents, and the couple is finally allowed to marry. A happy ending? Perhaps, but the story conveys a disturbing message about women's identity. Both Ariel's father and her lover treat her as a pawn to be traded back and forth in the war between their egos. Southesk views Ariel as a pleasurable object to be gazed on, remarking to himself when he first sees her: "What a charming little sprite it is."[5] The epitome of the good, dutiful daughter, Ariel can only plead "silently" (188) with her father when he separates her from her lover. Underneath this story lies a subtext in which silent, dutiful daughters are forced to live out the Father's dreams of vengeance, and then are passed onto husbands who view them as mere playthings or possessions.

This paradigm is played out in even greater detail in "The Marble Woman" (1865), a story with numerous incestuous overtones and a confusion (or perhaps equation) of the roles of father and husband. It concerns the relationship of Cecil Stein with her guardian, Bazil Yorke. Bazil has never forgiven Cecil's mother for marrying another man, and he decides to make the daughter pay for the mother's "sin." Bazil turns Cecil into a woman trained to "repress all natural emotions and preserve an unvarying calmness of face, voice, and manner."[6] He also forces Cecil "to bear in silence many things that perplex and annoy" her (152). Over and over, Cecil's lack of voice is emphasized: "Cecil performed her duties gracefully and well, but said little" (155); "though her heart was full of sympathy, she dared not show it, so sat silent till the clock struck ten" (154). To stifle her emotions and voice, Cecil even resorts to taking opium and becomes an addict.

However, Bazil falls in love with his young niece, and he begins to find her emotionless, drugged demeanor less than appealing. After transforming the woman into a statue, Bazil then sets out to turn the statue into a woman. His task is not easy, for he has trained Cecil so well that he cannot awaken her from her coldness, even after marrying her and buying her a fine new house near the ocean. He finally succeeds, and the story ends "happily," except for the disturbing overtones of incest and the violent erasure and silencing of Cecil's identity. The story's depiction of the attainment of feminine "power" is also chilling. Power for women can only be achieved through self-concealment and, finally, self-erasure. Cecil gains control over her husband by conforming to his dictates, by wearing "a mask so long, that she might subdue her guardian's proud heart" (235). But in the end, Cecil becomes the ideal woman she has been pretending to be; the "real" Cecil (like the real Jo) vanishes under the facade of the True Woman.

This concept of masking as a way to attain "power" but also as a form of self-erasure pervades *Behind a Mask* (1866). To trick an elderly heir into marriage, the heroine (Jean Muir) pretends to be a young, simple, chaste girl, when in reality she is an aging, far from innocent, alcoholic actress. The novella's full title, "Behind A Mask; Or, A Woman's Power" aptly illustrates Jean's dilemma by suggesting that "a woman's power" does lie behind a facade of femininity. Power lies in a skillful manipulation of the appearance of domesticity that does not break free from its parameters but that also necessitates the destruction of unruly voices and identities.

Jean Muir knows that to find a husband she must maintain "a charming picture of all that is most womanly and winning" (167); in other words, she must wear the mask of femininity. She confides to a friend that in a past scheme, "All was going well, when one day my old fault beset me, I took too much wine, and I carelessly owned that I had been an actress."[7] For a moment Jean lets her demure mask slip and gives voice to her unruly tongue and her unorthodox identity. Like the fiancé described by Margaret Coxe in *The Young Lady's Companion,* Jean's suitor, Sydney, is "shocked" to discover her unruliness and promptly abandons her. In her next attempt, Jean succeeds in producing and maintaining a more convincing imitation of the cult of femininity. With the Coventrys, Jean claims that she seeks "a home" (98), and she demonstrates all the domestic virtues that would embellish it. She plays the piano skillfully and sings sweetly, makes excellent tea, is a good nurse and flower-arranger, and is kind to children and animals. These qualities are all attributes of the cult of femininity; they mark Jean as having "modest, domestic graces" (102). She also imitates the personality of a True Woman: she presents herself as meek and resigned (99), timid and maidenly (108), girlish, gentle, and sweet (109, 116). Above all Jean presents herself as pure and chaste, claiming that her "good name" — her sexual purity — is "dearer than life" (155).

Jean thus imitates a True Woman and finally becomes one through her marriage to Sir John. Sir John protects Jean and gives her a home, and in return she gives him undying faithfulness. Jean seems to be in control of the outcome, but numerous echoes of *Little Women* suggest that fundamentally these two books contain the same masterplot concerning women's submission to masculine dictates. One suitor proposes to Jean by asking her to be "the good angel of his life" (125); moreover, Jean is repeatedly described as a "little woman" (105, 113, 135). Yet the most telling echo of *Little Woman* has to do with Jean's silencing. Jean creates many voices that she modulates and controls to help her achieve her ends. However, like Jo March, Jean Muir (whose initials she shares) must abandon her deviant voices and desires in order to fit into a patriarchal model of femininity.

Of course, Jean is adept at creating the voice of the domestic saint. This voice is "soft" (99) and "meek" (105), and at appropriate moments she is silent (128). At other moments, a "curious quiver" (123) is heard in Jean's voice, combined with "the look of one who forcibly suppressed some strong emotion" (123). In this instance, Jean is actually manufacturing the domestic saint's repressed voice. The quiver, like Mrs. March's folded lips, represents the trace of repressed and unacceptable emotions. Jean also has a stronger voice that is described as "penetrating" (100). More often than not, however, Jean alternates this powerful voice with a more submissive one. In one scene, Jean speaks out to Gerald and silences him: "For an instant Gerald sat dumb. Never since his father died had anyone re-proved him" (126). Yet Jean quickly returns to a more submissive pose: "She looked at him with eyes full of tears, and there was no coolness in the voice that an-swered softly, 'You are too kind'" (127). In a later incident Jean speaks with "a sweet, submissive intonation" (140), but then quickly transposes this meek voice into an "indignant" one in which "not a trace of her former meek self remained" (141). Jean tells Gerald this indignant voice is her real one: "I restrain myself as long as I can, but when I can bear no more, my true self breaks loose, and I defy everything" (141).

Is this Jean's "real" voice and her "real self," as she claims? In fact, Jean's pas-sionate voice is still a performance, a mask. Jean's "true" voice appears only twice in the novel. At the end of the first chapter, Jean removes her false teeth, hair, and makeup, and stands metamorphosed as "a haggard, worn, and moody woman of thirty at least" (106). Here Jean reveals her undisguised self/voice: "Come, the curtain is down, so I may be myself for a few hours, if actresses ever are them-selves" (106). This statement problematizes Jean's identity by suggesting that she may not have one true, core self. Actresses like Jean (and perhaps all women?) may never actually be "themselves" — they may always be enacting a role — and femininity itself may always be a performance. However, this statement also in-dicates that the self manifested here is Jean's *truest* self, the persona she wears when alone. This self/voice is also presented in the story's final "act" when Jean's private letters are read out loud. These letters give voice to such unfeminine emo-tions that one character exclaims: "She never wrote that! It is impossible. A woman could not do it" (195). Jean's letters, with their anger, cynicism, ruthlessness, and pessimism, seem to defy every norm of feminine expression. Nonetheless, this is her truest voice, for in these letters "Jean wrote freely" (194) to her accomplice. These private letters obviously present a danger, convicting Jean of "unwomanly" conduct and desires, so she burns them. Like Jo's burning of her sensation sto-ries, Jean's action is a sort of self-destruction, an effigy to the gods of patriarchy. After incinerating these letters Jean's voice becomes docile: "Here all the sarcasm passed from her voice, the defiance from her eye" (201).

In destroying this aberrant voice, Jean becomes fixed in an identity of dutiful daughter/wife to Sir John. Jean uses alternating voices with the Coventrys, but with Sir John she always manifests the submissive and bashful voice of the True Woman. For example, Jean cannot tell Sir John that she loves him, because this would violate the norms of feminine speech: "How can I make him understand, yet not overstep the bounds of maiden modesty?" (177). The "bounds of maiden modesty" do not involve direct expression of desire or even love, so Jean must find a way of showing Sir John what she feels: she kisses his portrait. Yet even af-ter Sir John understands, Jean is still silent: "She did not speak, but a little hand stole out from under the falling hair" (178). Jean feels "real humility" towards Sir

John and even stoops to "kiss the generous hand that gave so much" (179). Alcott's implication in this passages is clear: the subversive voices Jean has marshaled will not be used with Sir John. Rather, with him she will be dutiful and humble. Jean finds power, finally, by becoming a submissive True Woman.[8]

Jean loses her truest voice, but she also survives and even gains power. The alternatives for women who refuse to submit to patriarchal authority are far more catastrophic, as another group of Alcott's sensational stories demonstrates. "Pauline's Passion and Punishment" (1863) describes a woman who refuses to tame her strong will and voice. Spurned in love, Pauline decides that although her tale of woe "is an old, old story . . . it shall have a new ending."[9] She resolves to abandon the traditional patriarchal plot in which men control women's destiny, loving or leaving them at will. After marrying a handsome, wealthy man, she makes her former lover, Gilbert, horribly jealous and dissatisfied with his own marriage, using "her woman's tongue [to] avenge her" (124). Pauline wins this "tournament," yet loses the man she has fallen in love with — her husband — when Gilbert kills him. In the long run, her unfeminine behavior leads to great harm: "with that moment of impotent horror, remorse, and woe, Pauline's long punishment began" (152). She is condemned to a living death for her assertive voice and her refusal to conform to patriarchal masterplots.

Pauline is a nontraditional woman in her assertiveness, but "The Fate of the Forrests" (1865) demonstrates that even traditional women who overstep the bounds of feminine conduct and voice are destroyed. In this story, Ursula Forrest is blackmailed into marrying Felix Stähl. Stähl is a member of a murderous sect determined to kill the man she loves, her cousin Evan. Ursula marries Felix to protect Evan, but her health and energy are decimated by her loveless marriage: "the living face was already wan and thin, many tears had robbed the cheeks of color, sleepless nights had dimmed the luster of the eyes, much secret suffering and strife had hardened the soft curves of the mouth and deepened the lines upon the brow" (DL 90). "I am not what I was" (90), Ursula accurately observes. Ursula resists some of her husband's demands, but she lacks a voice of protest: "The captive spirit woke and beat against its bars, passionately striving to be free, though not a cry escaped its lips" (93–94). When Felix finally dies, Ursula is put in jail for his murder. Although innocent, she admits to one sin: wishing her husband dead. In terms of the story's mandates this is enough, for Ursula dies during a long and painful prison sentence.

Like Ursula, Sybil, the protagonist of "A Whisper in the Dark" (1863), has desires that do not fit into a subservient domestic profile. But whereas Ursula rarely expresses her desires, Sybil is extremely outspoken. Indeed, this story is Alcott's fullest treatment of the verbally aggressive woman and of the battle between patriarchal discourse and women's speech. Sybil initially describes herself as "a frank, fearless creature, quick to feel, speak, and act," a woman who "has had my way all my life, and can't bear to be crossed" (PC 264). Sybil's uncle determines to "tame" her, however, using both verbal and sexual harassment. For instance, when Sybil tries to coax her uncle into assenting to her wishes by "kissing him daintily," he retaliates by holding her fast and kissing her "on lips, checks, and forehead, with such warmth that I turned scarlet and struggled to free myself" (265). A moment later, Sybil's uncle gives her a narcotic cigarette that causes her to fall into a deep sleep. She awakens in her uncle's arms, and becomes aware that he is humming a French *chanson* about "love and wine, and the Seine tomorrow!" (266). The sexual implications here are obvious; as Lynette Carpenter argues, Sybil's uncle drugs her in order to take "a pleasure which is specifically sexual," establishing his sexual dominance (35). In the battle of the sexes, even the female body becomes part of the terrain of struggle.

But language is the most important terrain of struggle in this gender war. Sybil's "liberty of speech" (267) greatly perturbs her uncle. When she learns that her deceased father betrothed her to her cousin Guy, she resists violently and verbally, sparking her uncle's fury:

> "Do you intend to obey your father's wish . . . and fulfill your part of the contract, Sybil?"
>
> "Why should I? It is not binding, you know, and I'm too young to lose my liberty just yet. . . . What right had my father to mate me in my cradle? How did he know what I should become, or Guy? How could he tell that I should not love someone else better? No! I'll not be bargained away like a piece of merchandise, but love and marry when I please!"
>
> At this declaration of independence my uncle's face darkened ominously. (280)

With its eerie echoes of Bronson Alcott's chastening of his two-year-old daughter, this passage depicts the fundamental conflict of Alcott's fiction. The Law of the Father treats women as possessions to be bartered back and forth, silent objects with no subjectivity. Women use their voices to resist, but their efforts are often futile.

Sybil does oppose this Law. For example, when her uncle tries to marry Sybil himself (he was in love with her mother and sees the daughter as a substitute), Sybil refuses to submit to his imperious commands. For this disobedience, Sybil's uncle has her placed in a mental institution — the same institution where her insane mother is incarcerated. Sybil's hair is shorn, she loses weight and sleeps poorly, and finally becomes ill with a fever. Like many other of Alcott's defiant females, she becomes "a shadow of [her] former self" who feels "pitifully broken, mentally and physically" (290). Sybil's body and spirit are crushed, and she agrees to marry her uncle. Fortunately, Sybil's uncle dies and she is finally allowed to marry the man she now loves — her cousin Guy. Sybil's infidelity to the Law of the Father has been punished, and at last she is allowed to go free, broken mentally and physically.

The story's depiction of textual conflicts also invokes a generational pattern in which women's voices struggle futilely to escape patriarchal language. The Law of the Father is represented by documents that the father and uncle create to silence and confine women. For instance, as Sybil reads her father's will she notes that "a sudden bewilderment and sense of helplessness came over me, for the strange law terms seemed to make inexorable the paternal decree which I had not seen before" (279). The language of this legal text makes the Law of the Father explicit and inexorable. Sybil initially resists this Law; despite the fact that she loves Guy she does not wish to be treated as a piece of property, an item in a legal text. But in the end, she succumbs to this text, marrying Guy, fulfilling the paternal decree. Sybil's uncle also uses texts to control his wayward niece. When he wants Sybil to marry Guy, he writes a letter to her governess informing Sybil of his plans, but prefers "the girl to remain ignorant of the matter" (263). Sybil's uncle and father continually manipulate texts to gain control over her.

Set against these autocratic documents is the voice of the mother and daughter, of the woman trapped within the prison house of patriarchal language and society. This voice is manifested most clearly in the messages Sybil receives from her mother while both are incarcerated in the mental institution. Sybil's mother whispers through her daughter's keyhole: "Find it! For God's sake find it before it is too late!" (292). This message perplexes Sybil: "What was I to find? Where was I to look? And when would it be too late? These questions tormented me; for I could find no answers to them, divine no meaning, see no course to pursue. Why was I here? What motive induced my uncle to commit such an act? And when should I be liberated?" (292–93). The mother's discourse does not elucidate the daughter's situation, but instead leads to an endless circle of questions. In the center of this circle is a question the daughter asks but the mother is powerless to answer: "When should I be liberated?"

Responding to this and other perplexing questions, Sybil begins to produce enigmatic texts of her own. In a prophetic echo of Gilman's "The Yellow Wall-Paper," Sybil begins to cover the walls of her room "with weird, grotesque, or tragic figures" (293), but finally she retreats into silence, sitting "mute, motionless, and scared" (294). It is at this point that Sybil finds two letters from her mother that culminate in a warning: "Child! Woman! Whatever you are, leave this accursed house while you have power to do it" (297). Sybil interprets these letters literally and makes plans to escape, but the letters' injunction to "leave this accursed house" can be interpreted more symbolically. The mother is also encouraging Sybil to leave the prison "house" of patriarchal discourse. However, the only liberation the mother can find is death, and the story never answers the question of whether there is any other escape. Sybil herself does not leave the house — she does not find a way to escape the Law of the Father. In Sybil's rewriting of her history, she claims that "but for my own folly, [I] might have been a happy wife" (300). In fact, it was not Sybil's folly that placed her in a mental institution but her uncle's willful desire to control her. Furthermore, when Sybil and Guy marry, the couple agrees "to submit, to forgive, forget, and begin anew the life these clouds had darkened for a time" (301). Given the story's gender dynamics, however, it is hard to believe that it is Guy who will "submit."

Patriarchal discourse thus seems to have banished the mother's texts and the daughter's aggressive voice. Yet Sybil remembers her mother's message: "over all these years, serenely prosperous, still hangs for me the shadow of the past, still rises that dead image of my mother, still echoes that spectral whisper in the dark" (301). The mother's voice has been repressed but not silenced. We can interpret this to mean that the mother's voice is present within patriarchal discourse and language, but only as what Kristeva would call a semiotic presence. Kristeva argues that the semiotic, which she associates with the preoedipal and with the womb or *chora*, is not separate from symbolic language. Maturation into symbolic language involves repressing the semiotic *chora*, but the *chora* does not disappear. As Toril Moi explains: "Once the subject has entered into the Symbolic Order, the *chora* will be more or less successfully repressed and can be perceived only as pulsional *pressure* on symbolic language: as contradictions, meaninglessness, disruption, silences and absences in the symbolic language. The *chora* . . . constitutes, in other words, the heterogeneous, disruptive dimension of language, that which can never be caught up in the closure of traditional linguistic theory" (162). The voice of Sybil's mother has been repressed, but it returns again and again. And again and again Alcott revisits the scene of silencing, looking for the remainder, the trace of the feminine that cannot be caught up in the closure of the father's discourse. Later writers such as Freeman and Cooper unhinge patriarchal discourse by incorporating the voice of the mother into it, as the next chapter demonstrates. But for Alcott, this maternal discourse remains a presence that troubles, but does not undermine, symbolic language; finally the voice of the mother does not offer a viable theory of verbal or psychological resistance.

Alcott therefore wrestles with the question of liberation throughout her work, indicating over and over that women's voices and selves are censored by patriarchal discourses and definitions of femininity. Her later novels also continue to examine this question, reaching similar conclusions. In *Work* (1873), Christie Devon tries a variety of employments that might allow her to maintain an autonomous economic existence, only to fall ill, renounce her independence, and marry. Alcott's first version of *Moods* (1864) depicts a woman who considers divorcing her husband and finally dies unhappily, while the revised version of this novel (1882) shows Sylvia Yule finding happiness in marriage. Again, the alternatives are clear: autonomy from patriarchal norms and death, or survival by succumbing to these norms. Works such as "A Marble Woman," *Behind a Mask,* and "A Whisper in the Dark" subtly suggest that these choices are not so clear-cut. Yet even in these radical fictions the liberation of women's voices and selves remains a hope rather than a distinct possibility. However, that Alcott continued to articulate this hope throughout her long career indicates the impossibility of fully repressing women's unruly tongue once it has been released, and foreshadows the struggle of later nineteenth-century women writers not only to unearth but also to validate this subversive and troubling feminine voice.

Signifyin(g) on the Cult of Domesticity:
Harriet E. Wilson as Trickster

As this chapter has shown, Alcott's and Fern's female characters gain empowerment from within the ideology of domesticity, yet women such as Ruth Hall and Jo March Bhaer still are not able to achieve a voice of self-expression. Many women writers from the dominant tradition could not imagine viable alternatives to the domestic voice for their heroines before the 1870s and 1880s. However, writers on the margins of this tradition, such as Harriet Wilson, could — and did — imagine alternatives as early as 1859. Henry Louis Gates has painstakingly demonstrated that the plot of Wilson's *Our Nig* has striking parallels to the domestic novel (Introduction xliii), and Hazel Carby has argued that Wilson adapts this form to fit an African American woman's experiences (*Reconstructing Womanhood* 45). And yet, Wilson does more than adapt conventions. Unlike other African American writers from this time period who "use a conventional narrative form . . . in unconventional ways" (Carby, *Reconstructing Womanhood* 43), Wilson uses a conventional narrative form — the domestic novel — to deconstruct it.

In fact, Wilson is "signifyin(g)" on the cult of domesticity. As Gates explains in *Figures in Black*, in the African American tradition signifying can involve formal parody, the suggestion of a given structure or trope by a failure to coincide with it, or "repetition of a form and then inversion of the same" (243). Thomas Kochman argues similarly that signifying depends upon the signifier reporting or repeating what someone else has said in order to undermine it (32). Wilson signifies on the cult of domesticity to show that its reality is far different than its rhetoric; moreover, she both repeats and inverts its structure, casting Frado as the "true" domestic saint and her white mistress as her savage and subhuman antithesis. Ironically, Wilson's inverted system of signification also casts Frado as the *silent* true woman, and like Jo March and Ruth Hall, Frado is only partially successful in finding self-expression. Through the documents that frame the text, however, Wilson creates an alternative identity for herself. By using an ethnic discursive tradition, Wilson achieves a voice as an articulate, signifyin(g) trickster who can manipulate and even deceive her readers when it suits her narrative purposes. Wilson is therefore a far more subversive and accomplished writer than critics have previously suspected, and her inversions indict the fundamental belief systems of her time period.[10]

The cult of domesticity was an image promoted primarily for white, middle-class women, and fictional texts by Anglo Americans often excluded African American women from it. As Frances Smith Foster explains in *Witnessing Slavery*, "If the 'negress' were not a hot-blooded, exotic whore, she was a cringing terrified victim. Either way she was not pure and thus not a model of womanhood" (131). Carby confirms this, arguing that "figurations of black women existed in an antithetical relationship with the values embodied in the cult of true womanhood, an absence of the qualities of piety and purity being a crucial signifier" (*Reconstructing Womanhood* 32). The consequence of such narrative devices, as Carby astutely notes, was that African American female characters were made to speak their own exclusions from the definition of "womanhood."

Given this cultural and literary background, we might expect African Americans writing in the 1850s and 1860s to reject the cult of domesticity and forge their own conceptions of womanhood. Yet the reading public was still predominantly white, and perhaps for this reason authors such as Harriet Jacobs and Martin Delany do not abandon True Womanhood. Jacobs criticizes the cult of domesticity in *Incidents in the Life of a Slave Girl* (1861), stating "that the slave woman ought not to be judged by the same standards as others" (56). Yet she also uses this ideology to gain the sympathies of her white, female audience. Similarly, Martin Delany's 1852 treatise *The Condition, Elevation, Emigration, And Destiny of the Colored People of the United States* argues that: "Until colored men attain to a position above permitting their mothers, sisters, wives and daughters, to do the drudgery and menial offices of other men's wives and daughters, it is useless, it is nonsense, it is pitiable mockery, to talk about equality and elevation in society" (43). While agitating for greater equality and employment opportunities for African American men, he restricts African American women to one role: teachers of children—preferably their own (196). In fact, Delany sees women's desire to work outside the home as evidence of "the deep degradation of our race" (198). He implies that when women assume their place within the home as educators of children, as true ladies, the race will be elevated.

Delany's position parallels the dominant thought of many African American writers during this time period. African American periodicals such as the Augusta-based *Loyal Georgian* published articles on "Women as the Helpmeet of Man" (3 February 1866) and encouraged African American women to define themselves primarily as wives and mothers. After an extensive survey of such periodicals, Bess Beatty argues that they portrayed the ideal nineteenth-century African American woman's highest mission as "caring for her home and children, serving as her husband's helpmate, and maintaining the highest standards of morality" (47). Many African American novelists also attempted to empower their female characters by portraying them as True Women (Foster, "Adding Color and Contour" 34). Yet there were limitations to the empowerment that could be achieved through this image.

Harriet Wilson, conversely, deploys the ideology of domesticity to hollow it out. Jane Gallop states that "Infidelity…is a feminist practice of undermining the Name-of-the-Father. The unfaithful reading strays from the author, the authorized, produces that which does not hold as a reproduction, as a representation" (71). Wilson's unfaithful portrayal of the cult of domesticity actually deconstructs it. Wilson subverts the cult of domesticity, for instance, through her treatment of white women such as Mrs. Bellmont, Frado's mistress. Mrs. Bellmont sees Frado and all blacks as subhuman, commenting that "you know these niggers are just like black snakes; you *can't* kill them" (88). Yet ultimately Mrs. Bellmont (the "saint") turns out to be a "she-devil" (17), and Frado (the "black snake") emerges as more human and saintly than the supposedly superior white mistress. Wilson continually sets up the code, the racist binary opposition of <white = human = civilized> over <black = subhuman = bestial>, then inverts and subverts its oppositions, thereby suggesting that it is both arbitrary and hypocritical.

Indeed, throughout the novel Wilson's characterization of Mrs. Bellmont reverses the codes associated with the domestic saint. The mistress of the household is not submissive or silent. Rather, in a striking inversion, Mrs. Bellmont uses her tongue to silence her husband and is described as being "a *scold,* a thorough one" (25). Mrs. Bellmont's voice is an instrument of harassment, and she spices Frado's work with "an incessant torrent of scolding and boxing and threatening" (66). Mrs. Bellmont's verbal and physical harassment of Frado also involves a high degree of sadism that violates the domestic saint's requisite of purity: "[Mrs. Bellmont] suddenly inflicted a blow which lay the tottering girl prostrate on the floor. *Excited* by so much indulgence of a dangerous *passion,* she seemed left to unrestrained malice; and snatching a towel, stuffed the mouth of the sufferer, and beat her cruelly" (82, my emphasis). A kind of rape occurs here, as Mrs. Bellmont symbolically "penetrates" Frado by stuffing her mouth and then taking her pleasure. Mrs. Bellmont also feels "satisfied" (66) or "relieved" (41) after beating Frado. Given these innuendos of sadism, it is clear that Mrs. Bellmont does not exhibit the necessary attribute of purity. Her piety is also undermined. Although she is a professed Christian, she values Frado's economic utility over her possible spiritual destiny (90). Finally, the novel also parodies and subverts her domesticity. Mrs. Bellmont considers herself a perfect housekeeper, but a typical morning's work for Mrs. Bellmont involves only brutality: "It was her favorite exercise to enter the apartment noisily, vociferate orders, give a few sudden blows to quicken Nig's pace, then return to the sitting room with such a satisfied expression, congratulating herself upon her thorough house-keeping qualities" (66). This image unites Mrs. Bellmont's sadism, vocality, and domesticity in a searing parody of the meaning of "housekeeping."

Throughout the text it is also Frado—not Mrs. Bellmont—who comes nearest to embodying True Womanhood. Frado demonstrates real domesticity: at the age of fourteen she is "able to do all the washing, ironing, baking, and the common *et cetera* of house-hold duties" (63). Yet she is also domestic in more than a literal sense. At the end of the novel, Frado gratefully comments that she has "at last found a *home*. . . . My cup runneth over" (135). When Frado loses this home she laments the fact that she is "homeless," that she has "no home to call my own" (136). Like Alcott's and Fern's texts, the vision of a happy family circle reunited in a home of one's own haunts the novel's ending. Frado's domesticity is also linked to her piety, as a private poem that she sends to her friend Allida demonstrates:

> Though I've no home to call my own,
> My heart shall not repine;
> The saint may live on earth unknown,
> And yet in glory shine.
>
> (136)

Although Gates (Introduction xlix) argues that Frado's conversion to Christianity is neither genuine nor complete, this poem clearly indicates her faith in at least some of its tenets. At the end of the narrative Frado is described as "reposing on God" (130). Frado is thus more genuinely pious than her white mistress, and she is also closer to the ideal of sexual purity. Frado's relationship with her husband Samuel suggests not sexuality but companionship: "Here was Frado's first feelings of trust and repose on human arm" (127). This language contrasts sharply with the florid rhetoric describing Mrs. Bellmont's passionate beatings of Frado.

In Wilson's reversed code, then, it is the African American maid, not the white mistress, who is pure, pious, and domestic. Frado also exhibits the "womanly" virtue of submissive silence. When Mrs. Bellmont cuts off Frado's hair, dresses her in rags, and works her nearly to death, Frado does not resist. Frado also does not protest Mrs. Bellmont's repeated cruel beatings until Mr. Bellmont tells her she may do so (104). With Mr. Bellmont's blessing, Frado tells Mrs. Bellmont "Stop! . . . strike me, and I'll never work a mite more for you" (105). Yet Frado lacks a language of resistance that is her own. Within Wilson's reversed code, Frado must be the antithesis to the vocal she-devil, Mrs. Bellmont; in short, Frado must fulfill the role of the silent domestic saint. For instance, she must weep silently because when she weeps aloud Mrs. Bellmont sees this as a symptom of discontent and beats her with a rawhide (30). Frado is "shut up," both linguistically and spatially: "Mrs B. and Mary commenced beating her inhumanly; then propping her mouth open with a piece of wood, shut her up in a dark room" (35). When Jack asks where Frado is, he is told that "Mother gave her a good whipping and shut her up" (36). A moment later Mr. Bellmont enters and inquires whether Frado " 'was shut up yet' " (36). Again and again, Wilson repeats the idea of Frado's being "shut up" in order to emphasize Frado's silence in the face of her all too vocal oppressor (66, 77, 93). No wonder, then, that Frado sees Mrs. Bellmont as "the cruel author of her misery" (83). Mrs. Bellmont will have no self-authoring; she controls Frado's language and tries to control Frado's very being.

Frado does resist this silencing. Like Wilson, Frado often uses witty inversions to "speak" her intentions and undermine racist systems of signification. When commanded to eat off Mrs. Bellmont's plate, Frado first has Fido, her pet dog, "clean" the plate with his tongue (71). This sarcastic gesture elevates Fido over Mrs. Bellmont, but Frado is later beaten and silenced for it (72). Frado's literacy is also an avenue of resistance. When she reads she "felt herself capable of elevation; she felt that this book information supplied an undefined dissatisfaction she had long felt, but could not express" (124). Despite these victories, Wilson suggests that Frado still does not control her self-representation. Frado cannot run away because Mrs. Bellmont's logic entraps her: "She determined to flee. But where? Who would take her? Mrs. B. had always *represented* her ugly. Perhaps every one thought her so. Then no one would take her. She was black, no one would love her" (108, my emphasis). This passage demonstrates that Frado has internalized Mrs. Bellmont's oppressive racism; she believes herself to be unlovable because of her race. She cannot represent herself but must remain the subject of others' ugly representations. Psychologically and linguistically, Frado is still "under [Mrs. Bellmont] in every sense of the word" (41).

Gates argues that Frado learns "to master the word" (Introduction liii–liv). However, as with the other writers discussed in this chapter, it is important to see both similarities and differences between Wilson and her semi-autobiographical character, Frado. In the documents that frame the text, Wilson achieves voice through a series of subversive narrative gestures, but Frado's victory is less certain. She never seems to escape Mrs. Bellmont's oppressive authoring. And crucially, within the narrative of *Our Nig*, Frado does not become an author. We learn of Frado's decision to write her history only through the letters written by others in the novel's appendix. Literally, Frado never becomes an author within her text, and on a metaphorical level, Frado remains entrapped within a system of signification that allocates her the place of a silenced, objectified, subhuman entity.

The novel also depicts Frado's subjectivity as fractured in ways that are never completely healed, and in ways her language reflects. Children sometimes respond to abuse by forming a series of separate and discrete selves, and Wilson represents a similar kind of fragmentation in Frado—a break between the self as active agent and passive observer, between the self as subject and object. This is made clearest by the novel's multiple points of view. The titles of the first three chapters are written in the first person: "Mag Smith, My Mother," "My Father's Death," "A New Home For Me." Yet the internal contents of these chapters are related through an omniscient, third-person point of view: "Frado... was a beautiful mulatto, with long, curly black hair, and handsome, roguish eyes" (17). From chapter 4 onward the chapter titles use the third person ("A Friend For Nig," "Spiritual Condition of Nig," "The Winding Up of the Matter," etc.), while the internal contents of the chapters are often related in the first person: "A few years ago, within the compass of *my* narrative" (126, emphasis added). It is unclear whether this first-person narrator is meant to be Frado, as in the titles of the earlier chapters, or another narrative voice altogether.

Although Gates claims that the gap between author and character is stabilized as the text progresses (*Figures in Black* 146), it should be clear from these examples that this is not precisely the case. I suggest that we should not read these inconsistencies as mistakes on Wilson's part or as a loss of textual authority (as some critics have done). Instead we should see these inconsistencies as Wilson's skillful portrayal of a character struggling toward—but not quite achieving—self-authorization.[11] Wilson depicts Frado as a divided and fractured self, attempting to take control of her identity through language, through the telling of a tale—her tale? Yet the splits in Frado's psyche are never completely healed, and her language reflects a fracturing between subject ("I," "my," "me,") and object ("Nig," "the matter"). Frado's multiple names (given to her by others) also reflect a fractured self not quite in control of its own representation. We learn in the appendix that her real name is Alfrado, yet she is referred to throughout the text as "Frado," and at one point, she is called "Fra." She is also referred to within the narrative as "Nig" and "our Nig." Where is the real voice behind these many pronouns and names: my, me, I, the matter, Nig, our Nig, Alfrado, Frado, Fra?

In the end, Frado cannot find a voice of self-representation because of the inverted system of representation that Wilson has designed. In the equation Wilson has set up, an equation designed to reverse the codes of domestic sainthood, Frado must fill the place of the silent and the silenced. Carby argues that "while the portrayal of black women as defiant, refusing to be brutalized by slavery, countered their representation as victims, it also militated against the requirements of the convention of true womanhood" (*Reconstructing Womanhood* 38). Simply put, to be active and vocal was not to be a True Woman. Wilson utilizes this ideology to deconstruct its racial politics, but her character remains trapped within its linguistic confines. Like Fern and Alcott's characters, then, Frado is constrained by the cult of domesticity's limited vision of "women's voice."

Unlike her character, however, Wilson is able to step outside this image and find a voice as an articulate trickster. Wilson's preface—which has her initials, H. E. W., attached—uses a sophisticated strategy to obtain control of the text. Wilson claims she writes for a black audience: "I sincerely appeal to my colored brethren universally for patronage, hoping they will not condemn this attempt of their sister to be erudite." Yet is *Our Nig* really intended for a black audience?[12] In 1859, would there be a large, literate, black population with the extra money to purchase a book? According to Martin Delany, there would not: "One of our great temporal curses is our consummate poverty. We are the poorest people, as a class, in the world of civilized mankind — abjectly, miserably poor, no one scarcely being able to assist the other" (204). Wilson's appeal to her "colored brethren," then, may be read as not entirely genuine, and numerous internal textual details also raise doubts about her intended audience. In discussing Frado's white mother's marriage to an African American, Wilson says: "You can philosophize, gentle reader, upon the impropriety of such unions, and preach dozens of sermons on the evils of amalgamation. Want is a more powerful philosopher and preacher" (13). In general, in this time period it was whites and not African Americans who would be more likely to preach sermons against miscegenation. Moreover, when Aunt Abby and James discuss the prevalent popular opinion that African Americans are inferior to whites, they soliloquize at length about the innate humanity of African Americans (73–76). At whom are these sermons directed? It seems likely they are directed at a prejudiced white reader who might buy the book because of its racist title but then be exposed to Wilson's hidden message — the humanity of African Americans.

Of course, we cannot know what Wilson's intentions were, but these details suggest that her claims about audience might not be entirely straightforward; she may have had an audience of whites and African Americans in mind, or even a predominantly white one. Yet why, then, does Wilson say her audience is African American? I believe this is a sophisticated narrative strategy on Wilson's part, a trick designed to make her audience believe they are voyeurs, secretively peeping at a book designed for other (or Other) eyes. Wilson's preface fools the white reader into thinking that he or she is in control, watching from afar, reading what is intended for African Americans. In reality, though, Wilson is in control, watching as her white readers pick up a text they think is for black readers but hear messages really designed for white readers. In short, Wilson tricks her readers into reading her text and then springs her subversive messages on them.

From Wilson's preface, then, we can discern the outlines of an author far more manipulative than her character Frado, one fully in control of her self-representation. The three letters that constitute the appendix to the novel also provide evidence for Wilson's identity as a trickster. These letters authenticate the veracity of Frado's narrative, yet neither Gates nor Barbara White has been able to find records that document the existence of the individuals who wrote these letters: Margaretta Thorne, Allida, and C. D. S. Wilson may, then, have taken the audacious step of authenticating her own narrative through three fictional personas, three alter egos, as certain circumstantial pieces of evidence suggest. Gates concedes that C. D. S. was a common abbreviation of "Colored Indentured Servant," and the initials double back on the narrative in a curiously recursive way, since in the novel Frado is a C. D. S., and in Wilson's real life she was informally, if not formally, a colored indentured servant. Margaretta Thorne's name is also rich with symbolic possibilities that resonate with the narrative. Although Frado claims that all of the Bellmonts died before the publication of the narrative, in fact several were still alive (White 42). Is Margaretta Thorne (a.k.a. Harriet Wilson) the "thorn" in the Bellmont family's side? Margaretta Thorne punctures the Bellmont's image by using the same kinds of inversions Wilson uses—inversions that cast Mrs. Bellmont as the she-devil and Frado as the True Woman: "I often wonder [Frado] had not grown up a *monster*; and those very people calling themselves Christians, (the good Lord deliver me from such,) and they likewise ruined her health by hard work, both in the field and house" (139). Who is the monster, here, who the true Christian? Margaretta Thorne has no doubts on this subject.

Finally: "Allida." Who is Allida? Allida has letters from Frado and poems Frado has written, and she is also apparently a poet herself. Is Allida Wilson? If so, what does this alter ego symbolize? Personal name dictionaries from England, the United States, and Africa contain no entries for this name. "Allida" is also not listed as a Hebrew name, a baptismal name, a surname, or a nickname in any dictionaries I have found.[13] Speculatively, I want to argue that Allida is a trick played by Wilson on her unsuspecting audience. "Allida" is an almost perfect anagram of a name Wilson's readers might be more familiar with: Delila (a common variant spelling of Delilah).[14] In the biblical narrative of Samson and Delilah, of course, Delilah disempowers Samson by cutting his hair. This image echoes back to the narrative's description of Mrs. Bellmont's attempt to disempower and humiliate Frado by cutting off all her glossy ringlets (68). In the appendix, is Wilson reversing or inverting the paradigm, making herself the Delilah who disempowers Mrs. Bellmont? If so, Wilson is a more consummate and skillful craftsman than has been previously suspected.

But Wilson is also more of a trickster figure than most critics have suggested. Delilah is the original unreliable narrator, lying to Samson again and again to trick him, to get what she wants. Yet Delilah's name also has positive connotations. Patrick Hanks and Flavia Hodges's *A Dictionary of First Names* states that Delilah was taken up enthusiastically in the seventeenth century by those consummate truth tellers, the Puritans, perhaps because Delilah was beautiful but also clever. If troping with this name, Wilson is suggesting both that she herself is a trickster but also that she is beautiful and smart—smart enough to outwit her former mistress, to disempower the disempowerer.

These details suggest that there are multiple ways of reading Wilson's appendix, ways that should influence our reading of the novel as a whole. There is a polyvocality in these letters that is in keeping with an identity for Wilson as a trickster, a chameleon-like shape shifter who vanishes as soon as we feel we have gotten hold of her. Gates tells us the quintessential trickster figure *Esu*, the Signifying Monkey, limps because one of his legs is shorter than the other; apparently he has one leg in the spirit world and one leg in reality (*Figures in Black* 237). Like Esu, Wilson is a trickster figure, a supernatural being with one foot in the autobiographical, realistic world of her own life and another foot in the imaginary world of narrativity and texts. Gates suggests that the Signifying Monkey is an inversion, a transformation of the image of the simian-like African American into a more positive term.[15] Wilson similarly takes the derogatory term "nig" and uses it in a subversive narrative gesture that grants her empowerment.

Nig, our Nig, Frado, Fra, Alfrado, me, my, I, the matter, Delilah, Allida, Margaretta Thorne, C. D. S.: Are these names all the shifting shapes, shifting alter egos of the trickster, of Harriet E. Adams Wilson herself? In the absence of evidence to the contrary, I would like to grant Wilson the ability to craft an identity for herself as an articulate trickster. I would like to grant Wilson the ability to shift shapes, to confound and confuse, to subvert, invert, and signify. But what is her ultimate purpose? Does this trickster have a purpose, or are the tricks just trifles, baubles to fill out the text? As a trickster, Wilson deftly undermines and reverses the system of signification put in place by white authors, asserting her own right to textual authority. For, if *Esu* is the ultimate trickster, he is also the ultimate, authoring subject, fully in control of his self-representation, his signifying practices. *Esu* is the god of style and the stylus, the divine linguist, keeper of the word that creates the universe (Gates, *Figures in Black* 237–38). In allying herself with the trickster, Wilson thus grants herself an identity that cannot be questioned. Yet it also cannot be known. For with her multiple and shifting shapes and guises, Wilson in the end eludes categorization. Who is the real Harriet Wilson? Is she the victimized Frado? Is she the lying but intelligent Delilah/Allida? Is she the thorny Margaretta Thorne? Perhaps we shall never know — which may be exactly how Harriet E. Adams Wilson (whoever she is) would want it.

This chapter has argued that fiction written by Anglo American and African American women from 1850 to 1880 reflects discontent, but not a decisive break, with the model of domestic sainthood and the historically specific practice of women's speech enforced by this image. Characters who attempt to move beyond this model are swiftly censored: Ruth Hall's writing is safely confined within a domestic discourse, Jo March's fiction is burnt, Jean Muir's deviant voice is repressed, and Frado is repeatedly "shut up" and beaten for linguistic resistance. Although these authors sometimes articulate the theoretical structures of patriarchal and racist discourses that silence women, they seldom present an alternative theory of voice that allows female characters in their texts to challenge these structures.

The late-nineteenth-century writers discussed in the next four chapters sometimes censor their female characters' unruly tongues or reinscribe their voices within the domestic realm. But on the whole, these writers are more committed to breaking with the cult of domesticity and embracing an unruly discourse that undermines the theoretical underpinnings of patriarchal and racist language systems. They deconstruct these systems by bringing a feminine or maternal voice into symbolic language. They would not agree, then, that "no happy woman ever writes." Instead, these writers reach toward a new frontier of language that can be worked by both men and women — a frontier that no longer codes women as silent, suppressed shadows but rather enables them to become subjects and speakers in their own right.

3

From the Law of the Father to the Law of the Feminine
Mary Wilkins Freeman's and Anna Julia Cooper's Revisionary Voices

It may seem unusual to pair Mary Wilkins Freeman and Anna Julia Cooper, and to argue for a common strategy in their writing of the relation between women and language. Yet the discontinuities between these two women — one a New Englander, one a southerner, one Anglo American, one African American — substantiate the argument that an important shift occurs in the late nineteenth century in Anglo American and African American women writers' understanding of the problem of voice. These two writers emblematize this change, and so this chapter examines in detail two of their works: Freeman's "The Revolt of 'Mother'" (1891) and Cooper's *A Voice from the South* (1892). These works articulate the theoretical basis of women's silencing in structures of identity that envision the speaking subject as inherently male (and for Cooper, white). This is not to imply that Freeman is concerned with problems of race; if Freeman is aware of the presence of race in her New England milieu, this awareness is not made manifest. Cooper, on the other hand, continually questions her marginalization because of her status as an African American and a woman within a culture that devalues and silences both.

Yet for both writers, gender is a primary category of analysis, and both employ a similar strategy to undermine patriarchal discourse or the Law of the Father: they recover a voice that is specifically feminine and maternal. Freeman works directly on the smallest elements of language (the word or sign), using a voice of the mother to build a new language. Cooper is more interested in larger structures of racial and gendered discourses, and she focuses on the assertion of a heterogeneous, musical, and racially mixed feminine "keynote" that liberates other voices within society. Unlike the writers discussed in the previous chapter, then, Freeman and Cooper use a feminine voice to theorize and finally displace patriarchal discourse. However, after invoking a feminine voice that breaks the links between the speaking subject and the masculine gender, they attempt to move beyond this voice into a new frontier where both men and women — and for Cooper, individuals of all races and classes — can be speaking subjects. Their use of essentialism is therefore only a means to an end. Freeman's and Cooper's ultimate purpose is the creation of a language of equality that can (they hope) be spoken by all.

Engendering Discourse in Freeman's "The Revolt of 'Mother'"

As the introduction suggested, women's writing of the late nineteenth century contains a growing interest in the theoretical basis of women's silencing, but the subversive voices present in these texts are not always successful in their revolts against patriarchy. For example, some of Freeman's stories indicate that no matter how powerful women's voices are, they sometimes fail to change social roles in any permanent way. In "Old Woman Magoun" (1909) the outspoken title character cannot save her innocent granddaughter from the rapacious and predatory patriarchal society of Barry's Ford. Ultimately, as Leah Glasser states, "although Magoun attempts to argue, language is not a tool that works in Barry's world" (14). In "A Village Singer" (1891), Candace Whitcomb speaks out to the minister, asserting her right to sing in the village choir, but her unruly tongue causes her death. And in "A Poetess" (1891), when Betsy Dole learns from a male minister that her writing is no good, she burns her poems and dies.

Betsy's burning of her poems may remind us of Jo March's effigy to the gods of patriarchy, but Freeman's stories do sometimes indicate that women can successfully craft alternative identities and voices. Works such as "Evelina's Garden" (1898) demonstrate that when women work together, over several generations, they begin to redefine the patriarchal roles that have constrained them; Evelina cannot find happiness in marriage, but she bequeaths this opportunity to her niece. Community and voice are also important themes of "A Church Mouse" (1891); when Hetty's voice falters, the town-women's voices ring out "clear and strong" in their support for her: "Of course you can stay in the meeting-house. . . . I should laugh if you couldn't" (424).[1] And in "Christmas Jenny" (1891), a meek woman named Betsey Carey speaks out against her town's attempts to deprive an eccentric but sane woman of her few sources of satisfaction. A community of women supports the unruly voice of individual members, understanding its fundamental connection to a liberation of feminine subjectivity.

"The Revolt of 'Mother'" (1891) is Freeman's most incisive and thorough examination of how an assertion of a feminine theoretical voice can undermine patriarchal discourse and create a new (and more supportive) community. Yet when the story begins, Sarah Penn seems to be the perfect housewife. Freeman gains the sympathy of her audience (as Anna Julia Cooper does) by employing the image of the domestic saint. Sarah seems mainly concerned with her family's well-being, and even as she plots her rebellion she continues making her husband's favorite mince pies for his lunch (453). Furthermore, her revolt begins with an entirely domestic goal — a more comfortable and spacious home for her family. Sarah's husband, Adoniram, has plenty of money to build such a home, and indeed he promised Sarah this home when they first married forty years ago. But in the interim, Sarah's husband has insisted on building more barns and buying more cattle, thereby confining his family to their meager, rundown "box of a house." So Sarah finally takes matters into her own hands. While her husband is away on a trip to buy a horse, she subverts his intentions by moving her family and all their possessions into his recently completed (but empty) barn. When father returns, Sarah tells him: "we've come here to live, an' we're goin' to live here. We've got jest as good a right here as new horses an' cows" (467). And father tearfully agrees.

On the surface, this story may seem comic, and indeed some critics have called it funny. Behind this folksy humor, however, lies a serious subtext. Sarah Penn is forced repeatedly to understand her powerless status, a status that stems from her position in a patriarchal, frontier society more oriented toward animals than people. Yet Sarah is also powerless within the language of this frontier society, and the story's real focus is her struggle to become a speaking subject. To escape the binary system of silent women/speaking men that entraps her, she must engender a new linguistic frontier that merges the conflicting value systems of father's and mother's frontiers through a radical restructuring of the process of signification itself. She must give voice to an unruly tongue that challenges not just language practices but the theoretical basis of language's functioning in the patriarchal world she inhabits.

In Freeman's fiction, women's power is often intertwined with the issue of language.[2] To understand why communication fails, however, we must first examine the different psychological orientations mother's and father's visions of the frontier reveal. Father values building barns, but what does this mean in terms of his view of the world itself? From the outset, father's vision seems peculiarly overdetermined. The story emphasizes that he already has more than enough barns, more than enough cows, to provide an adequate source of income for his family. As mother says: "You've built sheds an' cow-houses an' one new barn, an' now you're goin' to build another.... You're lodgin' your dumb beasts better than you are your own flesh an' blood. I want to know if you think it's right" (457). To mother's question, father's "response" is only, "I ain't got nothin' to say" — a nonresponse he repeats three times in rapid succession when mother asks him about the purpose of the new barn:

"I want to know what you're buildin' that new barn for, father?"

"I ain't got nothin' to say about it."

"It can't be you think you need another barn?"

"I tell ye I ain't got nothin' to say about it, mother; an' I ain't goin' to say nothin'." (455)

Father is concerned only with making more money for the sake of the money it-self. Like the logic of his speech, his version of capitalism is peculiarly circular: he translates the wilderness into cattle, the cattle into money, and then the money into more barns to house more cattle.

Father's main symbol of success is his barn, and it is in opposition to the sym-bolic realm of the barn that mother counterpoises the actual and symbolic realm of the home. Mother values the home not as a symbol of wealth or social status but rather as a place for the generation and regeneration of human life. The Penns' daughter Nanny is engaged, and Sarah believes that her daughter will not be able to live with the Penns after her marriage unless the family lives in a larger house. Mother is concerned partially because she wants to keep her small, limited com-munity together. But more important, Sarah also believes Nanny's own life to be threatened: "She wa'n't ever strong. She's got considerable color, but there wa'n't never any backbone to her. I've always took the heft of everything off her, an' she ain't fit to keep house an' do everything herself. She'll be all worn out inside of a year" (457). Sarah has endured her home for forty years, but with Nanny's upcoming marriage the need for the new house becomes dire. Monika Elbert claims that Sarah's ultimate goal is the growth of her domestic economy and that mother's goals are as materialistic as father's (265–66). However, Sarah's desire for a larger house has more to do with the nurturing and preserving of life than with capital-istic values, or with acquiring money and property for its own sake.

As Alice Glarden Brand argues, "by contrasting father as antagonist with mother as protagonist, Freeman points to skewered [sic] priorities; father's are for ani-mals; mother's are for the human and relational" (91). These different priorities may be related to socialization practices described by nineteenth-century historians. For instance, children's books from this time period taught young boys to value competition, material success, and achievement, whereas young girls were taught to value cooperation and relationships.[3] Mother clearly demonstrates the affilia-tion motivation, centering her concept of morality on preserving human relation-ships in the family. Father is more interested in achievement, in getting ahead, in becoming wealthy. Across and against these gender differences, mother must find a way to communicate her values to father.

However, ordinary language does not provide her with a tool for communica-tion, since patriarchal discourse systematically excludes women as speakers. We do not need Lacan's idea that the Name of the Father acts as a linguistic enforcement of patriarchy to see patriarchal discourse at work in Freeman's fiction. In "The Revolt of 'Mother'" we have, literally, the name of the Father — "father" who jealously guards language so that "there was never much conversation at the table in the Penn family. Adoniram asked a blessing, and they ate promptly, then rose up and went about their work" (453–54). This description demonstrates that father is the only one allowed to speak on a regular basis, and it also depicts father's habitually rigid and miserly control over the flow of conversation. Similarly, father can refuse to speak if he wants to, as he repeatedly does at the opening of the story: "The old man said not another word" (449), "he shut his mouth tight," "He ran his words together, and his speech was almost as inarticulate as a growl" (448). Through his words, father can order that more barns be built, for he controls not only language but also commerce and commercial power, and yet he also frequently refuses to answer even the simplest question. Furthermore, he never has to explain himself; he merely does what he wants and responds when questioned: "I ain't got nothin' to say" (which he says repeatedly throughout the story).

It should be emphasized that although Adoniram Penn is terse, his terseness comes from a repression of language rather than the inability to speak. Father's mouth literally becomes full with the discourse he is controlling: "there was a sudden dropping and *enlarging* of the lower part of the old man's face, as if some heavy weight had settled therein; he shut his mouth tight" (448, my emphasis). Father's refusal to speak is part of the stranglehold he keeps on language: "he shut his mouth tight, and went on harnessing the great bay mare. He hustled the collar on to her neck with a jerk" (448). It is no coincidence that father is harnessing a mare, that he is hustling a collar onto her neck with force. Adoniram treats his wife like a dumb beast, in refusing to engage in any meaningful discourse with her, and he treats the dumb beast like his wife, in collaring, jerking, forcibly repressing any power the mare might have. As Joseph Church notes, "obviously, and especially given the French homonym, the mare stands in for 'mother'" (197). Anna Julia Cooper will also emphasize this point: that patriarchal subjectivity and language are founded on a silencing of the mother, an erasure of her human presence and her potentiality for voice.

Worse yet, Adoniram has taught his son Sammy to behave in like manner — to guard language vigilantly and refuse women's access. Freeman shows a distinctly gendered and generational pattern of discourse replicating itself. According to this pattern, women (Sarah and her daughter Nanny) question the men, but their inquiries go unanswered; and men (Sammy and Adoniram) carefully guard access to the citadel of power and knowledge: language. Even specific topics of conversation are replicated. When Nanny asks whether Sammy knew about the new barn, he turns, showing "a face like his father's" and responds "reluctantly" and tersely, "Yes, I s'pose I did" (450). No wonder he has "a face like his father's": both literally and symbolically, he replicates the old man, the Father. Raised under the Father's Law, Sammy will become the Father: an individual who believes in the silencing and objectification of women.

Freeman's fiction, then, manifests an understanding of not only the historical foundations of women's oppression in specific socialization practices but also its transhistorical and theoretical basis. Sammy's and Adoniram's commitment to repressing women's discourse and denying their subjectivity is crucial to their patriarchal status. For as Luce Irigaray has argued, representation and discourse are irremediably founded on the oppression of women's subjectivity: "Subjectivity denied to woman: indisputably this provides the financial backing for every irreducible constitution as an object: of representation, of discourse, of desire. Once imagine that woman imagines and the object loses its fixed, obsessional character. As a bench mark that is ultimately more crucial than the subject, for he can sustain himself only by bouncing back off some objectiveness, some objective" (133). Denial of subjectivity to Nanny and mother is crucial to Sammy's and Adoniram's power, and this denial operates most explicitly through language. The men carefully control speech and knowledge, sharing it with each other but only reluctantly allowing women to possess any information. Sammy, it seems, has known about father's proposed new barn for three months, but he has kept this information from his mother since he "didn't think 'twould do no good" to tell her (450). Sammy believes in the Father's logic: that women are absent and disempowered within systems of patriarchal language.

Telling his mother about the barn, then, might not be of any use; Sarah seems to be locked out of language and power, and changing this status is difficult. But Sarah does try. She does something she has not done before, as she says: "I'm goin' to talk real plain to you; I never have sence I married you, but I'm goin' to now. I ain't never complained, an' I ain't goin' to complain now, but I'm goin' to talk plain" (455). Sarah, further, adopts male patterns of language; she "pleaded her little cause like a Webster; she . . . ranged from severity to pathos" (457). Yet in adopting masculine models like Daniel Webster and plain speech, she falls into patriarchal discourse, and this ultimately renders her silent. As Adrienne Munich explains, "discourse — linear, logical and theoretical — is masculine. When women speak, therefore, they cannot help but enter male-dominated discourse; speaking women are silent as women" (239). And indeed, it is as if all of Sarah's eloquence is silent, unheard; Adoniram merely responds "I ain't got nothin' to say" (457) and goes out to get a load of gravel. In assuming that she can speak like a man, Sarah presents no challenge to the Father's rule, for father knows very well that she is not a man. As Stephen Heath argues, "any discourse which fails to take account of the problem of sexual difference in its enunciation and address will be, within a patriarchal order, precisely indifferent, a reflection of male domination" (53). Father is indifferent to Sarah's plea because the plea itself is indifferent, undifferent, undifferentiated; it fails to take account of sexual difference. Mother's fall into patriarchal discourse ultimately reinscribes her silent and powerless status, a status she acknowledges when she disparagingly tells her daughter, "You ain't found out yet we're women-folks.... One of these days you'll find it out, an' then you'll know that we know only what men-folks think we do, so far as any use of it goes" (451). Sarah's access into patriarchal discourse is a fall into powerlessness and defeatism.

Mother's inability to communicate, then, stems from her inscription within the institution of patriarchal society and her construction as a silent object within patriarchal theories of subjectivity. And yet the problem may lie even deeper than this, in the fact that her signification system itself is different from father's. To father, value resides in money, commerce, and getting ahead, and all this is symbolized by one thing for him: barns. Father's transcendental signifier—the item around which he organizes his entire concept of language and identity—is symbolized by "Barn," and by all that "Barn" represents. In effect, for father "Barn" figures forth what Lacan has called the phallus, the transcendent symbol of male potency that can never quite be attained. To mother, however, value resides in people, family, generation—all of the values symbolized for her by the transcendental signifier "Home." For both mother and father, value resides in different spatial locations and in different symbolic realms or registers. No wonder mother cannot convey her meaning to father. Their linguistic universes are structured around entirely opposed and mutually inaccessible notions of value. And mother has no way into father's universe of signification.

But if there is a language of "The Father" in this story, there is also a language of "The Mother"—a language that reenacts cultural mythologies about the origins of language in feminine terms. Josephine Donovan argues that Freeman presents only two options for female characters: "either they may remain in the prepatriarchal world of the Mother (the world of nature), which means they remain silent, or they enter the patriarchal world of language (culture) and are forced to submit to its misogynist exigencies" ("Silence or Capitulation" 44). I would argue, however, that Freeman tries to elude this binary choice of silence or capitulation to patriarchal language. Through actions that speak, through spatial reinscription, and through a renaming of objects, mother revises, reassigns, the fundamental oppositions that structure her and father's systems of signification, thereby developing a theory of language that allows her to be a speaking subject, a system of discourse that is feminine, but not silenced. So unlike Fern's or Alcott's female characters, Sarah is able to break the generational, gendered discursive patterns that constrain her. Mother begins her revolt, then, as a good domestic saint, but by the time it ends she has become someone altogether different: an unruly, unlawful feminine subject willing to retheorize language in order to re-create her world.

Mother's rebellion begins with a re-creation of language itself. Since mother cannot use patriarchal discourse to tell father what she wants, she creates a new language—a system of signs—based on interpretable actions, actions that function as words. She moves the house into the barn, she empties "all their little household goods into the new barn" (463). She dumps all the value of "Home" into "Barn," and she thereby takes an action that indicates that to her "Home" is as important, if not more important, than "Barn." And Adoniram finally understands, saying: "Why, mother, ... I hadn't no idee you was so set on't as all this comes to" (468). Sarah finds an action, in short, that can speak louder than words but can also *be* words. She creates a sort of sign language that bridges the gap between different systems of signification, and she makes father understand her feminine value system.

Sarah also uses space as a communicative tool, creating a physical expression of her feminine values. She manages to speak to her husband by co-opting his "barnyard" terminology, by replacing it with a feminine discourse of the home. Thus where father sees "box stalls," Sarah sees "better bedrooms than the one she had occupied for forty years" (463); where father had planned to have a harness room, mother "would make a kitchen of her dreams." She physically co-opts the space and plan for his new barn: "Sarah looked at the row of stanchions before the allotted space for cows, and reflected that she would have her front entry there." Ultimately, it is Sarah's architectural design for the barn as home, not Adoniram's plan for the barn as barn, that is enforced by the story's ending and that reduces father to tears: "after supper he went out, and sat down on the step of the smaller door at the right of the barn, through which he had meant his Jerseys to pass in stately file, but which Sarah *designed* for her front house door, and he leaned his head on his hands" (468, my emphasis). By architecturally redesigning the barn so that it is a home, Sarah imposes the muted feminine culture of the home onto, and over, the dominant masculine culture of the barn. Sarah forces Adoniram, quite literally, to see houses where he has previously seen only barns; in so doing she forces him to recognize her language, and to see her world view. And it is this change in vision that causes father to finally understand what Sarah wants: "I'll—put up the—partitions, an'—everything you—want, mother" (468).

Finally, Sarah also achieves a radical renaming that underscores the arbitrary nature of naming itself. Like Adam in the Garden of Eden, she points and names. Pointing to a green growing thing, Adam said, "Tree," and so it became a tree. Pointing to a barn, Sarah says, "Home," and so it becomes a home. But Sarah's action is more complex than this; where Adam sees one tree, with one name, Sarah sees something that has been called "Barn" and renames it as its opposite: "Home." This revolutionary linguistic act emphasizes the arbitrary nature of signification and undermines the fundamental oppositions father has used to structure his system of discourse, as well as his entire universe. In breaking the established pattern of discourse, Sarah undermines the Law of the Father, disrupting patriarchy itself, for as Nelly Furman explains: "A linguistic intervention which ruptures accepted (acceptable) discursive practices reverts us to the constitution of the social subject which is predicated on the repression of the maternal. Through disruption of the symbolic function of language, we are able to give expression to the repressed, or to detect traces of repression, but in so doing we are, even if only momentarily, in breach of the Law-of-theFather" (74). So Sarah breaches the Law of the Father through her house/barn, which expresses the repressed maternal and feminine values in which she believes. Indeed, Sarah's renaming is so revolutionary in its breaking of the established pattern of discourse that the villagers see her as either "insane" or "of a lawless and rebellious spirit" (464). Further, Adoniram's amazed reaction testifies to the undermining of his authority: he turns to Sarah in a "dazed fashion" (466), exhibiting "his old bristling face [which] was pale and frightened" (467). As well it should be, for Sarah has used her feminine language to subvert the authority he has kept tightly in his control for the last forty years.

Sarah resignifies, reinscribes in order to create a new theory of language that allows her to be a speaking subject — this, not the new home, is finally the goal of her revolt. In so doing, she breaks the stranglehold of "The Father" on language. When father first sees the new house/barn, he is reduced to speech without sound; watching him, the family sees that "his lips moved; he was saying something, but they could not hear what it was" (466). Later, Adoniram is still speechless — so much so that mother must remind him to say prayers: " 'Ain't you goin' to ask a blessin,' father?' said Sarah" (468). This last tableau forms a striking contrast to Adoniram's early recitation of prayers, as well as to the prior scenes where he was silent. His previous silence was that of the possessor of knowledge, the possessor of discourse. Now, he is speechless ("the old man . . . shook his head speechlessly" [467]) or gasping for words (" 'Why, mother!' the old man gasped" [467]). His silence comes from being without words — from being at a loss for words. For the first time in the story, *father* asks *mother* to explain, to interpret, the meaning of events: " 'What on airth does this mean, mother?' he gasped" (468). And Sarah tells him: "we've come here to live, an' we're goin' to live here." Sammy backs up Sarah on this point, speaking out "bravely," and further demonstrating that the father's miserly and gendered control of language has been lost. Sammy and Nanny's support for their mother's actions also underscores the fact that Sarah has found a small community of speakers who support her unruly tongue, a community of men (Sammy) and women (Nanny) who participate in her discursive universe. And once Adoniram is without a discursive community and Sarah is with one, Adoniram's jealous guarding of the citadel of knowledge also collapses: "Adoniram was like a fortress whose walls had no active resistance, and went down the instant the right besieging tools were used" (468). Speech is the key to the tumbling fortress, but Sarah must redefine language, and break the father's stranglehold on it, before she can be heard.

And yet it is not just that Sarah has wrested control of language from her husband and placed it in her own hands. Nor has she simply displaced father to a marginal position, as Joseph Church argues (197). Adoniram is silent, or he weeps, because he finally understands what Sarah wants. Like Sammy, Adoniram joins Sarah's linguistic community when she succeeds in communicating that her system of values is valid. Sarah engenders a language that expresses the values of her gender but that can also be understood by father, a language that allows both father's and mother's participation. Adoniram agrees to Sarah's demands because he now understands them: "Why mother, . . . I hadn't no idee you was so set on't as all this comes to." In the end, the family lives in a House/Barn, or a Barn/House, symbolically suggesting the peaceful coexistence of father's and mother's systems of values. Rather than merely inverting the opposition between "Barn" and "Home," Sarah creates a new linguistic realm where the values of *both* "Barn" and "Home" can be spoken.

Through a physical act of revolt, through actions that speak, and through revolutionary renaming, Sarah *merges* masculine and feminine value systems and gains the power to be a speaking subject. As if to indicate this truce, the landscape at the end of the story becomes peaceful and possibly utopian: "The twilight was deepening. There was a clear green glow in the sky. Before them stretched the smooth level of field; in the distance was a cluster of hay-stacks like the huts of a village; the air was very cool and calm and sweet. *The landscape might have been an ideal one of peace*" (468; my emphasis). This story, then, enacts a truce, a temporary act of communication that is successful, that invents a system of discourse that slips free from the binary system of sexual difference, of patriarchal or feminine theories of language, of speaking men or silent women, of barn versus home. Like Derrida, Freeman perhaps imagines a world beyond binary oppositions, a world that could approach "the area of a relationship to the other where the code of sexual marks would no longer be discriminating" (76). When the barn becomes the home, and the home the barn, when men and women *both* engage in discourse, Freeman suggests that the chance for peace — linguistically and sexually — might also exist. Perhaps.

Speaking the Silenced Feminine Keynote:
Cooper's *A Voice from the South*

Sarah's act of merging the home and the barn finally creates a radical new language that can be spoken by both men and women, yet initially she appears to be a domestic saint more intent on making her husband's favorite pies than on plotting a linguistic rebellion. In *A Voice from the South*, Anna Julia Cooper also strategically marshals the ideology of the cult of domesticity while simultaneously coopting many of its principles. Like Freeman, Cooper undermines patriarchal discourse through the assertion of a feminine and maternal voice. Unlike Freeman, however, Cooper employs a musical, heterogeneous speech that releases the plethora of repressed discourses trapped within the Law of the Father. Finally, she replaces patriarchal and racist discourses with a language belonging both to "the Mother" and "the Father," and to speakers of all races and classes.

In form and content, *A Voice from the South* straddles a number of rhetorical and thematic divisions, adding to its ability to create new forms of language. The work is both autobiographical and expository; in the eight essays that make up the text, Cooper draws heavily on personal experience, but her overall focus is an argument about the equality of all African American women supported through the rhetorical practices of deduction, logic, and classical argumentation. The text is both oral and written; many of the essays in the volume were originally delivered as speeches, yet their dense, allusive, at times ornate prose seems equally comfortable within the written format of an essay collection. The voice marshaled is communal and individualistic; Cooper articulates her identity as a representative individual ("A Black Woman of the South" on the frontispiece) and as a specific person ("Anna Julia Cooper" on the facing copyright page). The text therefore represents a diversity of voices, genres, and formats.

Thematically, this diversity is matched by a manipulation of the consideration of both race and gender as categories of analysis. The first four essays of the text focus mainly on issues of gender, while the next four (in the second part of the book) focus mainly on issues of race, but throughout the text Cooper considers the conjunction of race and gender that constitutes her identity in a patriarchal and racist society. For example, in an essay in the first half of her book, Cooper speaks of traveling by train in the South and reaching a rest stop where she sees bathrooms labeled "FOR LADIES" and "FOR COLORED PEOPLE" (96); she wonders "under which head I come" (96). Cooper never does tell us which door she enters, which serves to illustrate the text's refusal to be caught up in either/or choices: Cooper writes either of gender or race, either personally or impersonally, either as a representative individual or a specific persona. As Elizabeth Alexander argues, the essays in the text are "at once allegory, autobiography, history, oratory, poetry, and literary criticism, with traces of other forms of address" (337); they also "stand in a new space between the first-person confessional of the slave narrative or spiritual autobiography and the third-person imperative of political essays" (338). These essays interpellate the multiple dilemmas felt by racially marked and gendered bodies, by individuals who must find their voices within both patriarchal and racial discourses that would silence them.

The first half of the text does not ignore political issues concerning race and racism, then, but its primary focus is African American women's claiming of voice. One strategy Cooper employs to validate this voice and gain an audience is placing her analysis of women's speech within existing discourses of Anglo American womanhood. For example, she deliberately references works by Grant Allen (66), a novelist who wrote about the New Woman, and she touches on the New Woman's political goals, emphasizing unity between women of all races in the struggle for equal rights (121).[4] Cooper melds her interest in the literary and political agenda of the New Woman with a concern for the moral influence of the cult of domesticity. She argues, for example, that women can uplift a morally corrupt and materialistic world (131). Yet Cooper deploys this rhetoric to suggest not that women should stay in the home but that they can reform the public world: "[Woman] stands now at the gateway of this new era of American civilization. In her hands must be moulded the strength, the wit, the statesmanship, the morality, all the psychic force, the social and economic intercourse of that era" (143). Hazel Carby argues that Cooper did not believe women should be confined to the domestic sphere; Cooper develops "a sophisticated analysis of the power that women could exert as intellectuals" (*Reconstructing Womanhood* 99). Unlike earlier writers, Cooper marshals the rhetoric of the True Woman not to widen women's domestic sphere but to undermine it.

The numerous times Cooper references the rhetoric of the True Woman, however, indicate that she is explicating a relationship that is both external and internal, both disempowering and ambiguously empowering. She gains an audience by using this image, but she also interrogates her own relationship to this ideology that has defined her as subhuman, as not a woman. Mae Henderson contends that:

> What is at once characteristic and suggestive about black women's writing is its interlocutory, or dialogic, character, reflecting not only a relationship with the "others," but an internal dialogue with the plural aspects of self that constitute the matrix of black female subjectivity. The interlocutory character of black women's writing is, thus, not only a consequence of a dialogic relationship with an imaginary or generalized "Other," but a dialogue with the aspects of "otherness" within the self. (145–46)

Cooper is in dialogue with the way she is constructed as an "Other" by discourses of white womanhood (the cult of domesticity), but also with the way those discourses function within her own subjectivity as an "othering" force. Cooper must contend with the way discourses of race and gender "other" and silence her both internally and externally, and these discourses intersect in the cult of domesticity.

She calls upon the cult of domesticity, then, to engage both the dominant (or "hegemonic") order (discourses of male patriarchy that silence the feminine "other") and the ambiguously nondominant, or ambiguously "non-hegemonic," order (discourse of white femininity that silence the racial "other"). As Cooper says, the African American woman is confronted by "both a woman question and a race problem, and is as yet an unacknowledged factor in both" (134). With its repetition of the word "both" at each end, the sentence emphasizes that African American women are (at least) doubly interpellated by discourses of race and gender. To find voice, to become an "acknowledged factor" in systems of subjectivity, they must situate themselves within multiple matrixes of racially inflected and gendered discourses and speak not only against but also *through* these discourses. Mary Helen Washington finds Cooper "disappointing" because she is "never able to discard totally the ethics of true womanhood" (Introduction xlvi). But, as I have argued, Cooper employs this ideology to gain the sympathy of her audience, to deconstruct her representation as an "other," to interrogate the "otherness" she finds within her own consciousness, and to articulate her complex subjectivity within both racial and gendered discourses. Cooper's use of ideologies of femininity is strategic and subversive; she manipulates them not to endorse them but to interrogate and finally dismantle them.[5]

A main focus of Cooper's work is therefore a theoretical investigation of the silencing of African American women and of how they can break this erasure not to become True Women but empowered subjects with voices of their own.[6] She argues that although woman has been written about, the " 'other side' has not been represented by one who 'lives there' " (ii). This passage clearly connects woman's lack of voice with her oppression within patriarchal society; the African American woman is a silenced "other," viewed as an object, not a speaking subject. With no language of her own, the African American woman has been viewed as having "no God-given destiny, no soul with unquenchable longings and inexhaustible possibilities — no absolute and inherent value, no duty to self, transcending all pleasure-giving that may be demanded of a mere toy" (64). Woman has been viewed as a silent possession defined through her relationship with men; thus "her value was purely a relative one" (65). Gilman phrases this another way when she says that women have led a wholly relative existence as prepositions within language (*Man-Made World* 204), but the sentiment is the same: women provide the foundation for male subjectivity but are not seen as speaking subjects in their own right. Or as Irigaray puts it: "Any theory of the subject has already been appropriated by the 'masculine' " (*Speculum* 133). And the white, Cooper would emphasize.

However, Cooper's text articulates a movement out of such limited concepts of women's voice. In the past, women had clearcut spheres in "the kitchen and the nursery" (142), but in the present era they are breaking from this limited role: "The woman of to-day finds herself in the presence of responsibilities which ramify through the profoundest and most varied interest of her country and race.... All departments in the new era are to be hers" (142–43). It is precisely by moving into this larger sphere of action that woman finds subjectivity and voice: "Woman [is] stepping from the pedestal of statue-like inactivity in the domestic shrine, and *daring to think and move and speak*" (122, my emphasis). This passage corroborates that Cooper's real agenda lies not in the limited domestic sphere/speech of the

True Woman but in a New Woman's agenda of subjectivity, voice, and agency. In stepping from the pedestal of the "domestic-shrine," African American women find subjectivity and a voice that breaks from patriarchal repression.

What will this voice sound like? Cooper is sure that it will not be the same as the voice of African American men, that only the African American woman can speak for herself (iii, 31). According to Cooper, "*the world needs to hear her* [the African American woman's] *voice*" (121). This voice may be "muffled" (i) and "broken" (iii), perhaps, but it is also not the voice of a woman speaking like a man (54), not a tongue that "parrot[s] over the cold conceits that some man has taught her" (55). Instead it will be a voice "musical with the vibrations of human suffering" (55). In using these musical metaphors, Cooper articulates a new theory of women's language, allying women's voice not with the cold, logical, linear, trajectories of written, patriarchal discourse but with an oral (or perhaps aural) speech that is more heterogeneous, more discontinuous, but also more sympathetic. Like Freeman (and later Chopin in *The Awakening*), Cooper acknowledges that when women "parrot" male speech — masculine models of language — they are silent as women. African American women must find an alternative form of speech that articulates the complexity of their identities.

As I argue later, in *Herland* Gilman also posits that a musical, feminine speech is better suited to an articulation of a feminine identity than patriarchal discourse. But Gilman situates this musical speech in a utopian text, whereas Cooper's text locates this speech within existing discursive structures. The first part of Cooper's book (which focuses on women's voice) is titled "*Soprano Obligato*," the overriding voice; this section asserts the presence of an African American, feminine, soprano voice that overrides patriarchal and racist discourses of oppression.[7] The second part of *A Voice from the South* (which focuses on racial relations in America) is called "*Tutti Ad Libitum*." This is a section of a libretto where all the voices come in together more freely than in the first section, and this part of Cooper's text focuses on the recovery of a multitude of discourses. The structure of Cooper's overall assessment of the role of heterogeneous discourses is thus twofold: first, an African American woman's voice is marshaled to override and overturn patriarchal discourse, but then all the other marginalized voices within society can come in together, with more freedom and equality. Overturning patriarchal discourse through a feminine voice finally leads to a diversity of voices that commingle freely within the discursive matrixes of society.

Cooper's use of this musical metaphor therefore creates what Mikhail Bakhtin has called heteroglossia. According to Bakhtin, a text is heteroglossalic when it permits "a multiplicity of social voices and a wide variety of their links and interrelationships" (263) to exist in tension and in accordance with each other (or "dialogically"). In a discussion of heteroglossia in African American women's writing, however, Mae Henderson argues that it must be composed of at least two elements: a kind of "babble" or "speaking in tongues" which she links to the semiotic, pre-symbolic world of mother and child and the "diversity of voices, discourses, and languages described by Mikhail Bakhtin" as heteroglossia (Henderson 149–50). In Cooper's text, the first element of this speaking in tongues — glossolalia — is represented by the *Soprano Obligato,* the feminine voice that overrides dominant discourses through the language of play, of the aural/oral, of music, of the semiotic chora. The second element of this speaking in tongues — heteroglossia — is embodied by the phrase *Tutti Ad Libitum,* which is meant to symbolize a textual space where all voices — male and female, white and black — are brought together freely. In the text as a whole a diversity of discourses or tongues are permitted to exist dialogically.

Although not radical from a stylistic point of view, then, the text provides an illustration of the commingling of diverse (or heteroglossialic) languages. The text also uses heteroglossia to work toward a release of the many voices that dominant discourses repress. For example, the preface begins with a passage that calls upon numerous discursive systems, and it is worth quoting at length to demonstrate the way these systems intersect and interact:

> In the clash and clatter of our American Conflict, it has been said that the South remains Silent. Like the Sphinx she inspires vociferous disputation, but herself takes little part in the noisy controversy. One muffled strain in the Silent South, a jarring chord and a vague and uncomprehended cadenza has been and still is the Negro. And of the muffled chord, the one mute and voiceless note has been the sadly expectant Black Woman,
>
> An infant crying in the night,
> An infant crying for the light;
> And with *no language — but a cry.*
>
> The colored man's inheritance and apportionment is still the sombre crux, the perplexing *cul de sac* of the nation, — the dumb skeleton in the closet provoking ceaseless harangues, indeed, but little understood and seldom consulted. Attorneys for the plaintiff and attorneys for the defendant, with bungling *gaucherie* have analyzed and dissected, theorized and synthesized with sublime ignorance or pathetic misapprehension of counsel from the black client. One important witness has not yet been heard from. The summing up of the evidence deposed, and the charge to the jury have been made — but no word from the Black Woman. (i–ii)

This passage begins and ends with a focus on the silencing of the African American woman, the "one mute and voiceless note," the "witness [who] has not yet been heard from." But as Cooper articulates this passage using a "Voice by a Black Woman of the South" (iii), other discourses within culture are released and allowed to commingle. For in addition to calling upon an African American women's voice that will be distinct from that of "the dark man" (iii), the passage also utilizes multiple language systems (French and English, for example) and diverse types of discourse: political ("our American Conflict"), literary ("And with *no language—but a cry*"), legal ("one important witness"), metaphoric ("the dumb skeleton in the closet provoking ceaseless harangues"), and classical ("the Sphinx"). These discourses commingle in a structure of dialogic equality. Yet threaded throughout the passage is a foreshadowing of the text's dominant musical metaphor—a metaphor in which the black woman's "note" is most able to "sensibly realize and accurately tell the weight and fret of the 'long dull pain' . . . [of the] voiceless Black Woman of America" (ii). When this keynote is sounded, it leads to the release of numerous other voices. Cooper initiates heteroglossia in this allusive, intertextual, multivoiced opening passage, and she brings it to fruition through the text as a whole.

This release of heteroglossialic voices is paramount for Cooper because society has been dominated by oppressive systems of patriarchal language and logic. Cooper argues that since the fifth century, "the civilized world has been like a child brought up by his father" (51). The results of this subjugation to the father have been deadly: "the self-congratulation of 'dominant' races, as if 'dominant' meant 'righteous' and carried with it a title to inherit the earth. . . . The scorn for so-called weak or unwarlike races and individuals, and the very comfortable assurance that it is their manifest destiny to be wiped out as vermin before this advancing civilization" (51). Cooper allies patriarchal domination, the reign of the father, with brutality, colonization, and oppression of "weak" races by the "strong." This is a reign of the father, but also of the Father: a phallic law that sees everything not masculine and white as weak, feminine, and Other. According to Judith Butler, male dominance is established socially and linguistically through a repression of both female and racial "others." Therefore symbolic language is "not merely organized by 'phallic power,' but by a 'phallicism' that is centrally sustained by racial anxiety" (*Bodies that Matter* 184). Cooper's work articulates a complex analysis of the interrelatedness of oppressive discourses of race and gender, of the way phallicism sustains itself through the interlinked subjugation of racial and sexual difference.

It is certainly true, as Carby argues, that Cooper's agenda was never confined to women's issues because she saw the dominance of the strong over the weak as the most crucial problem (" 'On the Threshold' "). But in the first half of *A Voice from the South*, although Cooper is aware of how phallicism suppresses racial "difference," she is most interested in how it suppresses feminine "difference." According to Cooper, under the Law of the Father, warriors rule based on strength, power, and patrilineal rights, and everyone else is silenced: "Our God is power; strength, our standard of excellence, inherited from barbarian ancestors through a long line of male progenitors, the Law Salic permitting no feminine modifications" (53). Cooper's reference to the "Law Salic" (with both words capitalized) may be a pun on the notion of the "Law Phallic" — the phallocentric Law of the Father. Cooper understands that women's voices are silenced under patriarchal systems of law and language, of male progenitors, of Salic Laws that literally exclude women from inheriting property and thrones of rulership but more symbolically imply that within a patriarchal society, maleness is a prerequisite for empowerment, for subjectivity and voice itself.[8] Cooper argues that this Phallic/Salic Law of the Father leads to the silencing of the "feminine" (the law permits "of no feminine modification"). Furthermore, she demonstrates that in this system women are identified with the real, with the literal, with what stands just outside of language. Women are seen as "constantly and inevitably . . . giving out our real selves into our several little worlds" yet their words are only heard as "feeble declamation[s]" (55). The symbolic order of law and language depends on the identification of women with the literal, a position where her "real self" is felt but her words go unheard.

Like the British writers discussed in Homans's *Bearing the Word*, Cooper here alludes to a drama of subjectivity in which "the death or absence of the mother sorrowfully but fortunately makes possible the construction of language and of culture" (Homans 2). But Cooper also subverts this drama by advocating a replacement of the Law of the Father with precisely the absent voice of the mother. According to Cooper, the world needs "the great mother heart to teach it to be pitiful, to love mercy, to succor the weak and care for the lowly" (51). The world must be brought into the reign of the mother, into the "great mother heart." Once mother's voices have been heard, once the "feminine half of the world's truth is completed," the world will no longer "find the law of love shut out from the affairs of men" (58). Indeed, Cooper sees this feminine law of love as the foundation of the twentieth century: "In the era about to dawn, [woman's] sentiments must strike the keynote and give the dominant tone" (132). Just as in "The Revolt of 'Mother'" Sarah's assertion of feminine voice silenced Adoniram's overbearing one, Cooper marshals a voice of the mother to curtail and even dominate patriarchal discourse. She also indicates an awareness that "the symbolic order is founded, not merely on the regrettable loss of the mother, but rather on her active and overt murder" (Homans 11), and she revivifies a feminine voice, a voice of the mother, to counteract this murder. Thus while earlier writers use a discourse of motherhood to sanitize the ambitions of women writers, to safely reinscribe these ambitions, Cooper uses this discourse to revise dominant cultural myths that present the voice of the mother as being outside of language. She brings the feminine voice into the realm of the symbolic to overturn the reign of patriarchal discourse and phallic oppression.

Thus Cooper begins with a system of sexually marked voices in which men and women play complementary but different roles, where there is both "a feminine as well as a masculine side to truth" that are "complements in one necessary and symmetric whole" (Cooper 60). This system is also essentialistic: "While we not infrequently see women who reason, we say, with the coolness and precision of a man, and men as considerate of helplessness as a woman, still there is a general consensus of mankind that the one trait is essentially masculine and the other is peculiarly feminine. That both are needed to be worked into the training of children, in order that our boys may supplement their virility by tenderness and sensibility, and our girls may round out their gentleness by strength and self-reliance" (60–61). This system of logic privileges one side of the equation: the feminine, which is to be the dominant note, the "keynote," of the new era.[9] After criticizing domination, Cooper herself seems to engage in it. As Karen Baker-Fletcher notes, using this "language of 'dominant tone' to describe the potential compassion in women's leadership is problematic in moving away from systems of domination" (125). Furthermore, Cooper's system seems merely to invert the structures of patriarchal culture so that the feminine voice, rather than the masculine one, is privileged.

Yet the ultimate function of this system that privileges the feminine "keynote" is to move beyond the binary. The keynote rises above patriarchal language and overturns it, releasing the multiple discourses it sutures over: *Tutti Ad Libitum*. Cooper uses a visual metaphor to make this point. Under patriarchy, the world has seen only half of the picture, the masculine half (a point Gilman will also emphasize). Because of this, the world has to "limp along with the wobbling gait and one-sided hesitancy of a man with one eye" (122). But suddenly, when woman's voice is heard, "the bandage is removed from the other eye and the whole body is filled with light. . . . The darkened eye restored, every member rejoices with it" (122–23). When the darkened eye is restored, when women speak, a plethora of voices are released, uplifted, as every member of the "body politic" rejoices. Kevin Gaines argues that gender "[does] not play a major role in Cooper's scenario for the resolution of racial and social conflict" (145), yet it is precisely the release of a gendered voice (an African American woman's voice) that enables the freedom of all other voices within the discursive system Cooper constructs.

Furthermore, Cooper also allies a racial, feminine voice with both linguistic and social emancipation. She argues that woman's lesson is only taught when "not the white woman nor the black woman nor the red woman, but the cause of every man and woman who has writhed silently under a mighty wrong" (125) has been enunciated. Woman's voice replaces patriarchal discourse with an egalitarian voice that moves across lines of race and gender: "It is not the intelligent woman vs. the ignorant woman, nor the white woman vs. the black, the brown, and the red,— it is not even the cause of woman vs. man. Nay, 'tis woman's strongest vindication for speaking that *the world needs to hear her voice*" (121). Cooper aligns women's voice not with a particular cause, race, or gender but rather with all voices that have gone unheard. She situates her theory of language within the struggles of feminist reformers to articulate women's voice but also within the larger struggle of speaking what has been silenced: "Hers is every interest that has lacked an interpreter and a defender. Her cause is linked with that of every agony that has been dumb—every wrong that needs a voice" (122). The "feminine voice," then, is not restricted to a feminine cause but becomes the instrument for an opening up of all that has been silenced, repressed, erased within patriarchal society and discourse.

The "feminine voice" finally becomes a language not of difference but of commonality. In her discussion of African American women's voice, Henderson argues that using a Bakhtinian model is only partially successful, since this model functions adversarially, through an assumption that verbal communication is primarily characterized by contestation with other(s). She suggests that this model needs to be combined with Hans-Georg Gadamer's model of conversation, which presupposes as its goal a language of "consensus, communality, and even identification" (147). Henderson does not discuss Cooper, but the above passage clearly elucidates Cooper's movement toward a language of consensus, a language of identification in which one claims to be able to understand and express the concerns of the "Other," who is not actually an other but more simply another. Particularly in the second half of her book, Cooper extends her argument for an egalitarian discourse, arguing that social harmony can only be achieved by moving beyond binaries and hierarchies to an area where racial and sexual differences no longer lead to subjugation. In a chapter titled "Has America a Race Problem?" Cooper states that "*equilibrium, not repression among conflicting forces is the condition of natural harmony, of permanent progress, and of universal freedom*" (160). An environment that contains equilibrium, social and verbal balance, will create a society committed to equality. It is this equilibrium that Cooper's work as a whole moves toward, extending freedom to men and women, the wealthy and the poor, African Americans, Anglo Americans, and all other races.

Finally, language is Cooper's primary mechanism for achieving equilibrium. Appropriating language is the foundation of freedom, of subjectivity, of agency, of power. As Bakhtin says, language "becomes 'one's own' only when the speaker... appropriates the word, adapting it to his [or her] own semantic and expressive intentions" (293). But Cooper takes this idea further, insisting that appropriating the word need not lead to domination of an "other" but to the commingling of diverse languages. She argues that the world is moving toward an era "in which every agony has a voice and free speech" (166), in which women are not beaten "because [they] can speak," the laboring man is not starved and ground to powder "because [he] can make himself heard" (167), and "races that are weakest can... make themselves felt" (167). Once patriarchal discourse has been unhinged through an assertion of a musical, dialogic feminine voice, the plethora of voices trapped within dominant discourses will be released, and individuals of all classes, races, and genders will speak. In *A Voice from the South* Cooper finds and releases the keynote, the muted, muffled voice of the African American woman, so that all the other voices can join in, but more freely.

This chapter has argued that Freeman's and Cooper's works contain a common strategy for liberating women from patriarchal theories of language and identity that gender language as masculine. Both writers marshall a voice of the Mother to undermine the Law of the Father; they then attempt to move beyond this feminine voice into a realm where language is not restricted to one gender, or for Cooper, to one race or class. Are they successful in this movement, or does their employment of a feminine voice irrevocably undermine that attempt to move beyond the binary? Although I find both Cooper's and Freeman's writing to be persuasive and inspirational, I admit to being troubled by their use of binarism and essentialism. On the other hand, their manipulation of the possibility of a feminine voice does free them in certain ways from earlier writers, creating a more experimental methodology for the revising of dominant theories of "women's voice." The use of a voice of the Mother, then, is fraught with dangers, dangers these writers themselves seem aware of ("the landscape *might* have been an ideal one of peace"). Yet this feminine voice actually creates the possibility of an unruly presence within language that first inverts, but finally seeks to overturn, not just men's speaking but the entire foundation of patriarchal oppression.

The Search for a Feminine Voice
in the Works of Kate Chopin

When Kate Chopin's novel *The Awakening* was published in 1899, it was condemned as vulgar, morbid, and unwholesome. The book was allegedly banned
from some libraries, and Chopin was ousted from social clubs. She eventually lost
the contract for her next collection of fiction, *A Vocation and a Voice,* and it was
not published until almost a hundred years later. About the whole furor, Chopin
commented ironically: "I never dreamt of Mrs. Pontellier making such a mess of
things and working out her own damnation as she did. If I had had the slightest
intimation of such a thing I would have excluded her from the company. But when
I found out what she was up to, the play was half over and it was then too late"
("Aims and Autographs" 612). Despite the flippancy of these remarks, according
to Per Seyersted the scandal "hurt her to the core of her being" ("Kate Chopin's
Wound" 73). After publication of *The Awakening* Chopin faded almost into
oblivion; as Seyersted explains: "At her death in 1904 she was nearly forgotten, and a
book published in 1905 on Southern Writers does not even include her name" ("Kate
Chopin" 153).

Why did *The Awakening* present such a radical challenge to Chopin's society?
Neither Freeman nor Cooper were rejected when, like Chopin, they demonstrated
that women's language has the potential to unhinge patriarchal discourse. Unlike
Freeman and Cooper, however, Chopin suggests that feminine desire is an aspect
of women's search for voice; Edna Pontellier drowns herself partially because
she can find no one who understands the new sexual and social identity she is attempting to articulate. Like the New Women described in chapter 1, Edna connects

an unruly feminine language of self-assertion to the enunciation of a self-defined desire. That Chopin's text speaks this new sexual and social identity made it shocking and also connects her to later writers like Cather and Fauset, who too insist that feminine desire plays a crucial role in women's struggles for identity, voice, and art.

The protagonist of *The Awakening* understands that the cult of domesticity offers her no viable mechanism for a self-defined subjectivity or voice, and she reaches beyond it toward a new theory of language and identity. But Edna seeks a feminine, maternal language that is represented as existing outside of patriarchy; therefore she never finds a voice that functions in the everyday world she inhabits. In her short fiction, however, Chopin mediates the conflict between feminine discourse and patriarchal language through assertion of a covert voice that attempts to undermine patriarchal discourse through mimicry and through hollowing out patriarchy from within its own structures. Thus while some of Chopin's characters still seek a purely "feminine" voice beyond patriarchal discourse, others have found a metalinguistic one that traverses and deconstructs patriarchal language, a voice that can be heard through the widening cracks of hegemonic discourse. This metalinguistic voice is, finally, one that Chopin (unlike mid-nineteenth-century writers) refuses to silence, repress, or erase.

In 1896, Kate Chopin wrote a short poem that was first titled "To a Lady at the Piano — Mrs. R - - n." It goes as follows:

> I do not know you out upon the street
> Where people meet.
> We talk as women talk; shall I confess?
> I know you less.
> I hear you play, and touched by the wondrous spell —
> I know you well —
> (731)

This poem implies that the commercial spheres of a patriarchal world ("the street") inscribe women within constricting roles, roles that mean that they cannot know each other well. Moreover, when women talk in a conventional, patriarchal mode ("we talk as women talk"), their conversation only means they "know" each other "less." Yet music creates a nonpatriarchal language that allows them to move beyond cultural and linguistic inscriptions: "I hear you play, and touched by the wondrous spell / I know you well."

Throughout *The Awakening*, the protagonist searches for a realm like that created in this poem by women's music — one beyond patriarchal stereotypes of femininity, beyond the realm of the symbolic (the established order of patriarchal language and culture). Edna attempts to undo her inscription within patriarchal language by returning to a maternal, pre-symbolic discourse. In the voice of the sea, in

Mademoiselle Reisz's piano playing, and in her own art, Edna seeks what Julia Kristeva has called a poetic or semiotic language. The poetic language that Edna seeks is disruptive, but because it is figured as existing outside of culture, its subversive quality cannot be maintained. *The Awakening* thus dramatizes, but finally rejects, the dream of a maternal, feminine, poetic discourse that is not already inscribed within hegemonic language.[1]

Edna's search for a semiotic voice and the text's final rejection of this concept have not received extended critical analysis. Of course, in the last fifteen years, the protagonist's struggle for language has been a central topic. In a linguistic analysis of the text, for instance, Paula Treichler states that "*The Awakening* charts Edna Pontellier's growing mastery of the first person singular, and . . . when 'I' has been created, the book has successfully completed its mission and comes to an end" (239–40). Using a Bakhtinian approach, Dale Bauer argues that Edna struggles "to make her internally persuasive voice—her impulses and desires—heard against the overpowering authoritative voices of her culture, her religion, her husband's Creole ideology" (141). Patricia Yaeger reads Edna's struggle for voice through a variety of poststructuralist lenses, but is less certain her resistance is successful: "Edna Pontellier has no language to help her integrate and interrogate the diversity of her feelings; she experiences neither world nor signifying system capacious enough to accommodate her desires" (219). Yet while Yaeger, as well as Mylène Dresser and Deborah Barker, employ psychoanalytical concepts, none of these critics apply Kristeva's concept of the semiotic to Edna's search for voice.[2] Using Kristeva's concept of the semiotic, as well as Judith Butler's critique of this concept, clarifies not only what Edna seeks in language and where she situates her moments of voice but, most important, why her search is finally unsuccessful.

Although the novel primarily investigates the theoretical basis of Edna's linguistic oppression, Chopin does not divorce this subject from a historical context. As Frances Harper will do, Chopin situates her character on the cusp between two historical stereotypes of femininity. The novel begins in 1892, when the controversy over the New Woman had not yet exploded in the *North American Review*, or in novels by Sarah Grand, Grant Allen, and George Egerton.[3] Edna is caught precisely at the moment when the True Woman had become outmoded but the new image had not yet reached popular consciousness. As Edna admits to Arobin: "One of these days . . . I'm going to pull myself together for a while and think— try to determine what character of a woman I am; for candidly, I don't know. By all the codes which I am acquainted with, I am a devilishly wicked specimen of the sex. But some way I can't convince myself that I am" (966). The codes surrounding Edna construct her as "wicked," but she finds no alternative "code" that can help her understand who she is. Harper's characters uses a liminal space between the True Woman and the New Woman to remake these ideologies, but for Edna this liminal space is less empowering.

Clearly, Edna is not a domestic saint, as the text explains: "In short, Mrs. Pontellier was not a mother-woman" (888). Edna is willing to give up her physical self for her children, but not her identity, as she says: "I would give up the unessential; I would give my money, I would give my life for my children; but I wouldn't give myself" (929). This statement shows how far Edna has come from the model of selfless domesticity embodied by characters such Fern's Ruth Hall or even Alcott's Jo March. Edna realizes that she has a self separate from others and desires she will not relinquish for others. Yet when Edna kills herself, it becomes apparent that she has not entirely forsaken her orientation to domesticity. As she walks on the beach before her suicidal swim, she repeats to herself, over and over: "To-day it is Arobin; to-morrow it will be some one else. It makes no difference to me, it doesn't matter about Léonce Pontellier — but Raoul and Etienne!" (999). Edna feels responsible for her children, and this is one of the reasons she kills herself. Of course, in the act of killing herself, Edna does try to preserve the essential part of her personality that will not be subservient to others. Edna is striving, as Chopin explains, to "becom[e] herself and . . . cast aside the fictitious self which we assume like a garment with which to appear before the world" (939). But her success in "becoming herself" is only partial, for she can formulate no concept of identity that allows her to move beyond the codes of her time period, codes that construct her as "wicked."

To dramatize Edna's incomplete process of casting aside her fictitious self and finding a new identity, Chopin uses ambivalent symbolism. At novel's end Edna stands naked before the ocean, "like some new-born creature, opening its eyes in a familiar world that it had never known" (1000). This imagery suggests a rebirth of self for Edna that is "strange and awful" but also "delicious" (1000). Yet this positive language is contradicted by the novel's last few lines: "She heard her father's voice and her sister Margaret's. . . . The spurs of the cavalry officer clanged as he walked across the porch. There was the hum of bees, and the musky odor of pinks filled the air" (1000). Edna's father, the spurs of the calvary officer, and Edna's harsh sister Margaret are all reminders of patriarchal forces that have entrapped Edna throughout her life. Furthermore, the hum of bees and the smell of flowers suggest the forces that would drag Edna down, into the soul's slavery: her children and her sensuality. The imagery suggests rebirth into a new world but also that even in death, Edna has not formulated an identity that escapes the old world of patriarchal inscription.[4]

Therefore, although Edna reaches beyond the selflessness of the domestic saint, she never quite replaces the "fictitious self" she has been wearing. At stake here for Chopin, also, is Edna's inability to find a voice that articulates her new identity. For Chopin, self-possession and self-expression are crucially interlinked. Edna never formulates a theory of voice viable in the world she inhabits; therefore her sense of self is constantly being eroded by the languages of the world around her. Furthermore, Chopin is critical of Edna's new theory of language because it locates the subversive potential of the "feminine" voice outside Edna's society. Finally, Edna speaks "a language which nobody understood"—a language that has no community of listeners.

The novel is structured around a gestation and birth (it begins in June, when Adèle Ratignolle is just beginning to feel her "condition," and ends nine months later, when she gives birth). Here form and content mesh, since the novel is centrally concerned with Edna's attempt to birth herself into an alternative, feminine, maternal discourse. As Chopin explains at the novel's start, Edna is attempting to create herself anew: "But the beginning of things, of a world especially, is necessarily vague, tangled, chaotic, and exceedingly disturbing. How few of us ever emerge from such beginning! How many souls perish in its tumult!" (893). Language is central to Edna's struggle for subjectivity, as the next few sentences of this passage demonstrate:

> The voice of the sea is seductive; never ceasing, whispering, clamoring, murmuring, inviting the soul to wander for a spell in abysses of solitude; to lose itself in mazes of inward contemplation.
>
> The voice of the sea speaks to the soul. The touch of the sea is sensuous, enfolding the body in its soft, close embrace. (893)

The ocean represents a maternal realm of language as it might exist in the pre-symbolic, libidinal world of the mother and child. Chopin's novel returns to the earliest stages of women's inscription within language, asking whether there is some other process of being birthed into language than the oedipal one, some way of achieving subjectivity and voice that does not involve total submission to the Law of the Father, total silencing of the unruly feminine self and the unruly feminine tongue. As Yaeger states, the voice of the sea frames and articulates "Edna's incessant need for some other register of language, for a mode of speech that will express her unspoken, but not unspeakable needs" (219). In the ocean, Edna seeks a maternal voice that avoids the repression of patriarchal language, its erasure of feminine identity and desire.

Such a voice is needed because of the way language functions in a patriarchal world, and in the realm of the symbolic. According to Lacanian theory, an individual enters the symbolic by repressing primary libidinal impulses (including the dependency of the child on the maternal body) and adopting a language structured by the Law of the Father. For women, there are several problems with adopting this language. First, symbolic language suppresses multiple meanings—which recall the libidinal multiplicity of the pre-symbolic realm—installing unambiguous and discrete meanings in their place (Butler, *Gender Trouble* 79). So entering the symbolic entails giving up the body of the mother as well as the multiplicity of discourse and identity that might be associated with this pre-symbolic realm. As Kristeva states: "Language as Symbolic function constitutes itself at the cost of repressing instinctual drive and continuous relation to the mother" (*Desire in Language* 136). Second, this process actually reserves the "I" position for men: "Women, by gender lacking the phallus, the positive symbol of gender, self-possession, and worldly authority around which language is organized, occupy a negative position in language" (Jones 83). Inscription into symbolic language is thus extremely problematic for women; as Ann Rosalind Jones explains, "in a psycholinguistic world structured by father-son resemblance and rivalry and by the primacy of masculine logic, woman is a gap or a silence, the invisible and unheard sex" (83). The acquisition of symbolic language, then, suppresses women's relationship to the maternal, solidifies identity and discourse, and forces women to occupy a negative position in language.

Chopin depicts this becoming "the invisible and unheard sex" — a sex without desire and language — through her characterization of Edna. Rather than being seen as a subject in her own right, Edna is seen as a possession to be traded back and forth between men. Edna's husband views her as an "object" (885) or a "valuable piece of personal property" (884), and she is also called the invention (971) of her father. Edna is also the object of male discourse; she is most often spoken to and of, rather than speaking herself. When Mr. Pontellier reproaches Edna for her "neglect" of the children, for example, he talks in "a monotonous, insistent way" (885), while Edna is silent: "She said nothing, and refused to answer her husband when he questioned her" (885–86). Edna's silence, here, is that of one who does not possess words: "She could not have told why she was crying. . . . An indescribable oppression, which seemed to generate in some unfamiliar part of her consciousness, filled her whole being with a vague anguish" (886). At this stage in the novel, Edna obeys her husband mechanically and silently, and this demonstrates her inscription within symbolic language, within a discourse that renders her voiceless and powerless. This inscription within the symbolic also involves a suppression of Edna's instincts and drives, a suppression that leaves her without any passion: "Edna found herself face to face with the realities. She grew fond of her husband, realizing with some unaccountable satisfaction that no trace of passion or excessive and fictitious warmth colored her affection" (898). Dr. Mandelet knows Edna as a repressed, "listless woman," and he is surprised later in the novel to see her transformed into a being "palpitant with the forces of life" (952). In the early stages of the book, then, Edna is inscribed within a symbolic language that renders her silent, passive, and passionless.

Yet the voice of the sea continually hovering in the background of these early scenes suggests there must be something more: "the everlasting voice of the sea . . . broke like a mournful lullaby upon the night" (886). The ocean (*mer*)/mother (*mère*) sings a crooning cradle song to Edna that suggests another relationship to language. As argued in the discussion of Alcott's "A Whisper in the Dark," Kristeva posits that the poetic or semiotic dimension of language is never completely destroyed by inscription into the symbolic. The semiotic therefore has the potential to disrupt patriarchal discourse. In Chopin's text, the ocean represents this semiotic, disruptive potential of language, a recovery of the maternal body that Edna believes will allow her to dislodge her inscription within patriarchal discourse.

Edna also seeks other physical and intellectual realms that might allow the recovery of a maternal, poetic voice. Chopin uses the image of the meadow in Kentucky, for example, to suggest that Edna was not always inscribed within the symbolic, within the Law of the Father. Edna recalls that as a young girl, she had a sense of limitless possibilities while traversing this meadow: "I was just walking diagonally across a big field . . . I could see only the stretch of green before me, and I felt as if I must walk on forever without coming to the end of it. I don't remember whether I was frightened or pleased. I must have been entertained" (896). This meadow represents a pre-symbolic realm in which Edna experiences a sense of freedom, instinctual drives, openness, and passion. When asked why she was traversing the meadow, Edna comments that "Likely as not it was Sunday . . . and I was running away from prayers, from the Presbyterian service, read in a spirit of gloom by my father that chills me yet to think of " (896). Edna is running away from the Law of the Father, from the father's harsh and repressive voice, a voice that still has the power to chill her. At this early phase in her life, Edna can still escape to the realm of the meadow, to the realm of impulses and drives: "I was a little unthinking child in those days, just following a misleading impulse without question" (896). This phase of Edna's life is also characterized by passion, by desire: "At a very early age — perhaps it was when she traversed the ocean of waving grass — she remembered that she had been passionately enamored of a dignified and sad-eyed cavalry officer who visited her father in Kentucky" (897). Edna had impulses, drives, passions that had not yet been repressed by the Law of the Father, and these impulses and passions are captured by the image of the meadow.

At Grand Isle, Edna once again feels as if she is in this pre-symbolic world of the mother: "sometimes I feel this summer as if I was walking through the green meadow again; idly, aimlessly, unthinking and unguided" (897). Edna also feels "flushed and intoxicated with the sound of her own voice and the unaccustomed taste of candor. It muddled her like wine, or like a first breath of freedom" (899). Grand Isle functions as a retrieval of the maternal realm, and a retrieval of a subversive maternal voice that exists before patriarchal discourse has repressed the semiotic, poetic dimension of language. The resort area is dominated by mother figures like Adèle Ratignolle, Madame LeBrun, and the storyteller Madame Antoine; it is a place where men come to stay for the weekend but are, at best, visitors, interlopers, not part of the central social structure of mothers and their children. The men permitted to function in this realm — such as Victor and Robert LeBrun — do so by becoming attached to some maternal woman (Robert) or by remaining in a perpetual state of childhood (Victor).

Perhaps this is why Edna and Robert can talk freely at Grand Isle: while there Robert seems to have not yet completely internalized the Law of the Father or taken his place within the patriarchal world. Mr. Pontellier commands his wife or is bored by her "nonsense" (882), but Robert participates with Edna in conversation: "They chatted incessantly: about the things around them; their amusing adventure out in the water . . . about the wind, the trees, the people who had gone to the *Chênière*" (884). Robert and Edna are on terms of discursive equality, and this certainly has something to do with Robert's placement within a maternal sphere. In fact, Robert rejects the patriarchal realm of the Father in favor of this maternal space and discourse. When Mr. Pontellier tries to convince Robert to go to Klein's — a club for men — Robert admits "quite frankly that he preferred to stay where he was and talk to Mrs. Pontellier" (882). For Edna (and possibly for Robert, too) Grand Isle figures as a maternal space that recalls a time when the social and sexual divisions of patriarchal discourse, of the Law of the Father, had not yet been introduced.

Chopin's novel investigates whether there is a way of entering language that allows this maternal world not to be entirely erased. Specifically, Chopin's text explores whether a maternal, semiotic dimension of language can be preserved through women's art — whether art can become a poetic language that disrupts symbolic language. Edna's awakening begins the night she first responds to Mademoiselle Reisz's playing: "The very first chords which Mademoiselle Reisz struck upon the piano sent a keen tremor down Mrs. Pontellier's spinal column. . . . [T]he very passions themselves were aroused within her soul, swaying it, lashing it, as the waves daily beat upon her splendid body. She trembled, she was choking, and the tears blinded her" (906). This passage suggests a kinship between Mademoiselle Reisz's music and the ocean: both are characterized by libidinal passions, instincts, and drives characteristic of the pre-symbolic realm. Chopin's description of Edna's response to this music is certainly sexual, and we might be tempted to read this passage as an awakening to what Lacan might call *jouissance* (if he accepted that women have a knowable *jouissance*). And later that evening, when Edna first swims in the ocean (under the maternal moon), she seems to be "reaching out for the unlimited in which to lose herself" (908) — to be experiencing a loss of self that we might associate with a sexual awakening, with a "little death." But what Edna awakens to through Mademoiselle Reisz's playing is not a specific sexual desire, directed to or at someone or something, but rather an understanding of how much of her desire has been repressed by her inscription into symbolic language. The music allows Edna to immerse herself in the realm of the maternal and to begin the recovery of the multiplicity of desire and discourse her inscription within symbolic language repressed. And this immersion enables her to find a subversive voice that disrupts patriarchal discourse through a reinstating of feminine desire, feminine wants. Later that evening when Léonce commands Edna to come inside, she responds: "Léonce, go to bed. . . . I mean to stay out here. I don't wish to go in, and I don't intend to. Don't speak to me like that again; I shall not answer you" (912). In the past, when her husband commanded she submitted, but now her "will had blazed up, stubborn and resistant" (912). Edna combats her husband's verbal harassment with a voice that calls upon her own desires: "I don't wish to go in, and I don't intend to." Mademoiselle Reisz's music awakens "strange, new voices" in Edna (946), voices that Edna uses to combat the silencing and erasures of symbolic language.[5]

Of course, Léonce is adept at coopting such resistance, and when Edna refuses to go in, he simply sits outside with her until she gives up. Edna feels "like one who awakens gradually out of a dream, a delicious, grotesque, impossible dream, to feel again the realities pressing upon her soul" (912). She awakens from her dream of a maternal language of desire that subverts patriarchal discourse and finds herself caught in the everyday world. Edna returns to the domestic discourse that she had used earlier in the novel, a discourse that focuses solely on others, asking her husband, "Are you coming in, Léonce?" (913). Certainly, the novel charts the growth of Edna's voice and her self-defined subjectivity and sexuality. By the end of the novel, Edna claims that she has gotten into the extremely "unwomanly" (990) habit of expressing herself and that she has resolved never again to belong to anyone (963). But as the above scene with Léonce demonstrates, Edna's voice continually falters. In the novel's penultimate chapter, when Dr. Mandelet asks whether Edna plans to go abroad with her husband, she cannot respond clearly: "Perhaps — no, I am not going. I'm not going to be forced into doing things. I don't want to go abroad. I want to be let alone. Nobody has any right — except children, perhaps — and even then, it seems to me — or it did seem — " (995). She finds herself "voicing the incoherence of her thoughts" (995), and she says: "Oh! I don't know what I'm saying" (996). By the end of the novel, Edna's voice of resistance has been eroded, and even her sense of subjectivity seems to be under attack.

Edna also seeks voice in her painting, only to have this voice undermined. Noting that "there are no words to describe [Adèle] save the old ones that have served so often to picture the bygone heroine of romance and the fair lady of our dreams" (888), Edna tries to capture her friend. Yet while old, patriarchal words do not capture Adèle, Edna is no more successful at portraying her on canvass: "The picture completed bore no resemblance to Madame Ratignolle. [Edna] was greatly disappointed" (891). Later in the novel, Edna comments to her friend: "Perhaps I shall be able to paint your picture some day" (937), but that day never arrives. Edna's art frequently focuses on women and is frequently sensual. It is possible that in her art Edna seeks a language unlike the "old" words of symbolic language, one that articulates, rather than erases, feminine desire. However, although Edna's teacher says her work grows "in force and individuality" (963), Edna herself remains dissatisfied with her painting and claims that she is not an artist (939). When Mademoiselle Reisz tells her that "the bird that would soar above the level plain of tradition and prejudice must have strong wings" (967), Edna remarks blandly, "I'm not thinking of any extraordinary flights" (966). And when Edna kills herself, it becomes clear that her art has not provided her with a voice of the sea that could break apart symbolic language or speak feminine desires. As Edna walks into the ocean, Chopin tells us that "All along the white beach, up and down, there was no living thing in sight. A bird with a broken wing was beating the air above, reeling, fluttering, circling disabled down, down to the water" (999). This image emphasizes Edna's isolation ("there was no living thing in sight") as well as her inability to find a new theory of voice that transcends patriarchal language. Rather than being the poetic artist who soars above patriarchal discourse, she is the woman who is silenced, alienated, and disabled by symbolic language — a reeling, fluttering, broken creature, rather than a triumphant creator.

Why does Edna's attempt to formulate a viable new theory of language fail? Edna seeks a voice that can disrupt patriarchy but also one that is apart from, or underneath, or before the symbolic — the voice of the ocean, of the pre-symbolic realm of the meadow, of Mademoiselle Reisz's semiotic music, of her own painting. But because this voice is constituted as being *outside* of patriarchy, its subversions cannot be maintained. Butler's critique of Kristeva can be applied to Edna's struggle for voice. Because Kristeva situates the semiotic outside of cultural practices, she limits its potential for cultural subversion: "Poetic language and the pleasures of maternity constitute local displacements of the paternal law, temporary subversion which finally submit to that against which they initially rebel. By relegating the source of subversion to a site outside of culture itself, Kristeva appears to foreclose the possibility of subversion as an effective or realizable cultural practice" (*Gender Trouble* 88). Edna sometimes finds a voice of resistance, but because it is located outside all her cultural and linguistic matrices, its subversions are only temporary. She is finally silenced by her own inability to find a theory of language that does not put her outside all existing speech communities.

Like the parrot who introduces the novel, then, Edna finally speaks "a language which nobody understood" (881). Or as Treichler puts it, "at the point of her final movement, [Edna] speaks and embodies a language which cannot be spoken. Only in solitude can the true self speak and be heard" (254). When Edna tries to explain her newfound sense of selfhood to Madame Ratignolle, the two women "did not appear to understand each other or to be talking the same language" (929). And when Robert returns from Mexico, he seems to have lost his earlier ability to "chat" with Edna. Robert has become caught within a patriarchal logic and discourse that sees women as possessions to be traded between men, possessions that lack subjectivity and voice. No wonder, then, that he does not understand Edna:

"You have been a very, very foolish boy, wasting your time dreaming of impossible things when you speak of Mr. Pontellier setting me free! I am no longer one of Mr. Pontellier's possessions to dispose of or not. I give myself where I choose. If he were to say, 'Here, Robert, take her and be happy; she is yours,' I should laugh at you both."

His face grew a little white. "What do you mean?" he asked. (992)

Robert blanches before Edna's assertion of personal and linguistic freedom. Edna has found an unruly voice that puts her outside of his comprehension, and, indeed, outside the comprehension of her culture as a whole. Edna truly becomes, then, what Chopin's original title for the novel ("A Solitary Soul") implied; she becomes a solitary soul, with a solitary voice that only she (and perhaps not even she) can understand. Finally, neither the voice of the sea nor Mademoiselle Reisz's music nor her own art or language provides Edna with a maternal discourse that can disrupt patriarchal language. These maternal discourses cannot be translated by Edna into a language that can be spoken to a listener.

In discussing the notion of a female body that exists beyond the Law of the Father, Butler comments: "If subversion is possible, it will be a subversion from within the terms of the law, through the possibilities that emerge when the law turns against itself and spawns unexpected permutations of itself. The culturally constructed body will then be liberated, neither to its 'natural' past, nor to is original pleasures, but to an open future of cultural possibilities" (*Gender Trouble* 93). Applying this idea to Edna's search for language, we might say that Edna dreams of a return to a maternal language that is outside symbolic language, that gives voice to her newfound subjectivity and sexuality. However, she learns that because this language is outside of patriarchy, it cannot subvert patriarchy. Edna discovers that "if subversion is possible, it will be a subversion from within the terms of the law," a subversion from within the terms of patriarchal discourse itself. Dale Bauer argues that Chopin's novel is dangerous because it suggests the possibility, however imprecise, "of a world beyond: the world of the body, perhaps the world under threat of erasure by a moving, returning ocean that sweeps [Edna] back to the beginnings and beyond" (154). Yet finally, the novel rejects this dream of a world beyond, of a retreat to a language that exists in the beginning, before the Law of the Father has been imposed. When Edna drowns herself, "the voice of the sea is seductive, never ceasing, whispering, clamoring, murmuring, inviting the soul to wander in abysses of solitude" (999). Chopin repeats the lines she had used earlier to suggest that the voice of the sea functions as a maternal realm *outside* culture, a solitary world beyond patriarchal discourse that cannot exist within the culture Edna knows. The voice of the sea does not provide Edna with a viable theory of feminine voice, and Chopin finally rejects the idea that music, or art, or anything but language itself can subvert language. In the end, Chopin suggests that if we wish to be comprehended, we cannot speak "a language which nobody understood" but rather must talk "as women talk," waging our linguistic struggles in the here and now, in the interstices and gaps of patriarchal discourse.

Despite the liberation engendered by the decline of domesticity, not all fictional characters can find a viable theory of feminine voice, as Edna Pontellier's struggle demonstrates. Indeed, as Yaeger argues, the novel describes "a frightening antagonism between a feminine subject and the objectifying world of discourse she inhabits" (211). This frightening world is also present in Chopin's short fiction, and yet a comparison of her early and later short works shows her moving toward a clearer understanding of how women can most effectively resist the Law of the Father. In her earlier works, Chopin frequently depicts silent, passive women — women who seem incapable of expressing themselves or their desires. Chopin also depicts Anglo American and African American women who attempt to enunciate their desires and experiences through a voice of overt resistance that is quickly labeled meaningless or "insane." Early works such as "At the 'Cadian Ball," "La Belle Zoraïde," "Désirée's Baby," "Wiser than a God," and particularly "Mrs. Mobry's Reason" depict a voice of pure resistance that attempts to locate itself *outside* of patriarchal discourse and culture. Like Edna's maternal voice, these resistant voices are quickly erased, negated, or labeled "insane" by patriarchal structures. In some of Chopin's later short works, however — particularly those written during or after 1894 — she moves toward depicting women who are more active and more vocal. Moreover, these stories' strategies of resistance often entail a covert, metalinguistic voice. Works such as "Her Letters" and "Elizabeth Stock's One Story" depict a discourse of insubordination that attempts to bridge the gap between women who speak, like Edna, "a language which nobody understood," and women who are silenced by patriarchal discourse. These later works therefore reject a feminine voice existing outside of patriarchal discourse, and instead find a metalinguistic voice that forces patriarchal discourse into a subversive dialogue, a dialogue that shows its categories to be nonabsolute.[6]

Chopin's short fiction does not reflect a linear movement from silence to voice; rather, as her career progressed Chopin continued to test the ways women could — and could not — achieve articulation. Given her own experiences as a writer, Chopin's development of a covert, metalinguistic voice seems logical. Early in her career, when she wrote charming Creole stories with happy endings, she had little difficulty finding publishers. And when she depicted women who were silent and submissive, the reading public readily accepted her works. But, as Emily Toth shows, after 1894 Chopin attempted to be more daring in her short fiction; concurrently she had more difficulty finding publishers (224; 232–33). Moreover, her most subversive works — stories that often involved female heroines with strong desires and voices — were repeatedly refused by publishers, and, of course, the public and literary critics alike condemned the unconventional Edna Pontellier. Toward the end of the short decade during which Chopin wrote, she did not even attempt to publish works that posited a direct challenge to the literary and moral standards of her time. Yet she did not give up on challenging these standards. Rather, her challenge went "underground": it became less open and direct, more covert and inscribed. These covert strategies of resistance were Chopin's most effective weapon, because they allowed her to slip subversive messages past the censoring dictates of her own society.

Early in her career, Chopin tends to depict women who are silent, women who seek but do not find a voice, or women who find a voice only to have it labeled insane or meaningless. In an early story such as "A No-Account Creole" (1888, 1891), for instance, Euphrasie becomes engaged to Placide Santien even though she does not love him.[7] When Euphrasie realizes she loves another man, Wallace Offdean, she takes no steps to end her engagement. Even when Offdean declares his love for Euphrasie, she still cannot enunciate her desire: "She could not speak. She only looked at him with frightened eyes" (98). Throughout the story Euphrasie remains incapable of expressing her marital preferences and embarrassed about her sexual attraction to Offdean. Similarly, in another early story, "Love on the Bon Dieu" (1891), Lalie's silence causes her great harm: "Because she had been silent — had not lifted her voice in complaint — [the village people] believed she suffered no more than she could bear" (162). For Lalie, speech is a great effort: "Lalie had spoken low and in jerks, as if every word gave her pain" (160). And like Euphrasie, Lalie seems incapable of articulating her desire; she almost dies with her secret — her love for Azenor — completely unspoken.

These female characters are relatively passive, so perhaps it is no surprise their voices seem ineffective. Yet even more aggressive women, such as Calixta and Clarisse of "At the 'Cadian Ball" (1892), have difficulty. In this story, Calixta exhibits verbal dexterity, swearing "roundly in fine 'Cadian French and with true Spanish spirit" (219) and wittily chiding Bobinôt for standing "*planté là* like ole Ma'ame Tina's cow in the bog" (224). Yet Calixta's society dislikes her linguistic proficiency, as the crowd's reaction to this sally demonstrates: "Madame Suzonne, sitting in a corner, whispered to her neighbor that if Ozéina were to conduct herself in a like manner, she should immediately be taken out to the mule-cart and driven home. The women did not always approve of Calixta" (224). Apart from her linguistic forwardness, Calixta also behaves aggressively, slapping her friend Fronie's face when insulted, and eventually forcing Bobinôt to marry her.

Clarisse, too, is aggressive. She rides out alone in the middle of the night to "rescue" Alcée from Calixta, and forces him away from her rival. Yet Clarisse plays the role of the soft-spoken, pure woman; she is shocked, for example, by the "hot, blistering love-words" (220) Alcée pants in her face one day. Eventually, Clarisse admits she loves Alcée, but Chopin switches to indirect discourse and narrates this moment through the eyes of Alcée: "He began to wonder if this meant love. But she had to tell him so, before he believed it. And when she told him, he thought the face of the Universe was changed. . . . The one, only, great reality in the world was Clarisse standing before him, telling him that she loved him" (227). For the delicate Clarisse to enunciate her desire for Alcée would break the narrative parameters established for her character—as well as for the series of women Chopin portrays in these early works. And as we know from "The Storm" (1898) (the sequel to "At the 'Cadian Ball"), more aggressively verbal women such as Calixta end up with boring men like Bobinôt, and have to wait five years for the consummation of their desires.

Like Alcott's writing, then, Chopin's earliest fictions sometimes reward women who accept their inscription into symbolic language and punish women who assert an unruly voice. Even as late as 1896, Chopin sometimes censors the unruly tongues of her female characters. "A Night in Acadie" depicts Zaïda Trodon, a woman who has "an absence of reserve in her manner" and "the air of a young person accustomed to decide for herself and for those about her" (487). Yet after Zaïda realizes her would-be fiancé is a drunkard, after she must be rescued by another man, she loses her self-control and even her voice: "Her will, which had been overmastering and aggressive, seemed to have grown numb under the disturbing spell of the past few hours. . . . The girl was quiet and silent" (498–99). The last phrase—that the girl is both "quiet and silent"—seems repetitive for the usually concise Chopin, yet it marks her double attempt to appease her editors, who complained about the story's first ending in which Zaïda forces another suitor to marry her. According to Toth, this ending offended Chopin's publishers, and she bent to the literary tastes of her time, silencing Zaïda.[8]

Zaïda is described as having the free carriage of "a negress" (487), but racialized women in Chopin's early fiction also have their voices censored.[9] In "La Belle Zoraïde" (1893), Zoraïde (a light-skinned slave) wishes to marry the man who attracts her rather than the one her mistress (Madame Delarivière) has picked. Zoraïde tries to express her desire and to reason logically with Madame Delarivière: "Doctor Langlé gives me his slave to marry, but he would not give me his son. Then, since I am not white, let me have from out of my own race the one whom my heart has chosen" (305). But like Robert in *The Awakening*, Madame Delarivière simply ignores expressions of subjectivity and language contradicting her understanding of the world. When Zoraïde becomes pregnant by her forbidden lover, Madame Delarivière has him sold and later tells Zoraïde her baby has died. Zoraïde goes insane, believing a dead bundle of rags is her living child, even refusing to accept her real infant. She also loses the ability to speak rationally, becoming inscribed under a label of insanity as "Zoraïde la folle" (307).

This story seems to indicate that for African American women there is no middle ground between sexist and racist repression of speech and a discourse that goes unheard because it is labeled "insane." And this pattern is replicated in the story's frame. Manna-Loulou, an African American servant, tells this tale to her mistress, Madame Delisle. But Madame Delisle misses the point of the story, sympathizing with the abandoned child rather than the silenced mother (307).[10]

Resistant feminine voices of racialized characters, then, simply go unheard. Eventually such voices are erased by madness or suicide, as "Désirée's Baby" (1892) depicts. An orphan, Désirée marries a man who claims not to care about her obscure origins: "He was reminded that she was nameless. What did it matter about a name when he could give her one of the oldest and proudest in Louisiana?" (241). Désirée's husband, Armand, will inscribe his wife under his own social and linguistic identity, under his linguistic law. But when Désirée bears a child that shows signs of being African American, Armand takes this social and linguistic protection away, telling her to go. Armand also refuses to hear Désirée's language once he knows of her racial status. "I am white! Look at my hair, it is brown; and my eyes are gray, Armand . . . And my skin is fair . . . whiter than yours, Armand" (243), Désirée says to her husband, but Armand ignores her arguments. Soon Désirée becomes silent: "She tried to speak to the little quadroon boy; but no sound would come"; "She was like a stone image: silent, white, motionless" (243). As Ellen Peel has pointed out, Désirée appears to be a blank screen onto which others project their desires, a screen with no identity of its own.[11] And no language, I would add, once patriarchal protection, the Name of the Father, has been removed. The story clearly depicts a repressive structure in which phallicism sustains itself through an erasure of the voices of feminine and racialized "others," but it presents no way of challenging this structure.

In Chopin's early fiction, Anglo American women are more likely to retain their identity than their African American counterparts, but not necessarily their voices. Discourses spoken by Anglo American women can easily be labeled as "insane" as Zoraïde's, particularly when they do not enunciate socially acceptable codes, as Paula Von Stoltz of "Wiser than A God" (1889) learns. Paula's suitor, George Brainard, talks fluently, utilizing the language of romantic passion, while Paula (a musician) is silent: "Say if you love me, Paula. I believe you do. . . . Why are you speechless? Why don't you say something to me!" (46). Paula does finally attempt to explain her emotions to George: " 'What do you know of my life,' [Paula] exclaimed passionately. 'What can you guess of it? Is music anything more to you than the pleasing distraction of an idle moment? Can't you feel that with me, it courses with the blood through my veins? That it's something dearer than life, than riches, even than love?' " (46). Paula's speech calls upon codes other than those of romantic love and articulates the view that to an artist — even a female artist — art is life. None of this is understood by George, who only exclaims: "Paula listen to me; don't speak like a mad woman" (46). Paula flees from George and pursues her art, eventually becoming a successful pianist. But Paula continually finds that her language is not understood; even her mother tells her not to "chatter" (40).

"Mrs. Mobry's Reason" (1891) also depicts Anglo American women trapped between patriarchal silence and a discourse labeled meaningless or insane.[12] The story concerns a generational struggle for voice in which the mother, Editha Mobry, acquiesces and is silenced, while the daughter, Naomi, resists and becomes insane. Editha is reluctant to marry John Mobry, but he is "of that class of men who, when they want something, usually keep on wanting it and striving for it so long as there is possibility of attainment in view" (71). Editha cannot resist such a superior force of "wanting," despite her own obvious lack of enthusiasm for the marriage: "Her tired face wore the look of the conquered who has made a brave fight and would rest. 'Well, John, if you want it,' she said, placing her hand in his" (71). Editha therefore enters the symbolic order of language only by internalizing male desire; she phrases her wishes in terms of the male's — "Well, John, if you want it" — even enclosing her body, her hand, within the masculine sphere of desire. Because Editha enters the symbolic through the masculine gaze she silences herself, making herself part of the "invisible and unheard sex."

Editha also tries to make her daughter part of this invisible and unheard sex. Mrs. Mobry is a firm believer in the late-nineteenth-century view that women should not develop their intellect and mind; she believes that "ologies and isms and all that for women" (72) are useless and possibly injurious to women's mental stability. She will not allow her daughter to engage in intellectual pursuits that might lead to a mastery of language or knowledge. However, Mrs. Mobry has a secret reason for her behavior. Her lineage contains a hereditary strain of insanity, and her reluctance to marry stems from fear of passing on this taint. She also tries to prevent the spread of insanity by keeping her daughter unmarried. Mrs. Mobry therefore attempts to shield her daughter from both sexual and intellectual knowledge, from learning and love.

Yet she is unsuccessful. Naomi falls in love with her cousin Sigmund, and caught between her desire for Sigmund and her desire for her mother's approbation, she loses her mind. Moreover, when Naomi loses mental self-possession, she begins to speak a language not grounded in any normative conception of meaning. She believes she has mastered all discourse and can even understand what nature is saying: "I know everything now. I know what the birds are saying up in the trees . . . I can tell you everything that the fishes say in the water. They were talking under the boat when you called me — " (78). Naomi's unrepressed language is also tied to a sexual liberation: " 'Sigmund,' she whispered, and drawing nearer to him twined her arms around his neck. 'I want you to kiss me, Sigmund' " (78). But Naomi speaks "a language which nobody understood" — a language that is so contradictory and illogical it can only be considered insane. Sigmund, for example, reads Naomi as a blank; looking into her eyes, he finds that "there was no more light in them" (78). Furthermore, by the end of the story, Naomi has become silent: "Naomi sat upon a lounge. She was playing like a little child, with scraps of paper that she was tearing and placing in rows upon the cushion beside her" (79). Naomi can finally only escape from patriarchal dictates by regressing to childhood and silence.

The discourse Naomi achieves in "Mrs. Mobry's Reason" is thus a form of escape from patriarchal repression that renders the escapeé insane and seems to erase her personality. Between the silent mother and the daughter's insane babble, there must be an alternative discourse. This is the discourse not of overt resistance but of covert subversion. As in *The Awakening,* in her short fiction Chopin finally rejects a discourse located outside patriarchal culture, realizing that linguistic struggles must be waged in the here and now, in the daily "chatter" of women. For as Bauer explains, "The feminist struggle is not one between a conscious 'awakened' or natural voice *and* the voice of patriarchy 'out there.' Rather, precisely because we all internalize the authoritative voice of patriarchy, we must struggle to refashion inherited social discourses into words which rearticulate intentions (here feminist ones) other than normative or disciplinary ones" (2). Chopin's later texts continue the struggle through a covert, dialogic theory of voice that refashions inherited discourses, rather than through a feminine language outside society or outside the Law of the Father.

These covert, dialogic voices are depicted most clearly in Chopin's portrayals of women who write. "Her Letters" (1894) tells of a dying woman unable to destroy her adulterous love letters. Upon her death, she compels her husband to destroy the letters unread. The husband does so but then finds himself consumed by curiosity about their contents. Unable to pierce the mystery, he eventually follows the letters to their watery grave, drowning himself. The unnamed woman's letters are therefore subversive of male control in the most literal sense: they drive a husband to question his perception of his wife and to kill himself.

However, these letters are also subversive in a discursive sense, both for the woman and for her husband. This forbidden discourse — not her husband's presence or counsel — has nourished the woman for the last four years of her illness: "they had sustained her, she believed, and kept her spirit from perishing utterly" (398). Moreover, the letters — not her husband, or even her lover — provide the story's one moment of erotic pleasure: "But what if that other most precious and most imprudent one were missing! in which every word of untempered passion had long ago eaten its way into her brain; and which stirred her still to-day, as it had done a hundred times before when she thought of it. She crushed it between her palms when she found it. She kissed it again and again. With her sharp white teeth she tore the far corner from the letter, where the name was written; she bit the torn scrap and tasted it between her lips and upon her tongue like some god-given morsel" (399). In this subversive revision of the Eucharist, the word becomes wholly sensual, yet wholly disembodied. It is not her lover's presence the woman relishes but the tokens of their mutual esteem, the words making up their dialogic intercourse. Discourse becomes a subversive replacement for the bodies of men.

For the husband, the letters function differently, forcing him into a subversive dialogue that completely undermines his sense of knowledge and subjectivity. His wife's secret letters irrevocably change his world, for he realizes their probable contents. Although he can find no other written evidence documenting that "his wife had not been the true and loyal woman he had always believed her to be" (403), the letters seem to prove his wife had a hidden personality he could not discover while she was alive, and cannot fathom after her death. These covert texts, these unfathomable letters, force the husband to question his monolithic perception of his wife. He continues this dialogue with other men who have known her but finds only that his friends also misperceive her: "Foremost he learned she had been unsympathetic because of her coldness of manner. One had admired her intellect; another her accomplishments; a third had thought her beautiful before disease claimed her, regretting, however, that her beauty had lacked warmth of color and expression.... Oh, it was useless to try to discover anything from men!" (404). Other men believe his wife to be cold and asexual, but the letters seem to tell another story. The husband thus finds that the letters enact a subversive dialogue undermining his perceptions of the woman he thought he knew so well.

The letters, besides creating a dialogic problem, also create a linguistic problem, causing the husband to question his own understanding of how words function. Previously, when his friends claimed to have seduced women, he has "heard the empty boast... and had always met it with good-humored contempt" (403). Now, however, he distrusts his perception that these words are empty: "to-night every flagrant, inane utterance was charged with a new meaning, revealing possibilities that he had hitherto never taken into account" (403). The letters alert the husband to levels of covert meaning in language he has previously believed he could fathom but now finds he cannot: "He was remembering how she had conducted herself toward this one and that one; striving to recall conversations, subtleties of facial expression that might have meant what he did not suspect at the moment, *shades of meaning in words that had seemed the ordinary interchange* of social amenities" (403; my emphasis). The husband seems to have an awakening into the unreliable and potential disruptive possibilities of language—an awakening that profoundly destabilizes his whole universe.

Ultimately, the husband's identity and sense of language are so destabilized he kills himself. If subjectivity is irremediably founded on the oppression of the Other, then endowing this Other with some unfathomable but private sense of self—as

Chopin's covert letters do — seems to undermine the construction of male subjectivity. As Luce Irigaray explains: "If there is no more 'earth' to press down/repress, to work, to represent, but also and always to desire (for one's own), no opaque matter which in theory does not know herself, then what pedestal remains for the ex-sistence of the 'subject'?" (133). Covert texts such as these letters take away the pedestal for the existence of the subject by suggesting men do not really know the women they marry, live with, and believe they construct. The wife dies, but her letters affirm the presence of an unruly discourse and an unruly feminine subject. And unlike earlier writers, Chopin refuses to contain this discourse, to repress it under the Law of the Father; ultimately, it is a force that cannot be denied.

Texts, it seems, have a life of their own, a life that begins to undo some of the silences of the patriarchal masterplot. This theme is articulated most clearly in "Elizabeth Stock's One Story," a complicated text that needs to be examined in detail to hear Chopin's subversive, covert message. Like the wife in "Her Letters," the title character of "Elizabeth Stock's One Story" dies, but she leaves behind a text that undermines patriarchal control of discourse by giving voice to her subjectivity.[13] Elizabeth is an independent woman who supports herself through her job as postmistress in the small village of Stonelift. Within the society Chopin depicts, however, an independent woman cannot be tolerated for long. When Elizabeth reads and delivers an urgent postcard that arrives late, officials dismiss her for "reading postal cards and permitting people to help themselves to their own mail" (590). Read on the level of discourse, she must be dismissed by an "official" text for her transgressive, unofficial textual practices, as she explains: "One morning, just like lightning out of a clear sky, here comes an official document from Washington, discharging me from my position as postmistress of Stonelift" (590). After her dismissal from her job she becomes ill and dies. Official texts turn upon her, depriving Elizabeth of her livelihood and her life. Males retake the mail.

According to the narrator who introduces Elizabeth's story, the physicians at the hospital where Elizabeth is sent to recuperate "say she showed hope of rallying till placed in the incurable ward, when all courage seemed to leave her, and she relapsed into a silence that remained unbroken till the end" (586). Yet Elizabeth's silence is not "unbroken to the end"; her silence is only the final battle in a long war for self-expression she has waged. She is not content with the limits a patriarchal society has placed on her access to texts. There is a certain "Bartlebyesque" kind of irony in her job as a postmistress: she is responsible for the care and sorting of *letters*, yet she is not supposed to read these letters. But, as she explains, it is human nature — especially feminine nature — to want to possess knowledge: "I leave it to any one — to any woman especially, if it ain't human nature in a little place where everybody knows ever one else, for the postmistress to glance at a postal card once in a while. She could hardly help it" (587). Elizabeth desires to do more than just read texts, however. She also desires to author them, as the narrator informs the readers: "In Stonelift, the village where Elizabeth Stock was born and raised . . . they say she was much given over to scribbling" (586). But again, patriarchal forces must attempt to control and limit women's voice; Elizabeth's writing, like her body, must be deemed hopeless and incurable. The narrator finds the story — Elizabeth's one and only story — in her desk, "which was quite filled with scraps and bits of writing in bad prose and impossible verse." Out of "the whole conglomerate mass" the narrator can discover only one item which "bore any semblance to a connected or consecutive narration" (586).[14] Elizabeth's one story, then, is a found narrative, and after this belittling introduction, the narrator disappears, letting the story speak for itself.

Perhaps influenced by certain masculine notions of literature current in the 1880s and 1890s, the narrator faults Elizabeth's writing for lacking a coherent, linear style. Elizabeth's Uncle William, on the other hand, derides her stories because they lack a unique and adventurous plot, as she explains: "Once I wrote about old Si' Shepard that got lost in the woods and never came back, and when I showed it to Uncle William he said: 'Why, Elizabeth, I reckon you better stick to your dress making: this here ain't no story; everybody knows about old Si' Shepard'" (586). Like the narrator, Uncle William believes Elizabeth's writing is "incurable," and he sends her back to more feminine pursuits like "dress making." Elizabeth's society extols masculine, heroic narratives that she finds herself incapable of producing: "I tried to think of a railroad story with a wreck, but couldn't. No more could I make a tale out of murder, or money getting stolen, or even mistaken identity; for the story had to be original, entertaining, full of action and Goodness knows what all. It was no use. I gave it up" (586–87). Elizabeth cannot come up with any original, action-packed, muscular design for a plot. Yet she still wants to write: "But now that I got my pen in my hand . . . I feel as I'd like to tell how I lost my position, mostly through my own negligence, I'll admit that" (587). Admitting the negligence of the story, itself, *as a story,* Elizabeth's tale nonetheless asserts its right to textual existence. If Elizabeth cannot tell the tale of an American Adam, she may be able to tell the tale of an American Eve — the tale of a woman who tastes of forbidden knowledge, forbidden discourse, and thereby loses a privileged status.

Elizabeth's content, then, violates patriarchal norms, as do her style and structure. Her story is fragmentary and nonlinear, moving far back into Elizabeth's childhood, plunging forward into the present, receding to the past events of Elizabeth losing her job. It vacillates, waffles, wavers, digresses, gives details unrelated to the "plot" of Elizabeth losing her job, and frequently draws attention to its own flaws. Furthermore, the style is personal, subjective, colloquial: "Often seems like the village was most too small"; "Anyway, the train was late that day. It was the breaking up of winter, or the beginning of spring; kind of betwixt and between; along in March" (587). Most important, at the heart of the story there is a mystery: was Elizabeth the victim of a plot to oust her from her position as postmistress? And is she aware of the details supporting such a reading of events? On this crucial point the text is silent; it remains a riddle, a structure that resists closure by asserting its own mysteriousness.

According to Ewell, Elizabeth's voice is "colloquial and elliptical"; furthermore, "the one story Elizabeth Stock finally tells...has no conventional plot" (166). Elizabeth's story emphasizes its difference from patriarchal forms of writing through its cumulative rather than linear structure, its multiple narrative viewpoints, and its open ending: "But indeed, indeed, I don't know what to do... After all, what I got to do is leave everything in the hands of Providence, and trust to luck" (591). Elizabeth also allies her writing not with masculine novelty and heroism but with the repetitive, nonlinear structures of piecing and quilting: "I laid awake most a whole week; and walked about days in a kind of dream, turning and twisting things in my mind just like I often saw old ladies twisting quilt patches around to compose a design" (586–87). So while Elizabeth's other scraps and bits of writing have been read as babble and discarded, the tale itself endures, pieced, patched, and puzzling, but uniquely expressive of her own voice. Thus Elizabeth's silence is not "unbroken to the end," as the narrator and critics such as Heather Kirk Thomas (26) have claimed. Sometime *after* losing her job, but *before* she dies, she describes her experiences in her own, unique way.[15]

In so doing, she finds a voice that is her own but that also hollows out patriarchal discourse from within its own parameters. In earlier depictions of women writers such as "Miss Witherwell's Mistake" (1889), Chopin shows women content to write about domestic topics such as " 'Security Against the Moth.' " But Elizabeth refuses to force her writing into the mode of domestic discourse. Her writing is also not totally outside the realm of patriarchal understanding, like the "scraps and bits of writing" the narrator finds in Elizabeth's desk and discards, like Naomi Mobry's mad voice, or like Edna Pontellier's "feminine" language. The unknown narrator does not see this one particular tale as insane scribbling; believing it to tell a connected, consecutive narrative, the narrator admits it to the sanctified halls of discourse. But Elizabeth's tale exists in a middle ground: it is neither a linear, masculine, patriarchal plot, nor an insane, illogical, fragmented feminine discourse.

In short, Elizabeth finds a covert voice that allows her self-expression but that is not entirely repressed by patriarchy. Elizabeth disarms her readers with her forthright, simple tone; in other words, she plays the fool. But she is no fool. She remembers the name on the postcard — Collins — well enough to repeat it to her readers three times (588) but apparently does not make the connection that the postman hired to replace her after her "negligence" is also named Collins. She blithely informs the reader that one reason for her dismissal was that she allowed people to help themselves to their own mail, while apparently forgetting that the only one who ever actually helped himself to his mail was Nathan Brightman. Nathan Brightman is also the only person who had other concrete evidence for her dismissal, and the only person in town who knew the Collins family. Does Elizabeth know that Nathan Brightman had her fired so his friend Collins could get the job of postmaster? She does not say. Instead, Elizabeth presents the reader with 2 + 2 but does not add them up to 4. She plays the fool, creating a subversive dialogue between the reader and the text, a dialogue in which we are left to ponder just how much Elizabeth actually knew. If, as Bauer argues, a fool represents "a resisting reader *within* the text" who provides "the means of unmasking dominant codes" (11), then Elizabeth fits this paradigm perfectly.

Moreover, Elizabeth's text, while seeming to conform to patriarchal dictates (at least in terms of being nonoffensive or noninflammatory) still asserts its difference. Though pressure is exerted on the tale externally, by a hostile narrator, and internally, by an unsympathetic interpretive community, the text does not succumb. Elizabeth refashions patriarchal discourse, making it take account of her own specific experiences, her own subjectivity. Elizabeth's greatest creation, finally, is her own voice, her own self, which, as Ewell argues, rises "well above any conventional characters she might invent" (167). "Elizabeth Stock's One Story" depicts its own exclusion from "proper" discourse, but in so doing nevertheless subverts male control of texts, and perversely insists upon women's right to write/ right their own stories. And once again, Chopin refuses to contain her character's unruly voice: Elizabeth's story lives on after her death, enunciating the subversive messages patriarchal society and discourse seek to repress.

Elizabeth's subversive message is that women are excluded from language — from reading and writing — and denied self-determination. Her story enunciates the theoretical mechanisms whereby patriarchal forces create speaking masculine subjects through a silencing of a feminine "other." But her story also presents another theory of language in which women become speaking subjects through the use of covert, dialogic methods. Elizabeth did not end her quest for a form of resistance to patriarchal norms; she only made it less overt. And neither did Chopin. Despite the "failure" of *The Awakening*, she is still looking for ways to subvert patriarchal control of women's subjectivity and voice.

Although Chopin sought a publisher for "Elizabeth Stock's One Story" she was not successful, and after the furor over *The Awakening* its publication in *A Vocation and a Voice* was delayed for almost one hundred years. Toward the end of her career, Chopin did not even attempt to publish some of her most daring works, such as "The Storm." Chopin's fiction as a whole thus depicts a distinct pattern of repression of women's voices — a pattern reflected within the lives of the characters she creates as well as within her own career as a writer. A patriarchal society denies women's right to control their destinies, their desires, and their discourses, and censors or erases unruly female voices that do not conform to its dictates. And yet authors like Chopin realize that to conform to patriarchal dictates is to be silent as women; as Xavière Gauthier has explained: "As long as women remain silent, they will be outside the historical process. But, if they begin to speak and write *as men do,* they will enter history subdued and alienated; it is a history that, logically speaking, their speech should disrupt" (162–63). How to speak in a voice that disrupts patriarchal discourse, without being censored by patriarchal structures? Throughout her career, Chopin confronts this problem, trying various strategies for creating a voice of insubordination: characters who are mostly silent, characters who use overtly resistant feminine voices that go unheard, characters who find a covert discourse. Like earlier writers, Chopin sometimes destroys the unruly voice of her female characters. However, the overall focus of her fiction is an investigation of the way patriarchal theories of subjectivity and voice silence women, and a resistance to this silencing that involves a release and a validation, rather than a repression, of a subversive feminine voice.

Clearly, for Chopin, certain voices (like Naomi Mobry's) sacrifice the self for a momentary eruption of language no one can understand. There is no subversion that can occur from "outside" the confines of dominant discourses; as Edna Pontellier learns, there is no feminine voice "out there" that can be used to disrupt the voice of patriarchy that is "in here." But some forms of discourse walk the delicate tightrope between "a language which nobody understood" and the silence that is patriarchal repression of women's speech. Some forms of voice successfully challenge patriarchal language through a covert, metalinguistic interrogation of its very premises. So stories like "Her Letters" and "Elizabeth Stock's One Story" may be paradigmatic texts for women's experiences with patriarchal language and their development of an unruly voice. In *Julius Caesar* Mark Antony states that "the evil that men do lives after them." But texts, too, have a life of their own, a life that may exceed the author's and one day *undo* the evil men do. Like Elizabeth Stock's one story and the messages of the wife in "Her Letters," Chopin's texts live on after her, graphically depicting the way women were silenced and effaced but also speaking the subversive message that women desire — and sometimes find — a subjectivity and voice that exceeds that granted to them by the Law of the Father. I think Kate Chopin would be pleased to know that today, her most daring works — works like *The Awakening,* "Elizabeth Stock's One Story," and "The Storm" — are widely anthologized, admired, and read. In the end, Chopin had the last laugh. She may have lost the battle for feminine self-expression, but she won the war.

5

Herstory in Hisland, History in Herland
Charlotte Perkins Gilman's Reconstruction of Gender and Language

Charlotte Perkins Gilman is best know for her semiautobiographical text, "The Yellow Wall-Paper" (1892), but she completed numerous other projects. For example, from 1909 to 1916 she published a magazine called the *Forerunner*. For each monthly issue, Gilman wrote a short story, a chapter of a serial novel, a chapter of a prose work, and miscellaneous essays, editorials, songs, and poems. In the first volume, she even authored the advertisements. Her humorously risqué endorsement of one product—Moore's Fountain Pen—can be used as a general illustration of the changing concerns of early-twentieth-century women writers. Gilman's advertisement describes a woman who wants to write but finds she has problems with her "pen":

> It is all very well for men, with vest pockets, to carry a sort of leather socket, or a metal clip that holds the pen to that pocket safely—so long as the man is vertical.
> But women haven't vest pockets—and do not remain continuously erect.
> A woman stoops over to look in the oven—to pick up her thimble—to take the baby off the floor—and if she carries a fountain pen, it stoops over too and spills its ink.

Moore's Foundation Pen, however, has a cap that screws on so that the ink does not leak; literally, this pen reconciles women's domestic role with her desire to write.

More interesting, however, is that Gilman's advertisement postulates a theoretical connection between men and pens, one that makes women's writing somewhat difficult. Gilman puns on the connection between pen and penis that numerous feminist critics have observed. Gilman says it is more difficult for women to control pens because, unlike men, women do not "remain continuously erect." Pens leak when women try to use them, or they "distribute ink where — and when — it wasn't wanted" (31). Gilman's solution is to endorse a redesigned pen, an instrument that does not require women to be "continuously erect." Gilman praises a product, then, that deconstructs the link between men and "pens," between a subjectivity as a speaking/writing subject and the masculine phallus. In Gilman's playful advertisement, both men and women can manipulate the pen "with joy, with comfort, [and] with clean hands" (31). No wonder Moore's Fountain Pen is a "constant satisfaction" (31).

With less sexual punning than this, many turn-of-the-century women writers try to undermine the theoretical structures that grant men an articulate subjectivity while envisioning women as silent objects. However, some of their characters find feminine voices that are ineffective because they are finally located outside patriarchal society. Gilman's fiction demonstrates a desire to find verbal strategies that can survive in patriarchal culture, in a world where women must sometimes contend with pens that leak, with ink that will not stay put. Gilman's early work "The Yellow Wall-Paper" depicts the oppression of patriarchal language but presents no way of escaping this subjugation. Her later fictions, however, find more effective ways of reconstructing gender and language. Gilman's feminist utopia *Herland* (1915) uses a maternal discourse to undermine those binary structures that have created constitutively masculine speaking subjects (such as the phallus as transcendental signifier), but it sometimes gets caught up in new oppositions that undermine this project. Gilman's *Forerunner* fiction (1909–16), on the other hand, does not postulate that a maternal or feminine voice can be retrieved. Rather, the unruly women in Gilman's most subversive works are metalinguists who strip bare the wallpaper of patriarchal history and create a place for their subjectivity and voice in a renovated discourse.

In *The Man-Made World, or Our Androcentric Culture*, Gilman begins a chapter by posing and answering a question: "History is, or should be the story of our racial life. What have men made it? The story of warfare and conquest" (216). For Gilman, history is literally his story — a record of the dominance of the masculine subject. And yet, what is the source of history's androcentric bias? As previously argued, Gilman believes that language is "androcentric," defining women only through a social and linguistic relationship to a male subject. Therefore "herstory in hisland" — women's stories within the structures of patriarchal discourse and culture — will be a record of desperate but failed attempts to escape from the debilitating structures of gender and language, an ambiguous text much like Gilman's own short fiction "The Yellow Wall-Paper."

As numerous critics have argued, "The Yellow Wall-Paper" concerns women's entrapment within patriarchal language. Forbidden to engage in any intellectual activity, the female narrator resorts to covert writing and then, more and more, to "readings" of the yellow wallpaper. Ultimately these readings reveal a hidden history of feminine suppression, for underneath the paper the narrator sees a woman behind bars, a woman who creeps, a woman who sometimes becomes many women. The narrator determines to free this woman, and she strips the wallpaper off the walls. In so doing, she becomes the other woman; by the end of the story she claims, "I've got out at last . . . you can't put me back" (36). Paradoxically, the narrator also has a rope to tie the woman, should she try to escape. Finally, the narrator uses this rope to tie herself securely (presumably to the bed, the only object of furniture left in the room). She creeps around the perimeter of the room, fitting her shoulder into a narrow groove that has been worn in the wall by a previous occupant. Claiming to be free ("I've got out at last"), the narrator seems all the more enchained, mechanically rotating on an umbilical cord tying her to the scene of entrapment and oppression, the patriarchal marriage bed.

If we read this story as Paula Treichler does, in terms of a clash between masculine and feminine discourse, its seems to depict a temporary escape from the repressive sentence of authoritative male language:

> I interpret the wallpaper to be women's writing or women's discourse, and the woman in the wallpaper to be the representation of women that becomes possible only after women obtain the right to speak. In this reading, the yellow wallpaper stands for a new vision of women — one which is constructed differently from the representation of women in patriarchal language. The story is thus in part about the clash between two modes of discourse: one powerful, "ancestral," and dominant; the other new, "impertinent," and visionary. ("Escaping the Sentence" 64)

And yet, the narrator's escape from "the sentence" does not lead to a permanent liberation: "Her triumph is to have sharpened and articulated the nature of women's condition; she remains physically bound by a rope and locked in a room" (74). According to Treichler, the social and material conditions the narrator has diagnosed must change before she can be free.[1]

I would also argue that the narrator "escapes" the sentence only through a radical deconstruction of her own self. The narrator is suspended between her husband's precise, rational discourse and the "discourse" of the yellow wallpaper, in which there is "a lack of sequence, a defiance of law" (12): "when you follow the lame uncertain curves for a little distance they suddenly commit suicide — plunge off at outrageous angles, destroy themselves in unheard of contradictions" (5). She is caught between her husband's written schedule for her — his written "schedule prescription for each hour in the day" (4) — and the unscheduled reading and writing of the yellow wallpaper that goes on at all hours because it is ultimately outside the linear structure of time. The narrator is trapped between her own subversive reading of the yellow wallpaper and John's coercive reading of texts to and *at* her, for when she has bouts of madness her husband, as she says, sits "by me and read[s] to me till it tire[s] my head" (10). Like Chopin, then, in this early work Gilman portrays a conflict between a patriarchal, masculine language that silences women and an alternative feminine speech that seems more liberating.

In depicting this conflict between masculine and feminine discourse, Gilman draws on her own autobiographical experiences. As Mary Hill argues, Gilman's personal writings indicate that she felt a conflict between the "feminine" and "masculine" elements within herself, "between her mother's 'implacable sense of duty' and her father's more independent drive" (46). Gilman believed she had to make a choice between these two sides of her personality. In a letter to her first husband she writes, "I knew of course that the time would come when I must choose between two lives, but never did I dream that it would come so soon, and that the struggle would be so terrible" (Hill 99). At first she chose the "feminine" side, suppressing her "masculine" wish for a career in favor of duty to husband and child. The results were disastrous, as Gilman spiraled deeper and deeper into a near suicidal depression. It was not until she abandoned S. Weir Mitchell's prescription of a "rest cure" and resumed her career as a writer and lecturer that she recovered.

Gilman was not destroyed, then, by the conflict between her "male" and "female" sides, between her desire for a voice that was "masculine" and a more traditional women's speech. However, her narrator is not so lucky. Like Gilman she is a writer, but she does not have the option of choosing her "masculine," independent side over her "feminine," domestic one. She is explicitly told that if she does not get better (that is, become a better mother), her "sentence" will be increased: "John says if I don't pick up faster he shall send me to Weir Mitchell in the fall. But I don't want to go there at all. I had a friend who was in his hands once, and she says he is just like John and my brother, only more so!" (18–19). The narrator seems to have no way of escaping the oppressive control of male medical authorities (her husband, her brother, and Weir Mitchell) who deny her voice, who attempt to cure her by forcing her back into an outdated model of women's identity and speech.

In the end, this "cure" actually destroys her. Caught between modes of discourse that are figured as binary opposites — the rational and the imaginative, the logical and the illogical, the sane and the insane, the "masculine" and the "feminine" — the narrator's personality splits; she forms two warring psyches that mirror the discursive modes that surround her. Through identification with the wallpaper and the woman in it, she creates a subversive personality that tries to help the woman escape, one that so identifies with the woman in the wallpaper that she *becomes* her. This subversive "feminine" self bites the mattress, strips off the wallpaper, and ultimately claims, "I've got out at last . . . you can't put me back" (19). This self works with the woman in the wallpaper to free all women: "I pulled and she shook. I shook and she pulled, and before morning we had peeled off yards of that paper" (17). This self opposes the Law of the Father and her rebellion seems to succeed, at least momentarily. When John sees this subversive self at the story's end, he faints dead away, and the narrator has to "creep over him every time" (19) she completes a rotation of the room.

But in addition to this subversive self, there is one that attempts to "escape" from the tyranny of the oppressor by incorporating the oppressor's views. Prisoners placed in positions of authority will sometimes tyrannize other prisoners more than the jailers; identification with the oppressor becomes a psychological strategy of self-preservation. So while the narrator forms a "feminine" personality matching that of the woman in the yellow wallpaper, she also forms a "masculine" one inculcating patriarchal values. This personality constantly wars with the wallpaper, attempting — and failing — to "master" it, to impose sequence on it: "You think you have mastered it [the pattern of the paper], but just as you get well under way in following it, it turns a back-somersault and there you are. It slaps you in the face, knocks you down, and tramples upon you. It is like a bad dream" (12). This self possessively desires to penetrate the wallpaper, to unveil its hidden meaning: "I am determined that nobody shall find it [the pattern of the paper] out but myself" (14). Finally, it is this oppressor self that agrees to the incarceration of the prisoner in the wallpaper, and to its own incarceration: "I've got a rope up here that even Jennie did not find. If that woman does get out, and tries to get away, I can tie her! . . . I am securely fastened now by my well-hidden rope — you don't get *me* out in the road there! . . . Here I can creep smoothly on the floor, and my shoulder just fits in that long smooch around the wall, so I cannot lose my way" (18). Rather than shaking the bars of the prison, the oppressor self understands the "justice" of her confinement and even treats it as enjoyable: "my shoulder just fits in that long smooch . . . so I cannot lose my way." As Linda Wagner-Martin comments, although the later half of the story seems to move toward the protagonist's liberation, this freedom is ultimately false: "The woman . . . does not dance or skip or fly, common images for the state of freedom. She only *creeps,* a derogation of the more positive word *crawls,* which is not itself a very positive movement" (61). The oppressor self accepts her confinement within the house of patriarchy and her creeping, imprisoned, alienated status.

Two selves have thus been made manifest by the end of the story; neither one can be "put back" (19). Perhaps, as Treichler argues, the narrator has gained control of her language but not of the material situation. But perhaps she has lost control of both herself and her discourse. Trapped between the subversive patterns of the yellow wallpaper and her husband's rational discourse, between the "masculine" and "feminine" sides of her personality, she has only formed two incompatible identities that mirror two oppositional discursive modes. Finally, in the warring between these two opposed linguistic modes, her own personality and voice are erased by madness.

The narrator of this story at times attempts to master the subversive, feminine "Other" that emerges in a confrontation with patriarchal discourse. She may also attempt to master the unruly, threatening, racial "Other" that emerges in such a confrontation. In a provocative reading of the text, Susan Lanser wonders whether the yellow wallpaper could symbolize a racial threat: "Is the wallpaper, then, the political unconscious of a culture in which an Aryan woman's madness, desire, and anger . . . are projected onto the 'yellow' woman who is, however, also the feared alien? When the narrator tries to liberate the woman from the wall, is she trying to purge her of her color, to peel her from the yellow paper, so that she can accept this woman as herself?" (429). Certainly, Gilman's views on race were puzzling and contradictory.[2] But rather than eliding these views, she structures them into her text. So the yellow wallpaper can symbolize both the narrator's desire to master and enchain a racial "Other" as well as her desire to liberate this racial "Other" who is really not other, her desire to free and liberate all women, whether they be "yellow" or white. Gilman's text articulates what were for her — at this time — unresolvable contradictions, unresolvable oppositions between the "yellow" and the "white," the "feminine" and the "masculine," between a language that is freeing and one that constrains. The text is honest in positing these contradictions but presents no solution. Finally, "The Yellow Wall-Paper" depicts the feminine subject's entrapment within masculine and racist constructions of language and identity but finds no way of undercutting the oppositions that create this imprisonment. As a portrait of how women can "escape the sentence," it is ambiguous at best, despairing at worst.

Herland reverses this plot; instead of telling "herstory in hisland" it tells the history of three men who wander into a world where their gender has no validity and into a language that seems alien.[3] Yet Gilman does not merely invert the gender and language politics of patriarchal culture, as some critics have argued. She also attempts to write "the other history" of which Hélène Cixous speaks: "Phallocentrism *is*. History has never produced, recorded anything but that. Which does not mean that this form is inevitable or natural. Phallocentrism is the enemy. Of *everyone*. Men stand to lose by it, differently but as seriously as women. And it is time to transform. To invent the other history" (96). In *Herland*, Gilman invents the history of a nonphallocentric language and culture, and she attempts to move beyond the binary oppositions that have structured patriarchal culture. Not surprisingly, then, the history of Herland is unlike standard histories of adventure and conquest, as the narrator, Vandyck Jennings, recognizes in a chapter aptly titled "A Unique History": "It is no use for me to try to piece out this account with adventures. If the people who read it are not interested in these amazing women and their history, they will not be interested at all" (49). Instead, the history of

Herland undermines standard conceptions of gender and language, and in undermining them throws them open, making them polysemous, fluid, capable of being revised.

Gilman begins by undermining stereotypes of femininity. All three of the men who visit Herland (Van, Terry, and Jeff) have different expectations about women's "essential" nature. Jeff idolizes women and expects to find a country "just blossoming with roses and babies and canaries and tidies," while Terry has visions "of a sort of sublimated summer resort—just Girls and Girls and Girls" (7). In short, Jeff believes the land will be peopled with domestic saints, while Terry believes it will abound with oversexed New Women. Van tries to take a "middle ground" on the subject of women, yet he "argue[s] learnedly about the physiological limitations of the sex" (9) and says, upon finding evidence of advanced technology: "But . . . why, this is a *civilized* country. . . . There must be men" (11). But Van eventually realizes that in the patriarchal world he inhabits, "femininity" is actually created by masculine conceptions of the feminine: "These women [in Herland] . . . were strikingly deficient in what we call 'femininity.' This led me very promptly to the conviction that those 'feminine charms' we are so fond of are not feminine at all, but mere reflected masculinity—developed to please us because they had to please us, and in no way essential to the real fulfillment of their great process" (58–59). Men construct women as deficient, incomplete mirrors of themselves—femininity is "mere reflected masculinity." So it is no wonder these men believe they can predict what they will find in Herland; as Van says (apparently without recognizing his pun): "we had been cocksure as to the inevitable limitations, the faults and vices, of a lot of women" (81). In fact, where the men expect to find pettiness, jealousy, stupidity, and hysteria, they find instead social consciousness, affection, intelligence and a high "standard of health and vigor" (81). Through these contrasts, Gilman illustrates that the limitations of "Woman" are caused by patriarchal society and by phallocentric ("cocksure") definitions of the "feminine," not by some intrinsic psychological or physiological feminine character.

Herland also undermines phallocentric notions of masculinity, illustrating that the "masculine" is a social construction rather than an intrinsic difference between the sexes. Gender boundaries blur in Herland; the women have short hair and wear unisex clothing. Finally, it is only the men's beards that can be clung to as outward symbols of their masculinity: "We began to rather prize those beards of ours; they were almost our sole distinction among those tall and sturdy women" (84). In a patriarchal world, the men's beards would be a crucial mark of social and physiological difference, but in Herland they mean little. Masculinity itself, then, is shown to reside in a facade, an external construction of "difference." Furthermore, Van begins to question whether this facade actually signifies anything. To Van, Terry Nicholson has always been a kind of hero, a "man among men," but when placed in a different context Terry's masculinity seems excessive: "At home we had measured him with other men, and, though we knew his failings, he was by no means an unusual type. We knew his virtues too, and they had always seemed more prominent than the faults. Measured among women—our women at home, I mean—he always stood high. . . . But here, against the calm wisdom and quiet restrained humor of these women . . . here he was all out of drawing" (75).

Masculinity is contextual; it takes on virtue or vice depending on what it is measured against. In Herland, Terry's "intense masculinity" becomes a caricature of itself, something of which Van is "ashamed" (130). Terry's "intense masculinity" also loses some of its intensity when measured against a culture in which women have aspects of the "masculine" (power, strength, self-determination, short hair, etc.), causing Van to question whether this "masculinity" is a true and irrevocable essence or a contextual, constructed difference. Furthermore, since the Herlanders reproduce parthenogenetically (by means of "virgin birth"), masculinity is not necessary for reproduction, and on a broader level the text indicates that it is also not necessary for social progress.

"History in Herland," then, presents a critique of patriarchal constructions of masculinity and femininity. In Gilman's text, however, the destruction of gender norms and the construction of a new theory of language are crucially interlinked. Therefore, after demonstrating that the men's theories of identity are disconcerted when they come into contact with women who refuse to play the role of objects in men's dramas of subjectivity, Gilman then shows that the men's language is also disconcerted. The Herlanders speak a maternal language the men must learn. In effect, the men must find their place within an alternative symbolic order. And having once found their place within this mother tongue, they have difficulty returning to the father tongue, to the patriarchal discourse of power. Gilman uses these changes to demonstrate that symbolic language can be overturned by a new theory of language that configures voice as an instrument of dialogue and understanding rather than mastery over others.

The Herlandian language has the ability to enact change partially because it is nonbinary. Binarisms create hierarchies in which women are usually equated with the lesser term, as Cixous explains: "The philosophical [order] constructs itself starting with the abasement of woman. Subordination of the feminine to the masculine order which appears to be the condition for the functioning of the machine" (92). But in Herland, Gilman implies that the "machine" of binary oppositions does not exist; there is no patriarchy, and the Law of the Father cannot be established in a land where fatherhood has never existed, either theoretically or actually. Furthermore, because there is only one gender, there is no sexual binarism, no man/woman dichotomy. Even the presence of three men does not introduce binary differentiation. As Jeff says to Van: "They don't seem to notice our being men. . . . They treat us—well—just as they do one another. It's as if our being men was a minor incident" (30). In fact, all traces of men have long since vanished; as Jeff exclaims, "we don't see any *signs* of [men]" (29, my emphasis). Even in literature this is the case; the men can find "no *signs* of [men] in the books they gave us, or the pictures" (44, emphasis added). Gilman's emphasis on "signs" is not coincidental, for she depicts a world in which both physical and linguistic phallocentric marks of difference have been forgotten. Herlandian civilization establishes itself based on collective action, as Van explains: "they had no wars. They had no kings, and no priests, and no aristocracies. They were sisters, and as they grew, they grew together—not by competition, but by united action" (60). In Herland, then, subjectivity is not founded on the oppression of an "Other," and sexual difference itself does not exist.

Binary sexual differences, then, do not seem at first glance to exist in an essential way in Herland. The men have penises, but this is a minor incident, not the foundation for a pejorative construction of subjectivity. And yet, it has been argued that it is precisely sexual difference that creates humans' relationship to language. As Julia Kristeva explains: "Sexual difference—which is at once biological, physiological, and relative to production—is translated by and translates a difference in the relationship of subjects to the symbolic contract which *is* the social contract: a difference, then, in the relationship to power, language, and meaning" ("Women's Time" 196). The question arises, then, as to how one can enter the symbolic in a land where sexual difference does not exist. The question also arises as whether this "language" of Herland can properly be considered a language. The answer to these questions lies in the fact that in Herland, difference does exist, but it ceases to function as a limitation, a perception of lack. Instead, difference becomes a positive process whereby the individual can be both separate and one with the larger community. Difference exists, then, but it is difference with a difference.

Naming practices, for example, reflect not a separation between subject and object, male and female, as they do under patriarchy, but an integration into the community as well as a defining of self. In a patriarchal society, patrilineal naming enforces phallic law, portraying women as objects of exchange between fathers and husbands. Terry argues that his future wife, Alima, should take his name after marriage as "a sign of [his] possession" (118). However, in Herland names do not express ownership; children do not take their mothers' names but rather are given ones that reflect their individual qualities. As Moadine (a teacher) tells Terry: "A good many of us have another [name], as we get on in life—a descriptive one. That is the name we earn. Sometimes even that is changed, or added to, in an unusually rich life. Such as our present Land Mother—what you call president or king, I believe. She was called Mera, even as a child; that means 'thinker.' Later there was added Du—Du-mera—the wise thinker, and now we all know her as O-du-mera—great and wise thinker" (75). Through names difference is established, but it is difference that does not exclude or limit, difference that allows for distinction without hierarchy. This type of difference does not separate the world into two categories: subjects who possess their own names (men) and objects who are named and defined as the possessions of others (women and children).

Gilman also uses naming practices to emphasize that difference can be based on individual strengths rather than weaknesses. O-du-mera receives her name not as the result of displacing or replacing others but as a result of her ability to lead and guide. The communal, collective vision of the world guides these women; they are relationally oriented, and they find their differences in how they help each other. And so children find they "were People, too, from the first," people in a world of connection where what they learn "widen[ed] out into contact with an endless range of common interests"; the things they learn are "*related*, from the first; related to one another, and to the national prosperity" (100). Although Gilman does not avoid the binarism common to most utopias—the binarism of the utopian world versus the "real" world—within the culture of Herland, Gilman tries to avoid binarism by creating a world based on communal and collective good rather than oppression of the "Other." Of course, one must wonder whether any society could exist without binary oppositions and whether difference can be present without becoming repressive (a point I will return to at the end of this section). But Gilman's utopia attempts to move beyond the binary through emphasis on the communal; these women find their differences in how they help the collective good rather than in how they oppress a silent, disempowered "Other."

The women's relationship to language, then, is also construed in this way: it rests not on binary hierarchies but on collectivity. And unlike phallocentric discourse, the language of Herland does not emphasize feminine lack or insufficiency. Generally speaking, psycholinguists mark the oedipal crisis as the point at which individuals make their entry into the symbolic and into language. But as Patricia Waugh points out, both Freud and Lacan fail to investigate "the pre-oedipal period or to examine the mother's position as a subject in her own right. She remains necessarily 'other'" (61). In fact, some theorists have posited that language may exist in the preoedipal phase; Anika Lemaire observes, for example, that "At the time of [the Oedipus] complex . . . linguistic communication has already been established . . . logically, therefore, the complex itself cannot bring about the primal repression which establishes language" (88–89). Sandra Gilbert and Susan Gubar also question whether language need necessarily be tied to the Law of the Father: "It is possible . . . that the Oedipal moment functions as a repetitive revision of an earlier moment, and that the power of the father, while obviously representing the law of patriarchy, need not be inextricably bound to the power of language" ("Sexual Linguistics" 96). In *Herland*, Gilman investigates the mother's position as subject, positing a specifically maternal discourse that does exist, despite the fact that in Herland, there are no oedipal crises, no phalluses, and no "Others" that act as inanimate matter for the existence of the subject.

In a land without a Law of the Father, without a transcendental signifier figured forth by the phallus, language comes to be organized around motherhood. In fact, motherhood has been elevated into an actual religion. The Herlanders have evolved what Van calls a sort of "Maternal Pantheism" that binds and unites them to each other, and to nature itself: "Here was Mother Earth, bearing fruit. All that they ate was fruit of motherhood, from seed or egg or their product. By motherhood they were born and by motherhood they lived—life was, to them, just the long cycle of motherhood" (59). Van has difficulty describing this Herlandian mother-love religion, and he suggests the possibility of a specifically maternal discourse: "It was beyond me. To hear a lot of women talk about 'our children'! But I suppose that is the way the ants and bees would talk—do talk, maybe" (71). In this pre-oedipal—in fact, nonoedipal—matriarchal world, the Herlanders evolve a specifically communal and matriarchal discourse, the language of the "ants and bees" in their hives. Like Cooper, Freeman, and Chopin, Gilman retrieves a language of the mother to undermine patriarchal discourse.

Although Gilman's text does not give a detailed illustration of this language, she does go further than these other writers in describing it. It will not be static and monolithic; rather, it will be a hum of sounds, continually growing, evolving, changing. It will also be a process, not a product. The written law of Herland, for example, is continually being revised; as Moadine says: "We have no laws over a hundred years old, and most of them are under twenty." Laws are not based on an old system of contracts but on the needs of a changing society. Indeed, Herland is always growing, as Van explains, "life to them was growth; their pleasure was in growing, and their duty also" (102). Language thus becomes a fluid instrument of growth, of evolution, of process. The language's style, then, mirrors this concern with growth. Herland speech is musical and heterogeneous; when Van first hears it he notes "a torrent of soft talk tossed back and forth; no savage sing-song, but clear musical fluent speech" (15). The talk is a playful, fluid torrent, continually revised and modified as it is tossed back and forth between speakers like a rubber ball. Furthermore, the language of Herland is, at the same time, both old and new, both complicated and simple, both scientific and pure, as Van's description makes clear: "It was not hard to speak, smooth and pleasant to the ear, and so easy to read and write that I marveled at it. They had an absolutely phonetic system, the whole thing was as scientific as Esperanto yet bore all the marks of an old and rich civilization" (31). Simplified, yet still beautiful and rich, the language can accurately record the continually evolving world of Herland. Literature can be "*true,* true to the living world around them" (103). Rather than the monologic, rigid, hierarchical product that is patriarchal discourse, the musical

Herlandian language emphasizes dialogue, transformation, and improvisation. Language truly becomes a heterogeneous signifying process.

This language, this mother tongue, also has the power to undermine patriarchal discourse and, more specifically, the phallus as transcendental signifier. Initially, the men seek mastery of the Herlandian language because they believe this will grant them power over the women. But the Herlanders teach the men their language to make them part of a beneficent social contract: "As soon as we learned the language — and would agree to do no harm — they would show us the land" (44). For the Herlanders, who have no phallic symbol around which to organize the "haves" and the "have nots," mastery and language do not go hand in hand. "History in Herland" is therefore not a scripting of a narrative of conquest onto the female body of Herland, nor a story of masculine discursive control, as the men originally suppose it will be.[4] Instead it is a history of three men who come to understand that mastery of language and mastery of an "Other" need not be inexorably linked.

As the novel progresses, the men also learn that even the phallus is a contextually defined mark of difference, not a transcendental signifier that grants them mastery in all discursive situations. The women of Herland do not understand, as Van says, "the male sex . . . its special values, its profound conviction of being 'the life force,' its cheerful ignoring of the true life process, and its interpretation of the other sex solely from its own point of view" (134). In Herland, the phallus does not grant men the ability to subjugate an "Other." It is no wonder, then, that Van, Terry, and Jeff find themselves having difficulty with speech in Herland. Lacking a transcendental signifier, as well as the traditional vocabulary of patriarchal society — for in Herland, the words "virgin" (45), "home" (61), "family" (94), "patriotism" (94), and "wife" (118) have no meaning — the men cannot control the discursive situation. The men are urged to give "public lectures" about their country, and Terry revels in the fact that he will be "an Authority" (65) to an audience composed solely of young women. But the men find the women control the production of information, as well as the entire discursive situation: "They had mechanical appliances for disseminating information almost equal to ours at home; and by the time we were led forth to lecture, our audience had thoroughly mastered a well-arranged digest of all we had previously given to our teachers, and were prepared with notes and questions as might have intimidated a university professor" (65). In Herland, then, the men learn repeatedly that they cannot rule with the phallic scepter of power and authority.

Gilman also uses the history of one man in particular — Terry — to illustrate more specifically how the Herlandian language undermines the phallus as transcendental signifier, as well as a commitment to sexual and linguistic mastery. Terry has a habit of engaging in bursts of masculine sturm und drang, but he curtails them because he is — literally — making a spectacle of himself: "At first [Terry] used to storm and flourish quite a good deal, but nothing seemed to amuse [the Herlanders] more; they would gather around and watch him as if it was an exhibition, politely, but with evident interest. So he learned to check himself" (65). Exhibitions of phallocratic language are turned into the object of the gaze and rendered impotent. Terry has always been adept at controlling verbal power, but in the face of this feminine discursive control he begins to stutter: "'Confound their grandmotherly minds!' Terry said. 'Of course they can't understand a Man's World! They aren't human—they're just a pack of Fe-Fe-Females!' This was after he had to admit their parthenogenesis" (80). Terry, the emblem of phallic power, begins stuttering when confronted with evidence of the women's parthenogenesis, their ability to be self-sustaining. In a world of parthenogenesis, the phallus—as transcendental signifier and as an instrument of sexual and linguistic difference and mastery—lacks meaning and power.

But when Terry's discourse is rendered impotent, he tries to assert phallocratic power in a more direct way. After his marriage, Terry tries to force his wife Alima to have sexual relations with him: "Terry put into practice his pet conviction that a woman loves to be mastered, and by sheer brute force, in all the pride and passion of his intense masculinity, he tried to master this woman" (132). However, Alima will not submit to Terry's mastery. She struggles with Terry until others come to her aid. Alima also strikes out against phallocratic power more directly. As Terry reports to Van, Alima "kicked me. . . . And of course a man's helpless when you hit him like that. No woman with a shade of decency—" (143). In fact, Terry's attempt to rape his wife is indecent, not Alima's hitting below the belt. Literally, Terry is a phallocrat out of control, focused solely on the "passion of his intense masculinity." Clearly, Terry equates phallic, linguistic power with the subjugation of a silent, passive, feminine body; he is surprised, then, when this body turns out to be active and resistant. As Irigaray postulates, men are disconcerted when they begin to imagine that the object is not actually an object: "Once imagine that woman imagines and the objects loses its fixed, obsessional character. . . . If the earth turned and more especially turned upon herself, the erection of the subject might thereby be disconcerted and risk losing its elevation and penetration. For what would there be to rise up from and exercise his power over? And in?" (133). When Terry learns that Alima is not complacent, he has nothing to exercise power over, and in. No wonder, then, that Terry is "sick" (142) of Herland; in more ways than one, his phallic mastery has been deflated.[5]

Perhaps this is why, before leaving, Terry is willing to renounce his phallic power, at least in relationship to the land of Herland (which he has always conceived of as a feminine body). The Herlanders ask the men, as "gentlemen," to promise not to betray the location of the country. At first Terry refuses: "'Indeed I won't!' he protested. 'The first thing I'll do is to get an expedition fixed up to force an entrance into Ma-land'" (146). But when Terry hears the alternative—"he must remain an absolute prisoner [in Herland], always" (146) — he does promise. Terry's urge for phallic power, his urge to rape the land and "force an entrance" into Herland, is finally controlled. As Gilman's sequel *With Her in Ourland* reveals, Terry never does return to Herland, nor does he disclose its location. In the end, the word is stronger than the phallus — especially in Herland, where words themselves are figured as communal agents of truth and freedom rather than elements of destructive and coercive patriarchal power.

Herlandian language transforms the men who enter Herland, inscribing them into an order where they can no longer control the world by controlling the word. Terry is disconcerted when he learns there are limits to phallocratic power, and Jeff, as Van reports, is thoroughly "Herlandized." Even Van, the middle man, the "everyman" figure of the narrative, changes profoundly: "I began to see both ways more keenly than I had before; to see the painful defects of my own land, the marvelous gains of this" (137). Van and his wife, Ellador, talk until "a common ground" (127) grows between them and Van's "ideas of what was essential" also change (128). Unlike Robert in *The Awakening,* who only pales before Edna's assertion of an alternative mode of subjectivity and discourse, Van is able to understand and accept changes in women's subjectivity and discourse. Gilman's goal is not only a New Woman but a New Man, and the ideal human society will be a place where both can coexist.

Gilman's utopian vision, then, does try to offer more than an inversion of the language/gender politics of the androcentric culture. By reconceiving the function of language itself, Gilman asks us to reconceive our relationship to "Others." Language need not be an instrument of coercive dominance; instead it can establish "common ground" — the knowledge of the subjectivity of both genders. Gilman's revisionary viewpoint ultimately encourages the reader to see both "his story" and "her story." In our land, women are excluded from history, as Van explains:

> When we say *men, man, manly, manhood,* and all the other masculine derivatives, we have in the background of our minds a huge vague crowded picture of the world and its activities. To grow up and "be a man," to "act like a man" — the meaning and connotation is wide indeed. That vast background is full of marching columns of men ... of men steering their ships into new seas, exploring unknown mountains ... building roads and bridges and high cathedrals, managing great businesses, teaching in all the colleges, preaching in all the churches; of men everywhere, doing everything — "the world."
>
> And when we say *women,* we think *female* — the sex (137).

In this vast catalogue of patriarchal history, women are a mere footnote. In Herland, of course, the situation is quite different, and Van and the other men learn that women, too, are part of humanity: "We were now well used to seeing women not as females but as people; people of all sorts, doing every kind of work" (137). The men understand that women can be more than just a preposition in language; in fact, they can be the subject of language, and subjects in their own right. In the sequel to *Herland*, Van and Ellador return to our land, and Van retains his new-found vision of women as subjects. And Ellador, too, learns to understand men as people.[6] It is the discovery of the subjectivity of *both* genders that Gilman believes will liberate the world. And for Gilman, language is the primary instrument of this discovery.

The language of Herland therefore transforms the men who travel there, but it is also meant to transform the reader's conception of language and gender. When we read the text of *Herland* we are encouraged to make the discovery of the subjectivity of both genders. While seeming to transport us to another world, the text actually asks us to reexamine our own world and to revise our conceptions of gender and language. Ultimately, then, in *Herland* Gilman presents a speculative vision of hope. "Herstory in Hisland" — at least as embodied by "The Yellow Wall-Paper" — is a destruction of the feminine subject. But "History in Herland" is meant to be a story of coming to terms with, and understanding, the subjectivity of both women and men. And language is a primary way of effecting this change; the world can change through the word. In her introduction to *Herland*, Ann J. Lane argues that "it is not the scientist, the warrior, the priest, or the craftsman, but the mother who is the connecting point from present to future" (xxiii). I would argue that for Gilman, it is not the *mother* but the *mother tongue* that offers hope for the transformation of our world and our word. The language the Herlanders speak resembles Esperanto — the cognate of which is hope, and like Herlandian society, Herlandian language offers a speculative vision of hope. *Herland* seeks to revise patriarchal discourse, the Law of the Father, by creating a new form of expression — a language of the "ants and the bees in their hive." Gilman's text first elevates this maternal language over phallocentric discourse, but ultimately it attempts to move toward a language that allows both men and women to be speaking subjects.

Of course, there are a number of limitations to Gilman's utopian project. For example, in Herland, where motherhood is privileged over everything, some women are deemed unfit for motherhood (82); these women would, of necessity, be devalued, Othered. Furthermore, given Gilman's views on race, one might guess that many of these "unfit" mothers come from a "primitive," "atavistic," racial (that is, darker-skinned) stock, rather than from the pure "Aryan" (54) stock of the more "fit" Herlanders. The Herlanders, in short, may practice a form of "negative eugenics" (69) that seems to contradict Gilman's commitment to finding a world in which no one is disempowered. The text might, then, attempt to undermine the masculine/feminine basis of linguistic disempowerment only to construct and maintain another set of oppressive binarisms in its racial politics. But finally, does *Herland* actually undermine the masculine/feminine basis of disempowerment, the foundation of an empowered subjectivity in the oppression of an "Other"? Perhaps not. After all, Terry, Van, and Jeff will never be mothers, and in a world where motherhood is the transcendental signifier, again, it seems that of necessity they would be (or would come to be) the disempowered, the "opaque matter which in theory does not know itself."

Although Gilman's achievement in *Herland* is impressive, then, her utopian vision is flawed by a number of contradictions. But as with "The Yellow Wall-Paper," Gilman structures these contradictions into her text rather than simply eliding them. After all, once the men come to Herland, the women do not give up their transcendental signifier in favor of one that melds maternity and paternity. To use an analogy, they do not, like Sarah Penn, create a house/barn; neither do they create a womb/penis, a mother/father, or a maternal/paternal language of (for example) the ants and the bees in their hive and the lions and tigers in their den. For Gilman, this might be a way of reconciling a contradiction her text has raised but also eliding it. The power of Gilman's text is actually found in such contradictions, in asking whether it is possible to have a language of the feminine that does not debase the masculine, in asking whether a maternal text of necessity must exclude a paternal subjectivity. It is precisely these questions that late-nineteenth-century writers, and current feminist theorists, return to over and over again. Gilman does not resolve these questions, but she does explore their multiple dimensions through the speculative vision that is *Herland*.

Herland's utopian framework enables a creative critique of patriarchal discourse, but in the end Gilman's attempt to create a language that moves beyond the binary is flawed by a new set of hierarchical oppositions that the text establishes and maintains. Perhaps this is why Gilman's *Forerunner* stories are situated in the "real world" of an early-twentieth-century patriarchal society: these stories reflect Gilman's understanding that subversion of patriarchal discourse must occur from within the terms of the discourse itself. In many ways, Gilman's later short fictions therefore have more in common with twentieth-century writers discussed in the final chapter of this book. Texts such as "The Widow's Might," "An Honest Woman," "Spoken To," "Mrs. Beazley's Deed," "With a Difference (Not Literature)," and "Lost Women" insert an unruly feminine subject into symbolic language. This angry subject breaks apart patriarchal discourse by traversing boundaries, by refusing to silence herself, and by telling metafictions that critique and rewrite the erasures of patriarchal history.[7]

In "The Widow's Might" (1911) when Mrs. McPherson makes the transition from a good domestic saint to an independent woman with a voice of her own, she begins to challenge the theoretical structures that have maintained her linguistic and social disempowerment. Mrs. McPherson has endured a marriage to a tyrannous man whose own children are not saddened by his death. After Mr. McPherson's death, her children plan to sell their father's ranch and care for their mother, who they believe will be dependent and infirm. Mrs. McPherson's children assume that like a good domestic saint, their mother has no identity outside of her relationship to her husband and family — that she is, in short, a "preposition" defined through others. But Mrs. McPherson does have an independent, self-defined identity, and she decides to assert it: "I have considered Mr. McPherson's wishes for thirty years ... Now, I'll consider mine. I have done my duty since the day I married him. It is eleven thousand days — today ... I'm tired of duty" (104). During her husband's illness, Mrs. McPherson has turned the home into a "ranchosanitarium" where sick people can recuperate. In so doing, she has earned enough money to travel and, as she puts it, "play with" (106). Mrs. McPherson has changed her material conditions; she now has the economic power to do what she wants.

But this economic power would be removed by her children if it were not for another change: she has found a voice that challenges her construction as a silent and submissive object. When her son rebukes her desire to travel, she speaks out emphatically, saying: "I'm going to do what I never did before. I'm going to *live!*" (105). Mrs. McPherson refuses to be silent in the face of her son James's attempts to use his male authority to control her. For what Mrs. McPherson has achieved, through the long years of suffering, is precisely a voice that refuses the Law of the Father (or son). Gilman makes this clear through the use of a synecdoche in which Mrs. McPherson's voice stands for her whole self. During most of the story, Mrs. McPherson wears a black veil, and because her children cannot see her face, she seems to become wholly voice. For example, when James speaks of carrying out his father's wishes "to the letter" (103), Gilman depicts Mrs. McPherson's response through the voice synecdoche: "'Your father is dead,' remarked the voice" (103). As in Alcott's "A Whisper in the Dark," the paternal will seems to inexorably establish the Law of the Father, but Mrs. McPherson resists this decree through language, through an insistence that she has overturned the Law of the Father: "Your father is dead." Mrs. McPherson eventually sheds her veil and presents her entire self to her children, saying: "No question of my sanity, my dears! I want you to grasp the fact that your mother is a Real Person with some interests of her own and half a lifetime yet. ... Now, I'm free" (106). Mrs. McPherson asserts the rights of a "Real Person," becoming an active subject with a forceful speaking voice. But it is specifically her refusal of the Law of the Father — her refusal to be a silent object in a masculine drama of subjectivity — that creates her enfranchised identity.

Gilman's story demonstrates a theoretical understanding of feminine linguistic and psychological oppression, but is not very specific about how this oppression can be overturned. Mrs. McPherson finds a voice that challenges the Law of the Father — but how? And where? What is the nature of this voice, beyond its being "defiant"? "An Honest Woman" (1911) is clearer about how women can become metalinguists—individuals who understand, and revise, the theoretical power structures undergirding patriarchal language. The story begins with a conversation that seems to reveal women's secondary status in language and culture. Two men discuss Mary Main, the owner of a successful boarding hotel. While one man—Abramson—talks and talks about Mary, saying, "There's an honest woman if ever there was one!" (75), the other man—Burdock—only feeds him an occasional question. Abramson treats women as if they are public property—some are good and some are bad, but all can be talked about and defined by men:

"I've got a high opinion of good women," [Abramson] announced with finality. "As to bad ones, the less said the better!" and he puffed his strong cigar, looking darkly experienced.

"They're doin' a good deal towards reformin' 'em, nowadays, ain't they?" ventured Burdock.

The young man laughed disagreeably. "You can't reform spilled milk," said he.

"But I do like to see an honest, hard-working woman succeed."

"So do I, boy," said his companion, "so do I," and they smoked in silence. (76)

Puffing on his cigar, Abramson uses phallocentric power to inscribe the entity woman with labels of "good" or "bad," "angel" or "whore." For Abramson, women are words in men's mouths, and men have the ability to construct them—to stereotype and define them. Indeed, this is precisely how they construct their own identity as subjects—through an othering of women, of the "feminine matter" that in theory does not know herself. Notably, however, Burdock is rather silent; he is aware that some women escape men's categorizations.

As Burdock knows, Mary Cameron Main is not, in actuality, a "good" woman. A flashback in the story reveals that Mary is a "fallen" women who had an adulterous affair and bore a child out of wedlock. After Mary's lover abandons her, she realizes she is "ruined": " 'I suppose I am a ruined woman,' she said. She went to the glass and lit the gas on either side, facing herself with fixed gaze and adding calmly, 'I don't look it!' . . . The woman she saw in the glass seemed as one at the beginning of a splendid life, not at the end of a bad one" (82). This moment of mirroring reflects a radical swerve from the patriarchal plot, a metalinguistic moment in which women are encouraged to comprehend the constructedness of the linguistic categories used to define them, and to break from these categories. "Ruined" is an arbitrarily imposed signifier that men would use to define Mary, but it does not correspond in any "true" way to her physical and psychological reality. Mary here realizes the arbitrary nature of the verbal categories used to contain women, as does an attentive reader who has been tricked into a naive reading of Mary's character by the story's opening dialogue, and then tricked out of this naive reading by the character's radical, metalinguistic swerve.

In this moment, Mary also comprehends the rules of her culture's "language game": men control and manipulate language, authoring women's destiny through their words; women are silent, passive agents within language—created by language rather than creators of it. But at this crucial juncture, Mary Main rejects the rules of this language game and begins using language to author her own destiny. For Wittgenstein, the language game of a society reflects a particular worldview but is also subject to change: "There are . . . countless different kinds of use of what we call 'symbols,' 'words,' 'sentences.' And this multiplicity is not something fixed, given once for all; but new types of language, new language-games, as we may say, come into existence, and others become obsolete and get forgotten" (11). Mary decides to take advantage of this "multiplicity." She dresses in black, and when asked about her husband she "press[es] her handkerchief to her eyes and say[s], 'He has left me. I cannot bear to speak of him' " (83). Literally, she classifies her husband as unspeakable, but on a more metaphoric level, this statement demonstrates that Mary has discerned that she need not be passively constructed by patriarchal words but rather can actively and consciously engage in the linguistic processes that shape how she is received, the language games of her culture. Mary has also obtained a sophisticated awareness of the constructedness of essential categories of "woman," of the play between truth and untruth in language, and of the means whereby communication becomes distorted and distorting. In short, Mary has become a metalinguist: a person who not only uses language but who also understands and intervenes in its functioning in radical ways.

Mary demonstrates her metalinguistic ability most clearly when her former lover returns and threatens to blackmail her by revealing her "fallen" status to her customers. Like Abramson, Mr. Main believes women are defined by *what men say*; he claims that he could "shatter [Mary's life] with a *word*" (85, emphasis added). Mary merely smiles patiently at Main and states: "You can't shatter facts, Mr. Main. People here know that you left me years ago. They know how I have lived since. If you try to blacken my reputation here, I think you will find the climate of Mexico more congenial" (86). Mary takes a calculated risk, asserting that her actions have constructed a world that transcends the linguistic categories that would normally be applied to her. The battle is played over and within language. Mr. Main tries to force Mary to abide by the rules of the old language game, while Mary asserts a new reality in which she is judged by her actions rather than by patriarchal linguistic categories. Mary's confidence in her own abilities as a metalinguist finally convince Mr. Main that her reality is more credible, and he gives up his plan. Furthermore, Mary's new reality is affirmed by the external frame of the story, in which a silent observer—the male character Burdock—overhears the entire story yet does not reveal Mary's secret to anyone (86). Representing the voice of the town, Burdock's final promise to keep Mary's secret demonstrates that she has created not just a possible world but also an actual reality, in which women devise new and more empowering linguistic and social categories for themselves.

The story's final message is that masculine language may claim to construct women but that a metalinguistic understanding of language's functioning gives women the ability to reconstruct themselves and create a supportive community. But women also need to begin a renovation of language itself. In "Spoken To" (1915), Gilman shows how women can create new systems of signification that unite their deeds and language. Lucille, the protagonist of this story, is an independent New Woman. Despite the protests of her mother and aunt, True Women who believe in "the theory of the weakness and dependence of women" (29), Lucille insists on walking alone. The harm her mother and aunt fear, however, seems to be mostly verbal: "You do not know the dangers you so recklessly court. . . . Why you might—you might be *spoken to.*" In fact, several times while walking Lucille encounters men who try to use language and phallocentric power against her. One evening a man comes out of a dark side street and stands waiting for Lucille, but she is not frightened: "Lucille, seeing that he wished to speak to her, drew up and turned her friendly face to him. He seemed a little surprised and somewhat lamely asked the way to the best known street in the vicinity" (31). This incident indicates that, like Mary Main, Lucille understands how language is supposed to disempower her, and she consciously refuses this disempowerment. Lucille turns the gaze on the gazer, speech on the speaker, and in so doing undermines phallocentric linguistic power.

Although Gilman was fond of walking, this story does not advocate that women place themselves in situations of evident danger. Instead, it analyzes the way women are confined by a fear of phallocratic discourse. Aunt Marie, who is from Paris, has been frightened of walking alone ever since she was "spoken to," as she explains: "I was hurrying along, looking at no one . . . and there stepped up from behind — a man! He was close — almost touching my elbow, and he — spoke to me! He said — I cannot bring myself to tell you what he said! Oh, it was terrible! . . . Oh, my shame" (32). After this event Marie submits to the fear of being "spoken to," never walking alone. The man who insults Marie has a notorious reputation in Paris; he lays wagers on his ability to make women blush. Because of his actions, Marie believes that "No young girl is safe in Paris" (32).

When Lucille visits Paris, however, she has a chance to revise this history of feminine disempowerment and to exercise her metalinguistic abilities. Lucille encounters the same man but deliberately misinterprets his words as a plea for money:

And then, of a sudden, a gentleman approached her with studied grace, came close, very close, murmured something in her ear, and swept off his glossy hat with a magnificent air. . . . A little group of well-dressed men drew near, with meaning smiles, their eyes on the girl's face.

And Lucille?

She halted promptly, as the gentleman spoke, took in his whole impressive appearance with one lightening glance; heard, and fully understood, the unmeasured insult of his whispered words; gazed on him with eyes of unmoved cheerfulness; drew from her pocket one well-gloved hand — and put two cents in his hat.

She passed on, quite undisturbed, as one who has performed a good action.

He stood there, the center of many eyes, of much laughter, and from the edge of his white collar to the top of his bald head the slow color rose — pink — red — purple. If he had never blushed before, he was blushing now. (33)

Lucille pretends the man is a beggar and gives him a coin, thereby using the signs of class to undermine the gender hierarchy. However, Lucille's gesture can also be read as her invention of a language that expresses her condemnation of this man. To respond in kind — using a phallocentric language of abuse — would only validate this man's use of language. Lucille's gesture speaks her contempt for this man, and overturns his phallocentric dominance.

In "Spoken To," Lucille's language and actions construct a revisionist history that shows women speaking and gazing, turning the men who have kept them silenced and confined into a spectacle, the object of the gaze. "Mrs. Beazley's Deeds" (1911) is also a metalinguistic story that critiques systems of language that disempower women, but in this text Gilman indicates even more clearly that women's voices can transform discursive structures (such as the system of law), as well as the world around them. The story concerns a woman completely cut off from discourse, so much so that she is reduced to getting information through holes in the floor, as the story's opening vividly depicts: "Mrs. William Beazley was crouching on the floor of her living-room over the store in a most peculiar attitude. It was what a doctor would call the 'knee-chest' position; and the woman's pale, dragged out appearance quite justified this idea. She was as one scrubbing a floor and then laying her cheek to it, a rather undignified little pile of bones, albeit discreetly covered with stringy calico."[8] Mrs. Beazley is reduced to a pale "little pile of bones" crouching without dignity before the superior linguistic power of the male. But Maria Beazley is also disempowered in her personal situation, for she is married to a lazy, tyrannical husband who overworks her and beats their children. Mr. Beazley forces his family to live over the store he runs rather than in the more spacious house his wife owns. Mr. Beazley is now on the verge of selling this home, Maria's last piece of property, and Maria is listening at the hole in the floor in a desperate attempt to get information about this transaction.

With the help of a clever female attorney, Maria is eventually able to subvert this transaction, retake her maternal property, and divorce her husband. Yet language is central to her struggle for control, for Maria must overturn both a patriarchal discourse that has been used to silence her and a patriarchal story that has erased her agency. Mr. Beazley is a discursive tyrant who exercises complete control over his wife's access to information and knowledge. He never tells his wife about any of his business dealings until it is too late for her to object, and he pays no attention to her protests. Similarly, Mr. Beazley tightly controls his wife's access to legal documents (to deeds), as this exchange shows:

> "You might as well tell me what you're doin' — I have to read the deed anyhow" [Mrs. Beazley says].
> "Much you'll make out of readin' the deed," said [Mr. Beazley] with some dry amusement, "and Justice Fielden lookin' on and waitin' for you!"
> "You're going to sell the Rockford lot — I know it!" said she. "How can you do it, William! The very last piece of what father left me! — and it's mine — you can't sell it — I won't sign!"
> Mr. Beazley minded her outcry no more than he minded the squawking of a to-be beheaded hen. (226)

Mr. Beazley refuses to let his wife read the documents, but he also ignores her speech; to him it is not language at all but merely the "squawking" of an imperiled animal. It is no wonder, then, that Mrs. Beazley's "voice rose in a plaintive crescendo, with a helpless break at the end" (226). She has little access to discourse, and language itself seems to be an ineffective means of protest.

When Maria Beazley confides this history to her friend Miss Lawrence (a lawyer), Maria states she is telling "no great story" (228). It is simply the sad tale of her life, a tale full of sound and fury but ultimately signifying little since, as Mrs. Beazley says, "girls don't know nothin'!" (170). And it is not even a unique story, for as Mrs. Beazley says, most of the women she knows are "near dead" (226) from overwork. Yet in telling this story, Maria begins to swerve from the patriarchal plot, the patriarchal language game that insists women remain silent and disempowered. The act of telling her story to a friend (which is, after all, an act of authoring her story) and the act of asking for advice (which is, after all, a way of asking how the story can be changed) destabilize the text's prior construction of Maria Beazley. Like Freeman's Sarah Penn, Maria Beazley makes disparaging comments about women but in the end puts faith in the power of her own voice.[9] When Miss Lawrence learns that Mr. Beazley has been putting his property in his wife's name in order to shield it from creditors, she helps Maria take legal action to gain control of it. So one day Mr. Beazley returns from a business trip to find that his store and house have been sold, his wife and children have left him, and his money has been withdrawn from the bank. Most important, Mr. Beazley no longer wields linguistic power over his wife, as Miss Lawrence informs him: "Any communication you may wish to make to her you can make through me" (231). Clearly, this is a legal change, but it is also a linguistic one. And language is the key to Maria's empowerment; becoming the author of her own story is the first step to her freedom, a step that enables all the other steps.

When Maria Beazley comments that she is telling "no great story" (228), she explicitly and metalinguistically comments on how language has functioned within the world she knows to keep women silenced and disempowered. Yet she tries to change this, and in so doing she swerves from the patriarchal plot itself, from a patriarchal story that constructs her as an object. Metatextual commentary, then, by a character within the story functions as a critique of patriarchal stories. Metalinguistic practices by another character — Miss Lawrence — create the possibility of a new story. Miss Lawrence understands that Maria's disempowerment is a product of language (of a legal discourse she does not understand), and she also understands that this discourse can be changed. Miss Lawrence gently prods Maria with questions, encouraging her to take actions that allow her to recuperate her property and her voice. Therefore, the metalinguistic and metafictional aspects of this story are used to rewrite the patriarchal story and to create a new reality in which women are active agents in the creation of stories and in the authoring of their destiny.

Metalinguistic stories (stories about language's functioning) such as "An Honest Woman," "Spoken To," and "Mrs. Beazley's Deeds" thus demonstrate that women must develop strategies to take control of language and renovate it; they can then use language to speak themselves rather than merely being "spoken of" or "spoken to." Yet in all three stories, a female character's speech has the effect of silencing a male character. Gilman's metafictions (her stories about stories) also demonstrate that women can renovate language, for in these texts women refuse patriarchal plots and create their own narratives. However, these stories also move beyond an inversion of the patriarchal plot. "With a Difference (Not Literature)" and "Lost Women" are more closely focused on story making than the texts previously discussed; not coincidentally, they offer a more radical reconstruction of language, narratives, and narrativity.

"With a Difference (Not Literature)" (1914) concerns the seduction and rape of an innocent young girl, Dora Holcomb. The story of Dora's "ruin," as the narrator states, is a familiar patriarchal tale: "We will begin and run along on the lines so sadly familiar, lines that fairly shine from constant use, like streetcar rails. Now we are off" (29). Dora is her parent's pride and joy, and they carefully guard her innocence. However, after a series of financial setbacks, Dora is forced to get a job in a factory, where she is befriended by a villain who makes it his business to ruin young women. Gilman alludes to what happens next in a way that directly calls upon the processes of reading and interpreting stories: "The sophisticated reader now follows with hopeless sympathy the pathetic tragedy which followed" (30). A sophisticated reader can predict the outcome of this particular story, and Gilman carefully plays into this "sophisticated" reader's assumptions. The villain drugs Dora's grape juice (she refuses to drink wine), takes her to his apartment, and rapes her. Although Dora is innocent, she does understand what has happened: "Innocent as was her mind, she had read in stories vague hints of a fate like this—

Gilman's Reconstruction of Gender and Language

and so by the light of fiction there suddenly burst upon her the awful Fact! She was ruined!" (30). In this ironic metafictional configuration, stories themselves are used to illuminate a story that the reader is reading, and stories are also used to explain what is happening to the character (Dora), what she is processing within the text through her own readings of texts. Dora is a reader within the story, placed on the same level as the reader of the story; both are trying to decipher events by reference to other narrative frames.

But for the reader (even a sophisticated one), the frames keep switching, as Gilman keeps intruding a voice into the story that unsettles the narratives we are attempting to impose. When Dora's mother hears her daughter's story, she is sympathetic, but Dora's father tells her to leave his home forever. Nat Holcomb's response is typical, but here the text switches abruptly from this typical, patriarchal tale. Gilman draws attention to the radical swerve her text is undertaking both linguistically and spatially — there is an actual gap in the text, and the next passage is separated from the prior one with six dots:

. . . . . .

There — that is the old story — so far.

Farther it leads the poor girl down the steps that grow steeper and narrower till she slips helpless into the abyss. The same old story.

But in this story something happened.

Witchcraft — revelations — inspiration — call it what you like; but this is what happened, in *this* story (31).

Gilman swerves radically from the patriarchal plot, emphasizing that in *this* story women take control of their own narratives. She also draws attention to her story's metafictional qualities by repeating the word "story" four times, and through the use of italics.

The effect of this radical swerve is to undermine patriarchal plots in which women are the passive victims of patriarchal discourse. First language itself is reclaimed from the patriarchal father, as both Mrs. Holcomb and her daughter speak up. Mrs. Holcomb reprimands her husband and contradicts his dictates: "You listen to me, Nat Holcomb. . . . This is my home and my child, and she stays here — with me" (31). Then Dora, no longer silent, begins telling her story: "What have I done — really done — that you should cast me off like this? . . . If you had told me that there were that kind of men in the world . . . *then* I'd have known what to look out for" (31). As Dora explains, she is not to blame, for it is patriarchal forces that conspire to keep women innocent, resulting in physical and psychological ruin of feminine potential. The story as a whole shapes a metafictional text that refuses the old patriarchal masterplot in which "ruined" women are condemned. Instead of dying in disgrace, as in the patriarchal plot, Dora becomes a teacher and redeemer of other women.

The metafictional qualities of the story thus undermine the "sentence" of the patriarchal story, but they also undermine the "sentence" of patriarchal discourse, the sentence suffered by the narrator of "The Yellow Wall-Paper." Both Dora and her mother find a voice of self-assertion, a voice that expresses their subjectivity, but they are not deemed insane, as is the narrator of "The Yellow Wall-Paper." This new voice is instead heard by the father, and it undermines his concept of femininity. Dora's linguistic assertion causes a response in Mr. Holcomb, as Gilman sarcastically explains: "Then the father saw a great light" (32). Mr. Holcomb acknowledges that he is partially to blame; specifically, Mr. Holcomb admits to depriving his daughter of sexual knowledge. Furthermore, Mr. Holcomb admits that women's submission and objectification are necessary to patriarchal dominance, that women act, as Irigaray says, as a pedestal for the existence of the subject. This is particularly true in terms of sexuality, as Mr. Holcomb indicates; his fury at his daughter was "pure selfishness and pride" (32) based on the reputed loss of the *tabula rasa*, the innocent and blank slate, the female daughter. As Mr. Holcomb tells Dora: "Why a man feels that his daughter is a—a sort of ornament and crown of glory, and if anything happens to her—to spoil the glory—he feels *himself* insulted" (32). Dora was the "opaque matter" which in theory does not know herself, the opaque matter out of which Mr. Holcomb constructed his own glory. This is the underlying tale hidden within the traditional patriarchal plot— a tale of women's objectification and erasure. Gilman reconstructs this tale through the female characters' assertion of their own literate practices of reading and speaking, and through a metafictional narrative voice that disrupts the traditional story, and the traditional reading of stories.

The world that Gilman creates in this work, then, and that the metafictional narrative commentary sustains, presents a more positive fictional pattern in which women reclaim their language, their stories, and their lives. This reclamation does not, however, lead to the silencing or disempowerment of men, as it does in "Mrs. Beazley's Deeds" and "Spoken To"; like the women, Mr. Holcomb finds a story of his own that breaks from the patriarchal masterplot. "With a Difference (Not Literature)" and the next story to be discussed, "Lost Women," therefore present a discursive universe in which both men and women can learn from each other's stories; male characters in these stories are vocal participants in the metalinguistic and metafictional processes that create a new reality.

"Lost Women" (1912) begins by focusing on an issue that seems, at first, to be only relevant to women: the disempowerment caused by patrilineal naming practices. This is a subject Gilman wrote about extensively in several prose essays. In "Names—Especially Women's" (1911), for example, Gilman argues that women are not seen as needing their names because they are not considered persons: "This is but one of the many invidious distinctions between men and women under an androcentric culture. Men, being persons, had names. They must be distinguished from one another. Women, being female belongings, needed no badge save that of the man to whom they belonged. When they left their father's possession, when he gave this woman to be married to this man, she took the name of her new owner, naturally" (262). On a more metaphorical level, the paternom (the husband's or father's name) reduces women to the status of possessions: "It [the man's name] is something like a collar on a dog, the license tag and name of the master" (263). Women are denied subjectivity through the Name of the Father, through patrilineal and patriarchal language practices.

"Lost Women" also illustrates that patrilineal naming practices deny feminine subjectivity. However, the story uses this specific issue to examine three larger questions: how do linguistic practices (such as wives taking their husbands' names) cause women's oppression? How do fictional practices (such as telling stories in certain, traditional ways) perpetuate feminine disempowerment? And what is the best way to change these practices — to create new stories rather than simply inverting or reversing patriarchal realities? To begin with the issue of how linguistic practices cause women's oppression, in "Lost Women" Gilman uses patrilineal naming as a signifier for both the actual and symbolic erasure of femininity. As the storyteller, Aunt Laura, says to her listener, "Don't you see we obliterate half the names as we go on?" (281). Aunt Laura is referring to specific women whose maiden names are lost, but her statement also suggests a more metaphoric collective destruction. Annabel, her niece and listener, does not catch the significance but merely says "Well, never mind that" (281), and urges her aunt to continue the story. Aunt Laura tells the story of Mary Jernigan, an heiress who never receives her inheritance because descent on the "spindle" (maternal) side is so difficult to trace. Mary is the friend of a wealthy woman, Nellie Clark, and a lawyer named Louis Robinson. Louis falls in love with Mary, but she rejects him because her good friend Nellie is in love with Louis. Louis is also unsuccessful in his professional goal; he has been sent to trace the spindle line of descent of a fortune. Mary Jernigan is the heiress, but Louis does not discover this. (And Aunt Laura never explains how she knows this piece of information.) So Louis returns to New York without having achieved success, either personally or professionally.

The story is highly contrived, but its contrivance does not create resolution; all the pieces are brought together, but they are never allowed to cohere. Annabel, a writer, continually tries to unify the story's subject, but Aunt Laura resists such efforts, as the following conversation illustrates:

> "There they all were, together — once — and then they all got separated. I wish I'd known 'em then!" My aunt laid down her rather perfunctory knitting work and looked into the fire. . . .
> "Do go on!" I said. "Which of 'em was the heiress? Mary, I hope."
> She looked at me in some annoyance. "You people that write do drag the vitals out of a story so prematurely! Yes, it was Mary — but much good it did her!"

"You don't mean to say she never got it!" I cried. "Oh, that is horrid—that spoils the story."

"I'm not making up one of your round, smooth, well-flavored, made-to-order stories, Annabel—this is what happened. And what's more, it's happening all the time." (282)

Although Aunt Laura insists that she is telling "what happened" rather than a story, her insistence on telling something that is "happening all the time" suggests that she reads these events metaphorically. She sees her tale as emblematic of the social and linguistic obliteration of women occurring continually in the greater "story" of history itself.

Like Gilman, Aunt Laura insists that what she tells is "not literature"; it is not a smooth, round, literary tale; it is merely "events." And these events continue in their pattern of noncoherence. Eventually, all three characters lose contact with each other, and because Mary Jernigan has become Mrs. John Smith and Nellie Clark has become Mrs. Thomas Brown, the three cannot be reunited. Ironically, Mary, Louis, and Nellie all live briefly in the same town in Texas; this is where Aunt Laura (who owns a hotel) knows them all—separately. But they never meet. Louis leaves the town, Mary lives on, poor and lonely (her husband has died), and Nellie lives on, wealthy and unhappy.

Annabel is appalled at this tale, and she and her aunt again have an exchange of words over the quality of the narrative, with Annabel calling the story "stillborn" and Aunt Laura insisting: "I never said it was a good story. . . . I'm telling you the facts, and I'll stop right now if you want me to" (283). Eventually, however, Aunt Laura does continue with her narrative, and it does achieve some degree of closure. After the death of her husband, Mary starts a small store under her maiden name. One day Nellie drives by, sees the store's name, and recovers her old friend. Then the women track down Louis; he is easy to find because, as Aunt Laura says dryly, "Men don't change their names" (284). The threesome is finally reunited and—apparently—lives happily after. Except that of course, Mary never gets her inheritance; the fortune cannot be traced to her because "there were too many lost women in between" (284). Only part of women's lives can be reclaimed; only part of their history can be recovered.

On a metalinguistic level, the story demonstrates that patriarchal language practices cause the economic, social, and personal disempowerment of women; both actually and symbolically, these language practices attempt to erase feminine subjectivity, to make all women "lost women." On a metafictional level, the story criticizes patriarchal literary practices. The main struggle of the story is between Annabel's versions of stories and her aunt's. A writer herself, Annabel wants stories to be smooth and well rounded, to move neatly and quickly toward closure, toward consummation of their narrative patterns. Aunt Laura relies on a colloquial and oral form of storytelling that is open-ended and participatory, rather than on the written, linear, "smooth" form of narration that Annabel favors. Aunt Laura also wants to tell her story in her own way, and to clutter it up with a lot of metafictional commentary ("It would go that way in a story, I suppose . . ." [284]). And finally, Aunt Laura wants her story to end with an ambiguous meaning rather than with closure and authority. Annabel strives to find a neat moral in the story, but her aunt only informs her that there are no easy resolutions:

> " . . . The moral of it is that I shall never marry" [Annabel states].
> "You'll be a fool if you don't," said Aunt Laura.
> "But then I'll have to give up my name."
> "You'll be a fool if you do," said Aunt Laura.
> "But what can women do, then?"
> Aunt Laura rose up and tucked away her knitting: "I'm only telling you a mean story," said she. (284)

Aunt Laura tells a story about "what . . . didn't happen" (284) and then refuses to provide a moral. Women are lost, erased all the time, and the point of Aunt Laura's "mean" nonstory, her metafictional anti-tale, seems to be that there is nothing they can do about it.

And yet the larger context of the story reveals a more positive pattern, one that answers the question of how women can change — rather than merely invert — the patriarchal practices of language and story making that disempower them. One clue is provided by Mary Jernigan's resumption of her maiden name. After Mary Smith returns to being Mary Jernigan, she is no longer "lost"; indeed, she is "found" by her friend and reunited with her lover. The unarticulated point of Aunt Laura's story seems to be that when women reclaim their names, they can begin to reclaim history; history is no longer a record of feminine erasure. Another unarticulated point of Aunt Laura's story is that men, as well as women, suffer because of oppressive patrilineal practices. Louis spends most of the story forlornly searching for his true love, whose social and linguistic presence has been erased under the paternom, Mrs. John Smith, and who is not restored to him until she returns to being Mary Jernigan. On a metalinguistic level, changes in language are portrayed as the key to women's social and economic empowerment, as well as to men's and women's personal happiness. There is also a metafictional point to Gilman's story, clues to which can be found in the character of Aunt Laura herself. Aunt Laura claims that what she tells is merely "events." But Aunt Laura knows more than she should. According to Aunt Laura, Mary Jernigan is the real heiress, but how does Aunt Laura (who is allegedly only relating what happened) know what Louis, Nellie, and Mary do not? Aunt Laura's knowledge belies the fact that she is merely retelling events and suggests that she is fabricating this story, this story about the creation of stories. There is good reason to believe that Aunt Laura herself is a metafictionalist, a creator of metafictions (of stories about the way stories are built up). Aunt Laura is not only a character within the story she tells — she is also its author.

But Aunt Laura authors her text in such a way that patriarchal linguistic realities are reconfigured. Aunt Laura's metafiction demonstrates that women are lost — silenced, effaced, and minimized — by patriarchal plots and language. However, Aunt Laura's story resists this erasure not through mere inversion. An inversion of patriarchal plots would make the female (Mary) the heroine and the male (Louis) the victim, but Aunt Laura's triangulated story is more complicated that this. All of the characters — Mary, Louis, and Nelly — are realistic individuals, neither completely heroic nor completely victimized, and no one (either male or female) emerges as completely victorious. Aunt Laura's metafictional story overturns patriarchal plots but replaces them with a new story that allows a fuller range of narrative possibilities and characterizations and a broader consideration of the problem of patriarchal discourse. Moreover, although Aunt Laura authors the story, she does not wish to speak in a voice of omniscient authority, and she does not provide a fixed meaning for her tale. Patriarchal naming practices, after all, insist on being authoritative, on fixing women's status. Androcentric language and literature, with its insistence on possession and conquest, must be resisted. Aunt Laura resists the all-knowing authority of the author, and she resists narratizing her story into a smooth, well-rounded tale with a definitive meaning.

Furthermore, Aunt Laura resists telling history — the story of men, conquest, and war. Nor does she simply tell "herstory": the story of women's erasure. Instead, she tells what I must call, for lack of a better term, "theirstory" — the story of two lost women and one lost man who eventually find their own stories, their own tales that deviate from the patriarchal norm. Aunt Laura also insists on her right to tell a mean tale, a tale that does not fit and that will not cohere, a tale that seems to have no hero or heroine and no ultimate moral. But in the telling of this tale she asserts the tale's right to existence; it may be a mean tale, but it must be told. Finally, Aunt Laura reclaims fiction and language from the androcentricism of the patriarchal world, creating a story that can enunciate the histories of both men and women, an ornery tale that is distinctly her own.

Aunt Laura makes the unspoken spoken, stripping bare the wallpaper of patriarchal discourse to give the silent, lost women (and men) a voice. It may be a "mean" voice — but why shouldn't it be? Why shouldn't this voice be an angry, jagged one? Annabel is an author who writes smooth, well-rounded stories, but given women's dispossessed status, Annabel may have merely adopted patriarchal language. Thematically and formally, Aunt Laura refuses to create androcentric literature. Gilman, too, refuses to tell conventional patriarchal tales in a conventional style. Gilman tells, instead, "not literature" — stories that draw attention to their thematic and aesthetic differences from patriarchal norms. In so doing Gilman finds a voice that resists patriarchal erasure, a voice that transforms both the language and the content of the patriarchal masterplot, freeing women and men from the prison house of androcentric discourse.

This chapter has examined Gilman's attitudes toward women and the "pen," toward women's ability to create a place for their subjectivity within the phallocentric structures of patriarchal language and patriarchal stories. Like Kate Chopin's writing, Gilman's earliest portrayal of this subject in "The Yellow Wall-Paper" shows a frightening antagonism between a feminine subject and the masculine world of discourse she inhabits. Gilman resided for part of her life in this frightening world, but unlike her protagonist she did not go insane. What saved her was, in fact, writing: the writing of "The Yellow Wall-Paper," as well as the writing of her later works of fiction. Gilman abandoned the Victorian medical establishment's prescription for women suffering from mental illness and became, in effect, her own physician, prescribing career and an independent life as the antidote to her mental illness.

Gilman's later writings — such as *Herland* and her *Forerunner* fiction — show women who attempt, like Gilman herself, to use language to escape the authoritative sentence of male discourse. In this sense, Gilman engages in an intertextual dialogue with her prior works, revising her earlier stance on women and language, a stance that diagnosed the problem of patriarchal discourse without providing a solution. And yet, not all of Gilman's "solutions" to the problem of women's linguistic oppression end up being solutions. *Herland* inverts the power structures that undergird "The Yellow Wall-Paper," elevating a feminine, maternal language over the paternal tongue of patriarchy. *Herland* thus occupies a prominent place in the imaginative process that frees Gilman to revise the history of the "manmade" world, for it allowed Gilman to see that phallocentricism was contextually defined and therefore could be contextually redefined. Yet finally, we must question whether *Herland* finds a language that moves beyond the binary, one that is viable in the real world of a patriarchal, early-twentieth-century society. Works such as "The Widow's Might," "An Honest Woman," "Spoken To," "Mrs. Beazley's Deeds," "With a Difference (Not Literature)," and "Lost Women" continue this imaginative process of recreating patriarchal language, but they also move beyond *Herland*'s speculative utopian vision through a renovation of structures of subjectivity and discourse that exist in the real world. Like Gilman herself, Gilman's unruly women finally insist on creating the language that describes the world around them rather than being created by it. In so doing, they engender a revised world where women, as well as men, are not prepositions in language but agents, authors, speakers, and subjects.

The Politics of Hybridity in
Frances Harper's *Iola Leroy*

Like Charlotte Perkins Gilman, Frances Harper engages in an intertextual dialogue with prior configurations of "women's speech" that moves women from object to subject, from being spoken about to speaking themselves. Published in the same year as "The Yellow Wall-Paper," Harper's *Iola Leroy* (1892) challenges and revises an intricate series of racial, textual, and cultural traditions. Unlike other late-nineteenth-century writers, Harper does not seek a "feminine" voice situated outside patriarchal or racist discourses, but she does conjoin a number of discursive strategies these writers have used. Like Chopin and Freeman, Harper unearths a "denied" language to overturn dominant discourses; like Gilman, she metalinguistically undermines the structures that have created silent feminine subjects; finally, like Wilson and Cooper, she investigates the subversive possibilities of a voice that is specifically African American. What Harper utilizes, then, is a hybridized voice: a voice that melds and also transforms a number of languages present in society.

Harper's text as a whole also utilizes a politics of hybridity that reconstructs the multiple ways within culture that gender and race are circulated. *Iola Leroy*, of course, concerns a "hybrid," a woman who quite literally meets the nineteenth-century definition of this term as an individual produced by the crossing of different races.[1] But the novel is also hybridized in terms of the genres with which it engages. Harper's novel transforms conventions from an earlier tradition of American women's fiction, exemplified by texts such as Lydia Maria Child's "The Quadroons" (1846). It also rewrites conventions from the slave narrative and the slave novel, as exemplified most clearly in William Wells Brown's *Clotel* (1853).[2] *Iola*

Leroy subverts prior textual constructions of African American women in order to create a new space where binary oppositions break down and a different theory of African American feminine subjectivity and discourse can be spoken.

Harper's text also employs a hybridized discourse that demonstrates not the triumph of one tongue over the other (male over female, white over black, intellectual speech over a folk dialect) but rather the impositions and superimpositions of different languages within culture. It is specifically through a crossing of languages that Harper achieves her aim of both analyzing and producing a politics of hybridity. Robert Young argues that the most productive paradigms for the understanding of hybridity have been taken from language theory. The structure of "pidgin" (the vocabulary of one language superimposed on the grammar of another), for example, suggests not a straightforward power relationship of colonizer over colonized but rather the way a vernacular (that is, disempowered) discourse, when enmeshed within a metropolitan (that is, dominant) discourse can tacitly decompose the dominant discourse's authority (5). Although *Iola Leroy* seems to be written in a hegemonic voice (one that is didactic and intellectual), a vernacular, African American voice of the folk interrogates the authority of this dominant voice. In the end, the text illustrates not the dominance of one particular form of discourse over another but the commerce and even fusion between discourses within a culture that is itself constantly circulating, intersecting, and mutating voices in an intricate web of interrelationships. Once this discourse is created within the space of the novel, it can become part of the constantly constructed and reconstructed social matrix that creates "race" itself.

To understand *Iola Leroy*'s intertextual revisions of American women's fiction, it is necessary to consider how an African American politics of hybridity might both adapt and subvert dominant discursive practices. In *"Doers of the Word,"* Carla Peterson argues that African American writers "constructed a productive discourse generated from within the community that borrows the vocabulary and categories of the dominant discourse only to dislocate them from their privileged position of authority and adapt them to the local place" (14). *Iola Leroy* deploys categories such as the New Woman and the True Woman not as a way of miming the dominant discourse, or as a counterdiscourse (as was the case with Harriet Wilson), but rather as a way of dislocating such categories from their privileged placement within Anglo American feminist discourse, as well as adapting them to the local place, and the local speech, of African American women's writing. *Iola Leroy* presents African American characters who can be read as both True and New Women: Iola's mother, Marie, for example, has characteristics of the True Woman, while Lucille Delany represents aspects of a "New Womanist" subjectivity.

Iola herself inhabits a liminal space between these images and hybridizes them in order to take power from both these ideologies, while simultaneously unmasking their racist underpinnings. Victor Turner has defined liminality as a space "betwixt and between the positions assigned and arrayed by custom, convention and ceremonial" (95), and Harper deliberately situates Iola between Anglo American images of femininity. Harper portrays a character whose subjectivity is not defined through a relationship to a male and whose discourse does not participate in the silencing of racial and sexual consciousness characteristic of prior generations of women, yet who also retains some of the True Woman's ideological power. In Iola, Harper also creates an African American female artist who can voice her race's cultural, artistic, and spiritual heritage. The female artist does not remain on the margins of the narrative, as in Harriet Wilson's *Our Nig*. Rather, she enters the narrative, transforming and renovating the fundamental power structures that have undergirded racist and sexist theories of "women's speech."

Iola Leroy thus represents a hybridized text not only in the sense that Peterson uses this term but also in the sense that Bakhtin uses it. Bakhtin argues that "the novelistic hybrid is *an artistically organized system for bringing different languages in contact with one another*, a system having as its goal the illumination of one language by means of another, the carving-out of a living image of another language" (361). For Bakhtin, hybridization is an activity involving contestation, one that has as its goal the setting of different voices against each other so that authoritative discourse can be unmasked. By introducing the notion of an African American female artist into the text, and into the codes of the New Woman and the True Woman, Harper dialogizes these codes and finally synthesizes aspects of them into a new whole that deconstructs the authoritative power structures that undergird them: man over woman, Anglo American over African American, intellectual over folk, and high culture over low culture.

Harper's contestation of the discourses of Anglo American femininity can be seen in her revision of Lydia Maria Child's "The Quadroons." The plot of Child's "The Quadroons" describes a common nineteenth-century image of an African American female: the "tragic mulatta," who has no access to an empowered subjectivity or voice. Child's text details the story of Rosalie, a light-skinned slave who marries a wealthy southern white man named Edward. This union is "sanctioned by Heaven, though unrecognized on earth" (62–63), since southern laws do not allow intermarriage between races. Unfortunately Rosalie lives on earth, and when Edward betrays her by marrying a white woman, Rosalie dies and her daughter Xarifa is remanded to slavery. The beautiful Xarifa is bought by an older man who beats and rapes her. She goes insane and in a frenzy of despair smashes her skull against a wall. Her death goes unremarked as well as unnoticed: "the slaves buried her; and no one wept at the grave of her who had been so carefully cherished and so tenderly beloved" (76).

Child's African American characters are disempowered in multiple ways: as slave women in the South before the Civil War they lack economic, legal, and social power; furthermore, as characters created within white, female novelistic discourses their adherence to a constraining image of women's identity limits their power even more dramatically. Child clearly situates Rosalie within the tradition of the domestic saint: she has a "pure mind" (66) and is pious and domestic, caring more for her child than for herself. Only able to protest Edward's treatment through a "mute appeal" of "heart-broken looks" (66), Rosalie clearly lacks a self-defined identity and language. Unfortunately, the second generation of women replicate the mother's identity and voice, as Edward notes: "To hear [his daughter Xarifa] play upon the harp, or repeat some favorite poem *in her mother's earnest accents and melodious tones* . . . seemed to be the highest enjoyment of his life" (71, my emphasis). Like her mother, Xarifa does not attempt to escape from slavery but rather hopes a male suitor will free her. When this fails, she becomes a "victim" (75) of both slavery and patriarchy. Unable to be a pure, domestic saint, and unable to formulate an alternative identity, she dies in silence and insanity. Child's text fuses the image of the "tragic mulatta" with that of the True Woman, but not as an activity of contestation: in the end, "The Quadroon" supports, rather than dismantles, the oppressive social and cultural power of these images.

Iola Leroy has numerous plot parallels with Child's story, but Harper's hybridization of "The Quadroons" indicates that African American women must struggle to formulate their own identities and voices. The novel creates a space where this struggle can be negotiated, despite its painfulness, as Iola affirms in a passage that foreshadows *The Awakening*: "fearful as the awakening was, it was better than to have slept through life" (274). Harper begins by illustrating the pernicious effects of adhering (like Rosalie and Xarifa) to patriarchal and racist visions of feminine subjectivity. Iola's mother Marie exemplifies this tendency. A light-skinned slave, Marie marries her white master, Eugene Leroy, after he educates and manumits her. Yet it is clear that Marie still regards Leroy as her master. Marie has ideas about the South and about how her family should be raised, but she mutes her voice at the behest of her master/husband. When Eugene complains that she discusses race too often, she remarks, "If it annoys you . . . I will stop talking" (78). Leroy also forbids Marie to tell her three children — Harry, Iola, and Grace — of the "cross" in their blood. Marie dislikes this silencing of race but participates: "Leroy had always been especially careful to conceal from his children the knowledge of their connection with the negro race. To Marie this silence was oppressive" (82). Marie never finds a voice that allows her to disrupt the codes around her, codes that construct her as a silent, oppressed object of patriarchal domination, a "tragic mulatta."

Furthermore, because Marie cannot find a voice that undermines the codes of domesticity, her character is continually portrayed as being contained within this stereotype. Marie is a good domestic saint, as Eugene Leroy notes: "She is beautiful, faithful, and pure" (66). Her submissive helplessness is emphasized over and over again by Leroy: "Although the law makes her *helpless* in my hands, to me her *defenselessness* is her best defense" (65, my emphasis; also see 70). Marie seems to accept Leroy's definition of her and to work from within it to attain "power." But this is an externally imposed, white, patriarchal vision of subjectivity. So it is no wonder that when Leroy dies and Marie is remanded to slavery she is left with nothing: "[Marie] seemed a statue of fear and despair. She tried to speak, reached out her hand as if she was groping in the dark, turned pale as death as if all the blood in her veins had receded to her heart, and, with one heart-rending cry of bitter agony, she fell senseless to the floor" (96). Unlike Rosalie, Marie does not literally die; however, this passage clearly depicts a symbolic death. Marie is destroyed because she never begins the complicated process of finding a voice that overturns patriarchal and racist ideologies of African American feminine subjectivity.

However, through characters such as Iola and Lucille Delany, Harper demonstrates that African American women can hybridize the codes of the True Woman and the "tragic mulatta" in order to formulate new identities. Unlike Child's text, *Iola Leroy* does not show daughters simply replicating the mistakes of their mothers. Iola refuses to be cherished for her victimization, as a good True Woman would. When Dr. Gresham (a white man) proposes to Iola, he does so partly out of pity that she is from the "despised race." Iola refuses his proposal and his pity, saying, "Thoughts and purposes have come to me in the shadows I should never have learned in the sunshine. I am constantly rousing myself up to suffer and be strong. . . . I am a wonder to myself" (114). Although Dr. Gresham tries to construct Iola as being within the passivity of the Cult of Domesticity, Iola resists. She first unmasks the codes by emphasizing that they do not lead to victimization but rather to self-knowledge ("thoughts and purposes have come to me in the shadows I should never have learned in the sunshine") and then transforms them by articulating a new vision of herself as subject ("I am a wonder to myself"). Iola also unmasks the oppressive authority of Dr. Gresham's claims of friendship and equality, saying "To-day your friendship springs from compassion, but, when that subsides, might you not look on me as inferior?" (114). Unlike Xarifa, Iola learns from — and revises — the mother's history. After all, Eugene Leroy claimed to regard Marie as his equal, yet silenced her when he did not like her opinions. Iola dialogizes (unmasks and transforms) the images of the True Woman and the "tragic mulatta" to show that they create only unequal, disempowered identities.

Iola also dialogizes the oppressive verbal authority of these images, revising the rhetoric of silence endorsed by stories such as "The Quadroons," as well as by the Cult of Domesticity. Unlike Marie, Iola insists on speaking about her race. She tells Dr. Gresham: "I have too much self-respect to enter your home under a veil of concealment" (117), and "the best blood in my veins is African blood, and I am not ashamed of it" (208). Again Iola unmasks the codes (by refusing to conceal her race under a veil of shame) and reconstructs them (by insisting that her race is something of which she can be proud: "the best blood in my veins is African blood"). She also resists the authority of patriarchal language. When Dr. Gresham argues that African Americans will not appreciate her efforts to educate them, for instance, she flatly contradicts him (234).

Iola also introduces the notion of an African American woman artist into the text, and she thereby transforms the social and psychological codes that have denied African American women's potential to be speaking subjects. Iola hints that she might eventually do more than teach her race; she might also write about it, creating a book that would be "of lasting service to the race" (262). She first comments that she might write this book if she had leisure, money, and enough skill, for "it needs patience, perseverance, courage, and the hand of an *artist* to weave it into the literature of the country" (262, my emphasis). Although Iola seems unsure whether she could be this "artist," by the next page of the novel her desire to write a book has gone from the conditional tense (I would like to write a book) to the imperative ("When I write a book" [263]). In these crucial sentences, Harper paves the way for later writers (such as Jessie Fauset and Zora Neale Hurston) who will more explicitly develop the notion of a unique African American women's art. Once again, we must note Iola's liminal status, her placement between visions of women's identity that restrain women's artistic production (the True Woman, the "tragic mulatta") and those that endorse it (the New Woman, the female artist/heroine of the Harlem Renaissance).

As should be clear from this example, the text dialogizes codes surrounding not only the True Woman but also the New Woman. Iola's insistence on the importance of women's work outside the home would seem to mark her as a self-defined, career-minded New Woman. Iola argues repeatedly that women should have careers: "I have a theory that every woman ought to know how to earn a living" (205); "I think that every woman should have some skill or art which would insure her at least a comfortable support" (210). She grants women the right to be more than "a flotsam all adrift until some man has appropriated her" (242) and pursues several types of employment that are situated outside the home.[3] Yet when Iola marries she gives up her job in order to support her husband's career; as Tate notes, "Dr Latimer assumes the traditionally male-designated role as leader, and Iola assumes the complementary female role of helpmate" (148).

Iola would seem, then, initially to endorse, but later to reject, a New Woman's role in the public realm for a private or domestic role in the home. However, the distinction of private versus public realm may have functioned differently for many African American women than it did for Anglo American women. As Peterson argues, because many African Americans were automatically excluded from public institutions (education, politics, social spaces) by virtue of their race, the domestic realm often contained aspects of these institutions; for example, when public education was prohibited to African American children, the domestic sphere would become a site of schooling (15). In fact, *Iola Leroy* constructs a hybrid space that intermeshes the public and the private until they cannot be disentangled; without deviating from her sphere of influence in the "private" realm of the home, Iola performs a very "public" function: the education of African American children. Iola constructs a third space — an ethnic community sphere — that acts as an intermediary between these realms. This space hybridizes the True Woman's and the New Woman's spheres of action and empowerment. Harper creates a character who engenders a new vision of agency and a new sphere of power for African American women.[4]

Another example of the text's creation of an ethnic community sphere that mediates the True Woman's and the New Woman's realms of action is provided by Lucille Delany. As Hazel Carby (92) and Marilyn Elkins (50) have pointed out, the role of true intellectual leadership belongs to Lucille, for she is college-educated, whereas Iola has only a high school degree. Lucille is also more confident than Iola about speaking in male/female groups. She opens a school to train women for their domestic duties (199) but does not give up this career when she marries (280). As Tate explains, Lucille "assumes the nontraditional role of woman-as-leader," disavowing "the code that middle-class women do not work outside the home" (148). It would seem then that in Harper's text, Marie represents the woman of the past, Iola represents the woman of the present, but Lucille represents the true "hope for the future of [the] race" (Harper, *Iola Leroy* 200). Where Iola advocates the education of mothers, Lucille comments that the great need of the race is enlightened mothers *and* enlightened fathers (253), and she works outside the home to achieve this enlightenment. Yet Lucille is also committed to the "private" realm of domesticity; her school trains women not to be lawyers and doctors but to be good mothers. Lucille, then, also adapts the codes of True Womanhood and New Womanhood, and of the private and the public, to create an ethnic community sphere from which to both undermine and reconfigure concepts of women's empowerment.

Therefore the simple dichotomy of Iola as the "present tense" of the race and Lucille as the "future tense" is first created, but later unmasked, by the text. The central character of Harper's novel — Iola herself — inhabits a space between the codes of the True Woman and the New Woman. Like Edna Pontellier, Iola moves out of the "private"/domestic realm but does not completely break from it in order to formulate a public identity. But unlike Edna, Iola successfully hybridizes these realms, thereby moving beyond the binary options, the either/or choices, society seemed to offer Chopin's character. Iola's identity remains part of the domestic realm, and this allows her to speak a double-voiced discourse that exercises power both from within and outside the ideology of the True Woman. The novel as a whole also speaks a double-voiced discourse that successfully negotiates a multiple audience of African Americans and Anglo Americans, while simultaneously unmasking binary oppositions such as True Woman versus New Woman, empowered white subject versus silent black object, and private versus public realms of action. *Iola Leroy* shows the necessity of unmasking ideologies that limit women but also of adapting these same ideologies so that they can function as the reconstructed basis for linguistic and social agency.

Harper's text represents a hybridization (unmasking as well as adaptation) of the codes, ideologies, and stereotypes of Anglo American femininity, but the novel also hybridizes aspects of the African American tradition of the slave narrative and the slave novel. Peterson argues that the discourse of black women speakers in the North from 1830 to 1860 "constitutes a particular form of hybridity in its disruption not only of the discourse of the dominant culture but also of that of the black male elite" (15). Peterson does not discuss *Iola Leroy,* but it too disrupts both the dominant culture's construction of African American women and certain aspects of African American males' construction of feminine subjectivity and discourse. Harper once again appropriates a discourse (the slave narrative/ novel) so that she can be a producer, rather than a consumer, of the ideologies this discourse contains.

Numerous feminist critics have argued that the slave narrative was defined according to male criteria for heroism and identity. Valerie Smith explains that "by mythologizing rugged individuality, physical strength, and geographical mobility, the [slave] narratives enshrine cultural definitions of masculinity" (34). The most well-known and frequently read nineteenth-century slave narratives were written by men and emphasized the struggle for manhood within the confines of an institution that attempted to strip slaves of this prized possession. Beyond being a genre dominated by male writers and generic markers crucial to male identity, however, the slave narrative often crucially interconnects masculinity and freedom itself. For example, Frederick Douglass's *Narrative of the Life of an American Slave, Written by Himself* (1845) connects Douglass's struggle for freedom with a struggle for manhood; in the famous scene where Douglass fights back against the overseer, Covey, Douglass comments: "You have seen how a man was made a slave; you shall see how a slave was made a man" (77). The text depicts a heroic, manly slave who fights for, and finally achieves, his freedom, in part because of his masculinity.

Like Douglass's text, William Wells Brown's *Clotel* intertwines masculinity with moving out of slavery. Some critics have argued that *Iola Leroy* is a mere "repetition" of *Clotel* (S. Brown 139), but in fact Harper intertextually revises this novel, as well as the slave narrative's trope connecting freedom and masculinity.[5] In order to understand these revisions, however, it is necessary to examine *Clotel*'s depiction of male and female subjectivity. Brown's novel is itself framed by an articulation of African American male subjectivity; the first forty pages of the novel are called *Narrative of the Life and Escape of William Wells Brown,* and we are told from the start that Brown is "the subject of this narrative" (17). Throughout this framing text, freedom and manhood are equated. In England, for example, Brown is recognized "as a man and an equal" (47). When Brown learns to read and write, he becomes a producer of texts "of which a *man* reared under the most favorable educational advantages might be proud" (54, my emphasis). Brown is a subject in his own right, capable of writing letters, capable of being a "freeman" (29).

Brown creates an identity for himself as literate free man, yet he continually presents women as the passive victims of slavery. When Brown escapes, his sister states that "there was no hope for herself, she must live and die a slave," and his mother comments that "as all her children were in slavery, she did not wish to leave them" (26). Portraits of female helplessness also continually spur Brown to obtain his freedom, as the following excerpt shows: "He saw in imagination his mother in the cotton-field, followed by a monster task-master, and no one to speak a consoling word to her. He beheld his sister in the hands of the slave-driver, compelled to submit to his cruelty, or, what was unutterably worse, his lust; but still he was far away from them, and could not do anything for them if he remained in slavery; consequently he resolved, and consecrated the resolve with a prayer, that he would start on the first opportunity [toward freedom]" (31). It is important to note that although Brown mentions having three brothers, the portraits of his mother and sister incite his need to escape. Brown's own narrative, then, is crucially focused on the drama of creating an identity for himself as a freeman. Unfortunately, this identity seems to construct itself through a continual portrayal of African American women as the silent victims of slavery rather than articulate subjects of their own narratives.

Similarly, although *Clotel* is the narrative of "The President's Daughter," it finally does not create viable identities for its African American female characters.[6] The novel tells the story of Currer, "a bright mulatto" slave woman and her two near-white daughters, Clotel and Althesa. When Currer's master dies, she and her two daughters are sold. Clotel is purchased by her white lover, Horace Green, but her mother and sister are taken away in a slave gang. At this point Brown appropriates Child's text: Green marries his slave Clotel (a marriage that is of course illegal according to southern law), and they have a child named Mary. Unfortunately, Green falls in love with a white woman who forces him to sell Clotel and enslave his child. Rather than being returned to slavery, Clotel ultimately commits suicide, jumping off the Long Bridge.

The other women's fates are no more heartening. Currer is enslaved for a number of years to a preacher named Mr. Peck who refuses to sell her, and she finally dies of "yellow fever." Currer's daughter Althesa marries a white northerner and has two children, Jane and Ellen, but when Althesa's husband dies she and her daughters are remanded to slavery. Althesa's daughter Ellen kills herself rather than be sexually abused, and her other daughter Jane dies of a broken heart when her lover/rescuer is killed. Jane's death is borrowed directly from "The Quadroons," for Brown says she "was buried at night at the back of the garden by the Negroes; and no one wept at the grave of her who had been so carefully cherished, and so tenderly beloved" (210). Of all the women in the book, only Clotel's daughter Mary survives, rescued by a French gentleman who takes her to Dunkirk and marries her.

This plot need not be, in and of itself, problematic; any one of the fates of these women could be constructed so as to allow for the possibility of feminine agency and heroism. However, as with Brown's own narrative, *Clotel* intertwines freedom, activity, and masculinity to formulate a definition of subjectivity, with the concurrent result that women often fill the place of the not-free, the passive, and the objectified. Brown's novel continually implies that women do not want or even need freedom, commenting that "A celebrated writer has justly said of woman, 'A woman's whole life is a history of her affections. The heart is her world; it is there her ambition strives for empire; it is there her avarice seeks for hidden treasures'" (244–45). Brown's point is that women's need for love supersedes the need for agency and freedom. This is aptly demonstrated through his character Mary, who switches places in jail with her lover so that he might escape. The result is that Mary's enslavement is worsened, while her lover goes free.

Mary's agreement to switch places with her lover is an interesting moment of activity, however, in a text that predominantly presents women as passive in the struggle for freedom. Currer earns good wages as a laundress, but she never considers buying her daughters' freedom or using her money to help them escape. Apparently, she sees marriage to a white man (not literacy or self-assertion) as the key to freedom, and she spends her time looking for suitable matches for her daughters. Clotel demonstrates a bit more agency than her mother, dressing "in the disguise of a gentleman" to escape. Again, there is an association between masculinity (or manliness) and freedom. However, Clotel goes back into slavery to rescue her daughter and becomes reenslaved. Finally, in the third generation, Mary can effect the rescue of a male slave, George, but she herself remains dependent on a French gentleman for freedom. Still, the question remains: if Mary is smart enough to free George, why doesn't she free herself?

In *Clotel* women are passive victims of slavery, and much of this passivity can be traced to their status as True Women. Brown's text is heavily invested in the iconography of the cult of domesticity, as well as of the Southern lady, as Barbara Christian points out (23). Clotel is explicitly described as a "True Woman" (112) and her daughters and granddaughters follow in her tradition — remaining in slavery for love, killing themselves rather than facing sexual assault, dying of broken hearts, sacrificing themselves (and their freedom) for others. The novel does not dialogize these codes or subvert them, and the result is that female characters emerge as powerless. The male characters, on the other hand, have no difficulty finding the autonomy, manhood, and voice necessary for freedom. As M. Giulia Fabi observes, "whereas Brown foregrounds the traditionally relational ideal of female courage as devotion and self-sacrifice, his male heroes loom in the background as powerful, cunning, and potentially violent freedom fighters" (641).[7] Mary's lover, George, makes an eloquent speech about freedom in which he says (among many other things): "I have heard my master read in the Declaration of Independence 'that all men are created free and equal,' and this caused me to inquire of myself why I was slave" (226). It is inconceivable to imagine Currer, Clotel, Althesa, Mary, Ellen, or Jane making such a statement. Its confident assertion of the right to freedom clearly belongs within a discourse in which all *men* are created equal and, apparently, are endowed with the capacity to want—and actively seek—their freedom. Enslaved women in the text not only lack the desire for freedom, they also lack voice. Appropriating the words of Child's character Rosalie, Brown tells us that Clotel can only protest her husband's marriage with a "mute appeal" of "heart-broken looks" (111). Compared to George's eloquence, Clotel's voicelessness speaks all too strongly to the way the text's presentation of African American male subjectivity effaces the potential heroism and voice of its female characters.

Brown published three other versions of *Clotel*, yet did not significantly change this characterization of African American women. In the final version of the novel (*Clotelle*, 1867) the female characters are still depicted as domestic saints; they are beautiful ladies who faint often (34, 35, 40). But, most problematically, they are still passive and silent; male heroism involves activity and voice, while female "heroism" involves the passive and silent "power to suffer and to love" (71). The novel's penultimate paragraph makes this point emphatically. An African American man who has purchased his wife's freedom tells her: "Shet your mouf dis minit, I say: you shan't stan' dar, an' talk ter me in dat way. I bought you, an' paid my money fer you, an' I ain't a gwine ter let you sass me in dat way. Shet your mouf dis minit: if you don't I'll sell you; 'fore God I will. Shet up, I say, or I'll sell you" (114). Three times in this short passage, the man tells his wife to shut her mouth. He has established his subjectivity through activity and heroism; in his logic, this "buys" him the right to objectify and silence his wife. Clearly, Brown's text is critical of this positioning. But finally, the text presents no alternative to this creation of an African American male subjectivity through an objectification of African American women.

It might be argued that Brown's representations of African American women are simply meant to be historically accurate. Yet we know from statistics that not all escaped slaves were men.[8] Moreover, we must consider the meaning behind such representations. Mary Helen Washington asks: "Why is the fugitive slave, the fiery orator, the political activist, the abolitionist always represented as a black *man*? How does the heroic voice and heroic image of the black woman get suppressed in a culture that depended on her heroism for its survival?" She responds by arguing that "the creation of the fiction of tradition is a matter of power, not justice, and . . . that power has always been in the hands of men—mostly white but some black. Women are the disinherited" ("'Darkened Eye Restored'" 32). We can see Brown's portrayal of this disinheritance in *Clotel*, but we can also see Harper's refusal of this disinheritance in *Iola Leroy*. There are a number of plot parallels between *Iola Leroy* and the various incarnations of *Clotel/Clotelle*, yet even a comparison of the novels' subtitles demonstrates that Harper is revising *Clotel* and the masculine tradition of the slave narrative/novel. Brown's subtitle defines his heroine through a man: Clotel is "the President's Daughter." Harper's title and subtitle (*Iola Leroy, or Shadows Uplifted*) hint at another theory of self-definition. If we read the shadows of the title as slavery, Iola is defined through the uplifting (the throwing off) of slavery. In the text as a whole, shadows also represent ideologies that limit feminine subjectivity. Thus "shadows uplifted" refers to the dismantling of damaging racist and sexist belief systems. Iola is defined not through her relationship to men (or to a male tradition) but through her attempts to escape the ideologies that have pressed her down and constrained her identity.

Harper's novel unmasks the concept sometimes present in the slave narrative that freedom is a gender-specific term; it also recoups and adapts certain elements of this tradition to further its portayal of African American women who assert agency and voice. Harper's text directly references *Clotel* in its description of a woman who "threw herself over the Long Bridge" (*Iola Leroy* 98) rather than be returned to slavery, yet the text as a whole focuses on female heroism. For example, Iola seems to have suffered both physical and sexual abuse under slavery, but unlike Brown's Ellen, whose rape and madness are simultaneous, Iola holds onto her sense of self: "I had outrages heaped on me which might well crimson the cheek of honest womanhood with shame, but I never fell into the clutches of an owner for whom I did not feel the utmost loathing and intensest horror. I have heard men talk glibly of the degradation of the negro, but there is a vast difference between abasement of condition and degradation of character. I was abased, but the men who trampled on me were the degraded ones" (115). Despite this treatment, Iola did not lose her integrity; she did not become a victim. Through psychological and linguistic resistance, she asserted an alternative definition of identity that emphasized heroism, self-determination, and survival.

Furthermore, in Harper's text survival and heroism do not belong only to near-white women such as Iola. Harper's Aunt Linda is a perfect contrast to Currer and to other of Brown's women who simply wait passively for men to aid them. Aunt Linda cannot read and write, but she is extremely intelligent, telling Robert Johnson: "ef you buys me for a fool you loses your money shore" (10). She actively strives for freedom, even calling a prayer meeting to discuss the progress of the war. Although Robert is clearly her superior in terms of book learning and education, she does not defer to him, telling him that "I ain't runnin' down my people. But a fool's a fool, wether he's white or black" (160; see also 176). Aunt Linda is also active and determined; when slavery is abolished she convinces her husband to purchase a valuable piece of land. Harper uses Aunt Linda to demonstrate that although some women of the older generation (such as Marie) have fallen into passivity, others exercise a great deal of autonomy and control. The novel thus unmasks the elements of the slave narrative that portray women as passive and provides powerful countermodels. Harper layers her novel over the discourse of *Clotel* in order to produce a hybridized, critical text that undoes the authority of the original novel.

Harper also grants women the right to do what Douglass, Brown, and so many other male narrators have done: to fight back, and in fighting back refuse their victimization. In the slave narrative's discourse, the spectacle of violence against women is sometimes portrayed as an incitement for men's claiming of manhood and freedom, but Harper subverts and transforms this spectacle. As already noted, Iola fights back against sexual abuse. Yet she has a forerunner in her maternal grandmother, Harriet Johnson. Aunt Linda approvingly remembers that Harriet was sold because "she snatched de whip out ob her [mistress's] hand and gib her a lickin'"(159). Aunt Linda further comments that "we women had ter keep 'em from whippin' us, er dey'd all de time been libin' on our bones" (159). In this extraordinary passage, the spectacle of violence against women as an inducement for male freedom is undone: violence against women provokes the resistance of *women*. This is indeed a daring move on Harper's part, one that might have alienated an audience who could only conceive of women as passive entities.

Is it coincidence that *Aunt Linda* tells this story about a woman named *Harriet*? Is Harper referencing Harriet Jacobs's pseudonymous slave narrative written by "Linda Brent"? If Harper consciously references Jacobs's text, she may do so because it offers an alternative to the masculinist tradition of the slave narrative. Like Iola, Aunt Linda, and Harriet Anderson, Harriet Jacobs resists her master's assumption that she will be passive in the face of his oppression. Jacobs does not literally pick up the whip Dr. Flint uses, but in other ways she picks up the master's tools (written language and false discourse) and uses them against him. Jacobs also transforms these tools to become the subject of her own narrative of agency and freedom.[9] By intertextually interpolating Jacobs's text, Harper creates a discourse that situates itself both outside of, and within, the tradition of the slave narrative. She adapts this genre to her own purposes, to her creation of a textual space for the speaking, active, empowered, yet still enslaved, female.

Furthermore, Harper contests the construction of the figure of the heroic, manly freeman through an interrogation of the categories of "heroism" and "freedom." For many male slave narrators "heroism" means escape, even if this involves abandoning one's family; furthermore, escape is presented as an autonomous, individualistic action. Harper calls Iola "a heroic woman" (59), but she redefines the meaning of "heroism." For the characters in *Iola Leroy*, heroism means understanding the bonds of community, and escape involves a group of individuals who aid each other. Ben Tunnel, for instance, longs for freedom but knows that his frail mother could not survive a difficult escape; therefore, Ben remains in slavery with his mother. This definition of "heroism" both subverts and reworks the codes of the slave narratives: Ben Tunnel, like Harriet Jacobs, defines "heroism" as a relational attribute.

Harper's text also challenges the intertwinement of "manhood" and "freedom." In this sense, *Iola Leroy* meets Bakhtin's definition of a "hybrid construction" as a text in which "one and the same word belong simultaneously to two languages, to belief systems ... and consequently, the word has two contradictory meanings, two accents" (304–5). Harper sets these contestatory beliefs against each other to unmask the authority of the dominant language. One particularly clear instance of this occurs just after emancipation, when Robert Johnson, Iola, Aunt Linda, and Uncle Dan discuss the meaning of "freedom." Robert begins by defining freedom as a masculine struggle: "But all the battles are not fought, nor all the victories won. The colored *man* has escaped from one slavery, and I don't want *him* to fall into another. I want the young folks to keep their brains clear, and their right arms strong, to fight the battles of life *manfully*, and take their places alongside of every other people in this country" (170, my emphasis). Three times in this short passage, Robert links freedom with manhood or the male gender. However, Linda and Uncle Dan quickly undermine this masculine discourse:

> "Dat's so," said Aunt Linda, "it's ralely orful how our *folks* hab been murdered sence de war. But I don't think dese *young folks* is goin' ter take things as we's allers done."
>
> "We war cowed down from the beginnin,'" said Uncle Daniel, "but dese *young folks* ain't comin' up dat way." (171, my emphasis)

Three times, Linda and Daniel link freedom with "our folks." Robert responds by adopting a less gendered discourse, saying, "It is not to be expected ... that these *young people* are going to put up with things as we did, when we weren't permitted to hold a meeting by ourselves, or to own a club or learn to read" (171, my emphasis). In the hybrid construction that emerges, freedom belongs exclusively to neither the masculine nor the feminine, the intelligentsia nor the folk, but to all "people"; at the war's end there stands "a race newly anointed with freedom" (138). Therefore, Harper's hybridization of the tradition of the slave narrative and the slave novel creates a new textual space where the link between freedom and masculinity can be broken, and then reconfigured as a link between freedom and the race as a whole. Furthermore, in Harper's text women are no longer shadows, but have become solid entities with voices and subjectivities of their own.[10]

Politics of Hybridity in Harper's Iola Leroy

So far this chapter has examined *Iola Leroy* using definitions of hybridity that have their predominant basis in literary and linguistic systems of thought. To understand how the text's use of a folk discourse creates a politics of hybridity, however, a more overtly social definition must be employed. In "Signs Taken for Wonders," Homi Bhabha defines hybridity as "a problematic of colonial representation ... that reverses the effects of colonialist disavowal, so that other 'denied' knowledges enter upon the dominant discourse and estrange the basis of its authority" (175). As previously argued, Aunt Linda and Uncle Dan estrange the basis of Robert Johnson's (intellectual, educated) authority through an insistence on the power of an alternative discourse of the folk. They thereby exercise what Paulo Freire and Donaldo Macedo have called "critical literacy": the ability to transform "the social and political structures that imprison [individuals] in their 'culture of silence'" (159). Aunt Linda and Uncle Dan's critically literate practices introduce a "denied knowledge" — the knowledge of the folk — into the dominant discursive domain; in so doing they both subvert and adapt this domain. A hidden discourse operates from within dominant discourses to undermine them, hollow them out, and finally produce a new discourse formed of discrete elements belonging to different languages, but contained entirely by none.

The novel's opening chapter, "Mystery of Market Speech and Prayer-Meeting," provides an example of Harper's deployment of a critically literate discourse of the folk to produce a new discursive form. As the chapter begins, two slaves seem to be "babbling" rather disjointedly in an "illiterate" dialect about the food at the market:

> "Good mornin,' Bob; how's butter dis mornin'?"
>
> "Fresh; just as fresh, as fresh can be."
>
> "Oh, glory!" said the questioner, whom we shall call Thomas Anderson, although he was know among his acquaintances as Marster Anderson's Tom.
>
> His informant regarding the condition of the market was Robert Johnson, who had been separated from his mother in his childhood and reared by his mistress as a favorite slave. She had fondled him as a pet animal, and even taught him to read. Notwithstanding their relation as mistress and slave, they had strong personal likings for each other. (7)

This passage illustrates Harper's use of a mixed dialect and her ability to "code-switch," to move easily between an "illiterate" discourse of the folk and a more intellectual discourse that seems to affirm dominant power structures (configuring the intelligent Robert Johnson, for example, as "a pet animal"). But it is also an excellent example of how a buried knowledge unhinges the power of the dominant discourse. For the "babble" of the folk is truly babble in the original meaning of this term; the language that develops after God's destruction of the tower of Babel is actually not one language but is comprised of many different discourses.

The language of the folk is heteroglossalic: it speaks on different levels, to different audiences. Hearing this "babble" about butter, Robert Johnson's mistress would no doubt conclude that the slaves were not discussing anything of value. But Robert Johnson and the other slaves know that such talk is a coded language, a way of spreading information about the progress of the Civil War. Harper explains that the slaves have "invented a phraseology to convey in the most unsuspected manner news to each other from the battle-field" (9). This "phraseology" conceals as it reveals, for beneath this "apparently careless exterior" of banter about butter, "there was an undercurrent of thought which escaped the cognizance of their masters" (9). This banter is a folk discourse, one that turns out to be a critically literate, formalized linguistic practice of empowerment.

Harper thus opens the novel with a scene that seems to present two separate discourses: the colloquial discourse of the "illiterate" folk, and a more formalized, intellectual discourse. The discourse of the folk is then shown, however, to contain elements of the other discourse: after all, this is not mere banter but a carefully constructed linguistic system for the conveyance of information about the war. The opening maps, then, not the separation of these systems of language, but the commerce between them. The opening scene also uses the hidden, "mysterious" discourse to overturn the dominant discourse's authority; Robert Johnson and Tom Anderson are shown not to be "pet animals" but rather sophisticated, critical users of language, and their information about the war's progress actually turns out to be *more accurate* than the information circulated by slave owners. Furthermore, Robert Johnson, the "pet animal" can himself code-switch, speaking in either the folk dialect or the dominant discourse, translating between the two languages. This translation subverts the oppositions between languages, for the difference between the folk dialect and the more formalized language is shown, as Barbara Johnson might say, to be not a difference between but a difference within. Thus binary oppositions are decomposed by this opening scene, and by the folk discourse that the text utilizes to subvert authoritative discourses.

Aunt Linda provides another example of how a folk dialect undermines the binary oppositions of dominant discourses. Aunt Linda recounts that her mistress tries to scare her by telling tales about how the Yankees will kill all the slave men. Linda does not believe these stories, but she knows that she must play a part: "An' when she war done she jis' set down and sniffled an' cried, an' I war so glad I didn't know what to do. But I had to hole in. An' I made out I war orful sorry" (11). On the surface, Linda seems to be a "good" slave, but her discourse reveals a powerful critique of the authority of the "mistress" and the mistress's discourse. Furthermore, she insists on the accuracy of her knowledge and her language, saying to Robert, "An' I want you to come Sunday night an' tell all 'bout the good eggs, fish, and butter. Mark my words, Bobby, we's all gwine to git free. I seed it all in a vision, as plain as de nose on yer face" (13). Linda here authorizes a knowledge (her vision) that is outside "rational," intellectual systems of thought and language. She insists on the power of a folk discourse and vision to undermine racist, hegemonic, and intellectual systems of language and thought. Once again, the text authorizes this discourse, for Linda's vision turns out to be accurate: she correctly predicts the ending of the Civil War and the emancipation of the slaves.

These are examples of the novel's deployment of a discourse of the folk to unhinge the binary oppositions of authoritative discourse. But finally, what the novel speaks is a heteroglossalic, composite discourse. While it may seem that the novel eventually privileges the discourse of the educated, intellectual population (as represented by characters such as Robert and Iola) over that of the folk (as represented by Linda and Daniel), this is not actually the case, for these discourses, as already demonstrated, overlap. Furthermore, as I have argued, the discourse of the folk is used as an important corrective to Robert Johnson's masculinist construction of "freedom" (171); it is no wonder, then, that Iola is described as learning much from the "shrewd intellect" of Aunt Linda (175). Certainly, as the novel progresses, the discourse of the folk is shown less frequently, but the folk wisdom of Aunt Linda and Uncle Dan is not erased from the book's final vision of an empowered speech. For example, the novel's last chapter reverses the structure of the opening chapter in presenting, first, a standard, intellectual discourse, but then, second, a discourse of the folk:

> It was late in the summer when Dr. Latimer and his bride reached their home in North Carolina. . . . Aunt Linda, who had been apprised of their coming, was patiently awaiting their arrival, and Uncle Daniel was pleased to know that "dat sweet young lady who had sich putty manners war comin' to lib wid dem."
>
> As soon as they arrived, Aunt Linda rushed up to Iola, folded her in her arms, and joyfully exclaimed: "How'dy, honey! Ise so glad you's come. I seed it in a vision dat somebody fair war comin' to help us. An' wen I yered it war you, I larffed and jist rolled ober, and larffed and jist gib up." (275)

This passages mixes an educated, intellectual discourse ("Aunt Linda . . . had been apprised of their coming") with less standard grammatical constructions, not only within individual paragraphs but also within individual sentences ("Uncle Daniel was pleased to know that 'dat sweet young lady . . . war comin' '"). Unlike the opening scene, where the discourses are kept as separate syntactical units, in this passage they are, quite literally, overlapping, imbricated within each other. Furthermore, unlike the opening scene, here the folk discourse does not overturn the more hegemonic one but rather supplements it, enhancing its knowledge. Aunt Linda's vision that Iola will arrive is not denied but in fact confirmed by the text's more formal discourse. Discourses are allowed to coexist in a composite construction comprised of both the intellectual world of Dr. Latimer and Iola and the folk knowledge and wisdom of Aunt Linda and Uncle Daniel.

As in Cooper's *A Voice from the South*, Harper's text moves away from a competitive model of the interaction of languages within society toward one that is more consensual. Harper acknowledges, however, that this coexistence is not always peaceful, that one discourse will often try to displace another. Aunt Linda is empowered in numerous ways, but Iola still feels the need to school her in traditional avenues of literacy. She tries to convince Aunt Linda to "get a pair of spectacles and learn to read" (276), to which Aunt Linda responds: "'Oh, yer can't git dat book froo my head, no way you fix it. I knows nuff to git to hebben, and dats all I wants to know.' Aunt Linda was kind and obliging, but there was one place where she drew the line, and that was learning to read" (276). Although Linda appreciates Iola's efforts to teach others to read (276), she does not herself need reading because she is already empowered without the dominant practices of literacy. Furthermore, Linda's spiritual reading is complete without written language; she has the Good Book in her head already and does not need to know more to get to heaven.

There are a number of ways of understanding Aunt Linda's refusal to read. She can be seen as outdated, refusing to adapt to the "modern" world by becoming literate in its reading practices. Or she can be seen as privileging a colloquial, spiritual form of reading over that of the dominant, written discourse. But I read this passage more metaphorically, as concerning a struggle over whose vision of the world will dominate — Iola's or Aunt Linda's, the intellectual or the folk, the hegemonic or the nonhegemonic — and as being about how this struggle can be resolved through hybridity itself. In many ways, *Iola Leroy* is a text about learning to read: learning to read texts and books, as well as learning to read faces and signs — the "butter" that is not butter and the "eggs" that are not eggs. Harper's text shows there are many ways of reading the word and the world and that *all* these ways are vital to the survival of the individual and the race. Iola insists that to read, Aunt Linda will need to wear "spectacles" — glasses that would correct her (apparently faulty) eyesight. But in a chapter that begins with Aunt Linda's perfectly accurate description of a prophetic *vision* of Iola, we must wonder whose vision is faulty. Who needs spectacles: the woman who has perfect twenty-twenty foresight into events that have not yet occurred, or the woman who believes that everyone must don spectacles and become schooled in traditional literacy? Harper's text finally suggests the necessity of combining heterogeneous reading and language practices to create individuals literate in multiple discourses, individuals who can code-switch in order to function effectively in a number of social matrixes. Harper uses this passage near the end of her novel, then, to show that African Americans need both types of literacy, both types of language. Iola's "vision" is incomplete without Linda's, and Linda's vision is incomplete without Iola's; the metropolitan discourse needs the denied knowledge, and vice versa.[11]

The novel also ends with a poem that synthesizes these conflicting notions of reading and discourse. The poem describes a time when African Americans will "grasp the pen and wield it as a power for good," creating a spiritual vision of the race's progress:

There is light beyond the darkness
　　Joy beyond the present pain;
There is hope in God's great justice
　　And the Negro's rising brain.
Though the morning seems to linger
　　O'er the hill-tops far away,
Yet the shadows bear the promise
Of a brighter coming day.
(282)

Although this poem is clearly the product of a literate pen, it articulates an oral folk vision very similar to that of Aunt Linda's, for Aunt Linda's faith always allows her to see the brighter day that is coming, even in the midst of darkness. The text shows, then, that a folk discourse continues to operate from within the structures of the more traditional discourse, dialogizing its visions, hybridizing its sources of authority, and allowing it to function effectively in a number of different linguistic and social matrixes.

Harper's discourse of the folk also needs to be seen as hybridizing the language of the texts with which *Iola Leroy* is in dialogue. Douglass and Child rarely represent the speech of the folk, or of anything but a literate, educated African American population; furthermore, in Brown's text, as in Douglass's, becoming literate in written language is portrayed as the pathway from slavery to freedom. Harper's text uses the example of Robert Johnson to show that traditional literacy is one avenue to freedom; Robert quite literally employs the master's tools against the master, using his ability to read newspapers "to help overthrow the institution [of slavery] to which [his mistress] was so ardently attached" (16). But Harper's text also dialogizes this trope so common to the slave narrative (literacy as the pathway from slavery to freedom) by suggesting there are other avenues to empowerment than learning to read and write standard dialect; standard literacy needs to be supplemented by the linguistic practices of the "denied" knowledge. A language of the folk is introduced, then, to heterogenize the language of the prior texts. This language of the folk finally illustrates that the most powerful discursive and political strategy is a politics of hybridity that privileges multiple languages and, in so doing, creates new ones that both adapt and undo dominant systems of authority and discourse.

Through a politics of hybridity and through intertextual dialogues with prior tropes and texts, *Iola Leroy* translates and transforms those ideologies that have constrained African American subjectivity and, more particularly, the voice of African American women. Harper transforms the discourse of the True Woman, the "tragic mulatta," and the New Woman to produce a new language that both overturns and adapts these ideologies. She also hybridizes the slave narrative's sometimes male-centered discourse with a less gendered discourse of the people. Finally, Harper retrieves a "denied" discourse — a language of the folk — in order to create a hybrid language that can be spoken by both men and women. In this sense, Harper is connected to writers like Cooper, Chopin, Gilman, and Freeman, who seek to retrieve a feminine discourse that can undermine the Law of the Father. In Harper's text, the folk discourse functions similarly to that of the feminine language in the texts of her peers: it is a buried discourse that Harper unearths to unhinge patriarchal and racist theories of language and to create a new theory of language.

However, Harper's language of the folk is never presented as being outside of dominant discourses, nor does it belong particularly to one gender. Harper thus finds a discourse that allows her to undermine sexist and racist discourses without moving outside of them, and without creating "a language which nobody understood." Because Harper does not rely on a language of the feminine or the mother, she also avoids a number of the theoretical contradictions found in texts such as *The Awakening, Herland,* and *A Voice from the South.* Harper is thus an appropriate author to end this section with because, in addition to utilizing discursive strategies similar to those of her contemporaries, she also foreshadows what will occur in the early twentieth century, in the fiction of Fauset and Cather. These twentieth-century writers employ an ethnic, metalinguistic discourse that works from within dominant languages to reconstruct those boundaries that have maintained patriarchal and racist systems of empowerment. In so doing, Fauset and Cather move beyond the preoccupations of late-nineteenth-century writers; they move, like Harper, beyond the feminine voice.

7

Jessie Fauset's and Willa Cather's Metalinguistic, Ethnic Discourses

Reviewing *The Awakening* in 1899, Willa Cather described it as "trite and sordid," the glamorizing of a "fanciful and romantic" personality (697–99). These remarks articulate a firm break with nineteenth-century traditions and tropes of femininity and, indeed, early-twentieth-century writers such as Cather and Fauset often dissociate their heroines from prior female characters.[1] Cather's and Fauset's protagonists contain characteristics of a twentieth-century New Woman ideology; they are autonomous, self-expressive, sexual, and even selfish about reaching their goals. Furthermore, art created by these characters speaks a metalinguistic, ethnic discourse that realizes the theoretical basis of women's linguistic disempowerment within structures of patriarchal discourse but also works on, and in, these structures to undermine them.

Although Fauset's and Cather's writing seems to represent a firm break with prior textual constructions of women's search for voice, these early-twentieth-century writers are nonetheless indebted to the previous generation's debates about the problem of voice. As has been argued, in late-nineteenth-century writing, there is a break with the concept of women's speech emphasized at mid-century, yet the figuration of the "ideal" woman as a domestic saint with a subservient voice is never completely erased from textual spaces. This image also does not vanish in the twentieth century. In the works of Cather and Fauset, however, the domestic saint and the domestic voice most often function as countermodels against which to measure a heroine's struggles toward a new subjectivity and voice. Fauset's *There Is Confusion* (1924) and *Plum Bun* (1929) and Cather's *The Song of the Lark* (1915) rewrite figurations of the female artist present in a text such as *The Awakening*, and they also revise the previous generation's theory of feminine voice. Cather's and Fauset's heroines uncover and validate a denied racial and sexual language that unhinges dominant discourses. Before discussing Fauset's and Cather's fiction, however, it is necessary to define the components of this metalinguistic, ethnic voice.

This section examines some of the ways Cather and Fauset build on but also revise the theory of women's speech present in earlier texts through their use of ethnic or "minority" representations of discourse, language, or art. I do not mean to suggest, however, that Cather and Fauset have the same concept of "minority" discourse. Instead, I trace continuities and disjunctions, both between writers and within their individual fictions. There are three crucial features of this metalinguistic, ethnic voice. First, it is fundamentally about boundary making and unmaking, about troubling the boundaries of patriarchal and racist discourses in order to overturn them. Second, it has a double function: the validation of a "denied" speech but also the critique of a dominant discourse. Third, it crucially interconnects a metalinguistic interrogation of the dominant discourse with the nature and function of "minority" discourse itself. Aspects of this discourse have been present in previously discussed texts, of course. But Fauset and Cather are more radical than prior writers in that they employ all three strategies of disruption of patriarchal discourse simultaneously, thereby creating a new synthesis, a new discursive formulation. Furthermore, they introduce the concept of desire into these strategies as a subversive way of breaking with patriarchal economies of desire and language.

To begin with the first of these components — Cather's and Fauset's use of a discourse that is fundamentally about boundary making and unmaking — it must be noted that the boundary is a space associated with subversion and revision, for a boundary is not actually a space but a space-in-between, a liminal place. As has been previously argued, according to Victor Turner it is precisely in such liminal spaces that social constructions can be remade. Cather and Fauset situate their heroines in boundary spaces — in spaces between cultures and languages — in order to trouble these spaces, to unmake and remake them. The art created by these authors' female heroines also has this boundary troubling function. Like their late-nineteenth-century predecessors, Cather and Fauset understand the theoretical basis of the construction of the masculine subject in patriarchal dramas of subjectivity that silence women, and they are interested in recomposing this story. But Cather's and Fauset's strategies involve not the creation of a feminine discourse located outside of patriarchal language but rather one that exploits the gaps, and remakes the boundaries, of dominant languages. For Cather and Fauset, the feminine voice is validated not because it is outside patriarchal discourse but precisely because it is a troubling presence situated *within* hegemonic structures. These writers do not, then, fall into the theoretical problem experienced by a writer such as Kate Chopin in *The Awakening*: the creation of a subversive voice that finally cannot subvert patriarchal discourse because it is situated outside of it. They also attempt to avoid the essentialism of writers such as Freeman and Cooper. Cather and Fauset validate women's speech not because it is spoken by women but because it can be nonhegemonic, and they attempt to claim these voices for women without dismissing the value of male nonhegemonic voices. Similarly, they validate a language of desire and an ethnic discourse because of their nonhegemonic qualities: their ability to exploit the gaps, fissures, and boundaries of dominant discourses.

This boundary crossing disrupts patriarchal conceptions of women's speech and women's subjectivity, but it is also meant to disrupt boundaries having to do with racial identities. In *Beyond Ethnicity,* Warner Sollors argues that ethnicity is often associated with boundaries and that "modern ethnicization is a form of symbolic boundary-construction which increases cultural vitality" (247). I would argue that ethnicization is also about boundary crossing and boundary troubling. One need only think of texts about "passing" to see how ethnicity and boundary crossing are often conjoined: a character who passes does not construct a physical or social boundary between the races but dismantles — or at least undermines — such boundaries. Indeed, in Fauset's *Plum Bun* (a text in which African American characters "pass" for white), the concept of passing undermines divisions between races and demonstrates that these divisions are the product of racist cultural and social formations rather than reflecting essential physical attributes of individuals. Moreover, in the texts I will discuss, ethnic discourses are often used to reveal how racial categories normally kept separate (such as "white" and "black," or "American" and "ethnic") are in fact imbricated in each other; "whiteness" or "Americanness" is often constructed through an erasure of race, of ethnicity or "blackness" — an erasure these ethnic discourses unmask. These discourses, then, undermine the boundaries of racist, hegemonic discourses.

It must be emphasized, however, that while Fauset actually dismantles (and then reconstitutes) racial boundaries, in Cather's text this dismantlement remains metaphoric. Cather's heroine Thea sings with the Mexican Americans, incorporating their music into her operatic performances, but the Mexican Americans do not become opera singers. Similarly, Cather calls upon a "dead" past of Native American artistry, ignoring the fact that Native American artists were still living who could have become the heroines of the text, or at least inspired the heroine. Cather uses an ethnic discourse to liberate a (white) female subject's voice, but there is little consideration of how the subjugation of an ethnic "other" within discursive structures might be undone.

Both Cather and Fauset therefore employ a metalinguistic, ethnic discourse, but Cather's challenge to dominant languages is not as radical as Fauset's. For both writers, however, this discourse performs a double function of articulating a metalinguistic critique of patriarchal discourse as well as validating other (forbidden or denied) discourses, and this is its second component. Cather's *The Song of the Lark*, for example, validates the art of ethnic cultures — the singing of the Mexicans, and the pottery making of the "dead" Native Americans — in order to suggest both that these cultures have a rich artistic tradition that has gone unrecognized by the dominant culture and that these ethnic traditions allow the heroine to find a metaphor for her own art, her own voice, that does not rely on patriarchal binarisms that limit and silence her. Fauset's *Plum Bun* suggests that its character, who is passing for white, can only become an effective artist when she accepts her racial heritage and uses it to speak what patriarchal discourse has denied, including the silencing of the feminine, African American subject. In these texts, then, ethnic discourses both critique the dominant discourse and enfranchise denied traditions and knowledges.

In Fauset's and Cather's texts, there is rarely a direct depiction of an ethnic "folkspeech," or of other ethnic speech patterns, as there is in (for example) *Iola Leroy*. However, figurations of ethnic discourse and art are recovered to validate the "minority" discourse as well as to inspect the dominant discourse. In a discussion of the language of the folk, John Lowe suggests that this double function is a characteristic of ethnic discourse: "Ethnic writers' pride in folkspeech stems from their joint awareness that dialect is rich, humorous, laden with metaphor, and therefore tactile and appealing. Since dialect, at least to the oppressor, is part and parcel of the negative stereotype, pride in dialect constitutes inversion, transforming an oppressive signifier of otherness into a pride-inspiring prism, one which may be used for the critical inspection of the 'other'" (448). The ethnic discourse ("folkspeech") both inverts and validates an oppressive signifier of "otherness," but it also enables a critical inspection of the oppressor, and the oppressor's language. These ethnic traditions foreground the inadequacies of the dominant discourse and demonstrate the way it erases, or at least covers over, discourses that could enrich it.

The use of a metalinguistic, ethnic language also allows these writers to articulate an alternative vision of what constitutes an "empowered" discourse within culture. The "marginal" discourse is foregrounded, and the dominant discourse is pushed to the edge, into the boundary. Margin and center exchange places, reverse and invert themselves, until one cannot be differentiated from the other. Finally, this double function (validation of the "minority" discourse and critique of the dominant one) dismantles some of the binary oppositions that separate languages (high and low, dominant and subdominant, hegemonic and ethnic) and (sometimes, at least in Fauset's works) the binary oppositions that separate the individuals who speak these languages.

This ethnic, metalinguistic discourse also has the ability to unearth and validate other kinds of language that can critique patriarchal discourse. For example, in both Cather's and Fauset's works, the use of an ethnic discourse is also associated with the recovery of a feminine desire that begins to undo patriarchal economies of desire and language. Traditional systems of representation figure women as objects of desire — what men want — rather than desiring subjects in their own right. For Lacan, for example, women are doubly alienated from desire because they are both objects in the symbolic order as well as subjected to the symbolic order: "That the woman should be inscribed in an order of exchange of which she is the object, is what makes for the fundamentally conflictual, and, I would say, insoluble, character of her position: the symbolic order literally submits her, it transcends her... [She is] placed as an object in a symbolic order to which, at the same time, she is subjected just as much as the man" (Seminar II, 304–5; quoted in Rose 45). In traditional systems of representation, then, women are alienated from desire. As Jaqueline Rose explains, "As the place onto which lack is projected, and through which it is simultaneously disavowed, woman is a 'symptom' for the man. Defined as such, reduced to being nothing other than this fantasmatic place, the woman does not exist" (48). Or as Hélène Cixous argues in more direct terms, woman is "matter subjected to the desire that he [man] wishes to imprint" (92). Most problematically, such phallocentric constructions of desire have the ability to silence and destroy women's actual desire, as Cixous further explains: "Because... there is so little place in society for her desire... she [woman] ends up by dint of not knowing what to do with it, no longer knowing where to put it, or if she has any, conceals the most immediate and the most urgent question: 'How do I experience sexual pleasure?'" (95). Patriarchal economies of language and desire ultimately deprive women of the ability to understand and articulate their own desire.

The discourses created in the art of Fauset's and Cather's characters retrieve a feminine desire elided or written over by such traditional (patriarchal) systems of representation. These texts also use this desire to critique patriarchal discourse and to articulate what patriarchal discourse makes unspeakable and unspoken. Desire becomes a central part of each heroine's art, but this desire is only retrieved through a language that is specifically ethnic and feminine. Upon seeing the artwork of the Native American women in the extremely sexual, and feminine, landscape of Panther Canyon, Cather's protagonist moves toward an understanding of how her own desire has been denied to her as a source of art. In *Plum Bun,* Fauset's protagonist begins to understand how her desire has been erased when she paints an African American woman; through her art she speaks what patriarchal discourse has made unspoken. The metalinguistic, ethnic languages created in these texts thus have a double function of allowing the retrieval of denied discourses (of race and feminine desire), as well as showing the limitations of patriarchal discourse and subverting its most fundamental oppositions.

This discourse also crucially interconnects a metalinguistic interrogation of the dominant language with the nature and function of "minority" discourse itself, and this is its third aspect. In "Ethnic Culture, Minority Discourse, and the State," David Lloyd argues that "minority" discourse is usually constituted along the lines of a struggle between a dominant discourse or institution that threatens to destroy or efface the nondominant language. For Lloyd, "minority" discourse registers this threat, as well as offering "the means to a critique of dominant culture precisely in terms of its own internal logic" (222). By registering the potential or actual erasure of ethnic voices and ethnic cultures, Cather's and Fauset's texts offer a means to critique patriarchal, racist culture precisely through its own sets of values. After showing that ethnic art is produced by valid cultures with developed artistic traditions of their own, Cather and Fauset then show how forces arrayed around these cultures systematically attempt to efface them. In *Plum Bun*, social forces suggest that the heroine's racial heritage is valueless and must be concealed to produce "successful" art, while in *The Song of the Lark* Cather depicts a society that automatically devalues all ethnic art as "primitive." Crucially, these authors validate ethnic cultures and languages in their own terms, as well as in the terms of the dominant culture, the dominant discourse. Thus the "minority" voices marshaled in these texts interconnect ethnic discourse with a metalinguistic critique of the dominant culture.

Finally, what these writers demonstrate is a relationship of reciprocity in which the ethnic discourse produces the metalinguistic one, and vice versa. Employing the discourse of ethnic "others" produces a metalanguage that can undermine patriarchal and racist discourses from within their own discursive paradigms. And metalinguistic investigation of dominant discursive paradigms reveals that they erase and silence the contributions of ethnic and female "others." Cather's and Fauset's metalinguistic, ethnic voices trouble discursive boundaries, validate a "forbidden" speech while also critiquing dominant discourses, and establish a relationship of reciprocity that interconnects the critique of the "minority" discourse with the critique of the metalanguage itself. In so doing, Cather and Fauset produce not only a new discourse but also a new theory for the understanding of language's functioning, one that demonstrates not the separation of discourses within culture (male from female, dominant from ethnic, hegemonic from nonhegemonic) but their enmeshment, overlap, and continual dependency.

Cather's and Fauset's earliest works sometimes remain mired in the same kinds of questions that stymied late-nineteenth-century writers, but their later works "pass" beyond earlier conceptions of women's voice into this metalinguistic, ethnic theory of language. The next section of this chapter examines two of Jessie Fauset's novels—*There Is Confusion* and *Plum Bun*—to illustrate this movement. Although *There Is Confusion* begins by telling the story of a self-defined female artist, it eventually swerves from this plot to depict an enshrinement within constraining formulations of feminine identity and voice. But Fauset's second novel, *Plum Bun*, moves beyond the domestic story and the domestic voice, foregrounding a feminine identity that undermines patriarchal ideologies. The third section of this chapter then demonstrates Cather's deployment of a voice that both rewrites figurations of the female artist present in the nineteenth-century but also invokes a new concept of the functioning of dominant and "minority" discourses in culture as a whole.

Passing Beyond the Domestic Story and the Domestic Voice: From Fauset's *There Is Confusion* to *Plum Bun*

As previous chapters have demonstrated, although the stereotype of the New Woman was less restrictive than the True Woman, late-nineteenth-century and early-twentieth-century literary texts often treat the New Woman with a certain degree of ambivalence. This is also true of texts by African American women, although for different reasons; as Claudia Tate explains, "while many late-nineteenth-century black women writers might have been sympathetic to the so-called 'new (white) woman's' rejection of traditional domestic roles and attendant radically revised gender constructions, their black heroines are not so extreme. After all, such heroines could hardly reject what had not been broadly within their domain to embrace" (138). According to Tate, a heroine created by late-nineteenth- and early-twentieth-century African American writers will accept "marriage as central to her personal advancement, central to the prosperity of her family and community, indeed central to the progress of civilization itself " (138).

Is this true of Fauset's early-twentieth-century heroines? Tate calls *There Is Confusion* "an upbeat domestic blues story about enduring racism with individual black heroism and sexual satisfaction" (228), but there is a great deal of dissonance in this novel. More specifically, the dissonance of *There Is Confusion* is generated by Fauset's dissatisfaction with models of subjectivity that emphasize that a talented heroine must eventually forgo a career in order to "accept marriage as central to her personal advancement" but also by Fauset's inability to formulate another model of subjectivity in this, her first, novel. An examination of the text's relationship to various stereotypes of femininity and its suggestive (but not fully formulated) concept of a metalinguistic, ethnic discourse reveals an attempt to move beyond limited images of femininity, an attempt ultimately overturned by desire itself.[2]

There Is Confusion initially seems to break with the codes of the True Woman by choosing an outspoken heroine who has no desire to marry.[3] The novel's protagonist — Joanna Marshall — knows that "love for a woman usually means a household of children, the getting of a thousand meals, picking up laundry, no time to herself for meditation, for reading" (95), and she resolves not to be like these "poor, silly sheep" (103). From a very young age she longs to be a great dancer or singer; as Deborah McDowell states, Joanna "has neither desire nor intention to accept or conform to conventional images of women" ("Neglected Dimension" 93). In fact, she is described as selfish by her more traditional sister Sylvia: "Joanna makes me sick . . . always talking of her lessons and how important she's going to be when she's grown-up. So tiresome, too, wanting to talk about what she's going to do all the time, with no interest in your affairs" (16). As Sylvia's complaint indicates, Joanna also possesses a voice that is self-defined and even self-centered. As a young child, Joanna climbs onto her father's lap and asks to be read a story about somebody great, "Great like I'm going to be when I get to be a big girl" (9). At this early stage, Joanna does not see any specifically female limits placed on artistic achievement, and she does not hamper herself with notions of feminine selflessness. Later in her life, she supports this independence with a discourse that does not defer to male authority. For example, when her fiancé, Peter Bye, tells her that he is "used to being waited on, not doing the waiting" (152), she responds by saying: "Peter Bye, you *are* spoilt . . . You're — why you're absolutely disgusting. . . . Whatever's come over you, Peter?" (152–53). Joanna does not defer to Peter's authority, and she contradicts him when she thinks he is in error.

Joanna's artistic "voice" also differs from that of prior female characters who followed the model of the True Woman. The novel explores the idea — developed more fully in *Plum Bun* — that the female artist's work functions as a metalinguistic, ethnic discourse that critiques patriarchal discourse. In a production called "The Dance of the Nations," Joanna plays a Native American, an African American, and an "American." When Joanna dances all three parts, she "speaks" to her white audience, telling them that African Americans should not be limited to narrowly defined racial roles. As Joanna puts it in an earlier scene discussing her dancing, "I am colored, of course, but American first. Why shouldn't I *speak* to all America?" (76, my emphasis). Symbolically, then, Joanna's dancing is meant to retrieve ethnic discourse and to authorize its presence within (rather than outside of) dominant discursive matrixes, within the discourses of "America." These matrixes will be altered and reconfigured by an assertion of ethnic voice.

The challenge of Joanna's metalinguistic, ethnic voice becomes even clearer when she has to defend her right to dance these parts in this production. The producers of the show initially insist that when she dances the part of an "American," her race must be hidden behind a mask. Literally, then, the "American" is shown to be constituted through an exclusion of the "ethnic." But Joanna's performance is so outstanding that the audience demands to see the face of the dancer; in front of an audience, Joanna must remove her mask. Fauset's text stages a radical scene of unmasking in which the "American" is shown to be contained within the "ethnic," and vice versa. So when Joanna removes her mask, she also unmasks those conventions that have forced her to be masked, those conventions that define the "American" as a separate category from the "ethnic." Joanna's statement in this scene also unmasks those codes that would force her race to be hidden to construct a facade of "Americanness." Joanna explains that dancing the part of an "American" is a logical and natural outgrowth of her heritage as an African American in America: "I hardly need to tell you that there is no one in the audience more American than I am. My great-grandfather fought in the Revolution, my uncle fought in the Civil War and my brother is 'over there' now" (232). Fauset's scene removes the sutures that create the hegemonic facade, indicating that Americanness (and "whiteness") are constructed through an artificial erasure of ethnicity; her scene also allows the ethnic and the American to reanimate each other.

However, when Joanna initially dances the part of the "American," she allows herself to be masked. Because of this, some critics have argued that Joanna's triumph in "The Dance of the Nations" is "mere accommodation, her temporarily 'safe' position proof that she has rewarded the audience's refusal to read her as anything other than the Other in a racial binary" (McCoy 112). But this "accommodation" is part of Fauset's ability to critique constructions of racial identity through a discourse that is both ethnic and metalinguistic. This discourse accommodates itself, or situates itself, *inside* of hegemonic discourses in order to remake them. The text obscures Joanna's racial identity, then, only so that its erasure within discourses of what constitutes the "American" can be unmasked and reconfigured. The text can therefore demonstrate both the erasure of ethnic identity by categories of whiteness or "Americanness" and how this erasure breaks down. This is not "accommodation" to a white norm but rather a form of disaccommodation that eventually shows precisely how racial binaries are constituted and how they can be dismantled.

Furthermore, Joanna's configuration of herself as "American" needs to be read as a subversion of this category that remakes it so that it can be more commodious; in Fauset's works "American" does not only mean Caucasian. Fauset's novel also demonstrates that African American art is a part of American art to further dismantle the binary division between white Americans and "black" (or foreign, or ethnic) "others." Central to Joanna's successful performance in "The Dance of the Nations" is an African American child's game that she translates into art for her white audience (229). Joanna thereby incorporates an "ethnic" folk art into what is considered to be "American" art — a mainstream dance production attended by an Anglo American audience. Carolyn Sylvander comments that "Black folk material as the basis for possible uniqueness in Black artistry is a nicely underplayed but repeated idea" (150), yet this theme is central to Joanna's development and to the novel as a whole. In insisting that she is American and that African American art and artists have a place in the "high" culture of "American" art, Joanna's dancing speaks her sense of racial, cultural, and social identity. Joanna's dancing has a double function, then, of both validating the ethnic and critiquing the binaries of the dominant culture that have separated the "ethnic" from the "American" and devalued the former while enfranchising the later.

Therefore, Fauset's novel creates a subversive feminine subjectivity that speaks through an unruly, metalinguistic/ethnic voice that deconstructs racial and sexual boundaries. However, after demonstrating the construction of this subject/voice, the text swerves rather abruptly to show its deconstruction. First, the heroine's self-defined voice is censured and erased. When Joanna's outspokenness causes her to lose her fiancé, she resolves to silence herself (202). The heroine also gives up the metalinguistic, ethnic voice she has marshaled, deciding that although it means something "to prove to the skeptical world the artistry of a too little understood people," the focus of her life should be "home, children, and adoring husband" (274). Finally, Joanna also sets aside her autonomous subjectivity. She learns to defer to Peter privately so that he can wield public authority: "In a thousand little ways she deferred to him, and showed him that as a matter of course he was the arbiter of her own and her child's destiny, the *fons et origo* of authority" (292). The novel suggests quite self-consciously that the sacrifice of female authority and autonomy is necessary for the achievement of African American male authority and self-reliance; Peter, not Joanna, eventually becomes "a great man" (296). In the end, Joanna gives up the new subjectivity and voice she has achieved in favor of a much less radical identity and discourse, figuring herself as a support for the patriarchal male subject.

What causes this shift from *Künstlerroman* to domestic novel, from a radical metalinguistic/ethnic voice to one that very much resembles the subservient, self-denying voice of the domestic saint? Deborah McDowell has suggested that Fauset is, finally, "a traditionalist regarding women's roles" and that Fauset is not secure enough in this novel to fully develop the radical and unconventional side of her female heroine ("Neglected Dimension" 98–99). However, there are specific textual clues as to what causes the derailment of the *Künstlerroman*, and it is not just Fauset's conservatism. Joanna's metalinguistic, ethnic discourse never considers the subversive role desire might play in her art, in her speaking of her presence as a female, African American artist. Fauset's text evokes the concept of feminine desire, but it does not find an alternative language that can incorporate this desire. Therefore, feminine desire can only be incorporated into patriarchal economies of desire that finally present no challenge to the structuring of the patriarchal world of discourse and identity.

Prior to this novel, the only text discussed that depicts female desire is Chopin's *The Awakening* and, as we have seen, many Victorian readers reacted with horror. In the early twentieth century, the idea that women lacked desire was being questioned, and Fauset and Chopin both ask a similar question: is there a textual or social or linguistic space in which this desire can become articulate? Furthermore, for Fauset there is the vexed question of how to represent an African American feminine desire in a society that has always pejoratively labeled these women as oversexed "Jezebels." Perhaps this explains why, in *There Is Confusion*, Fauset does not deny her character's desire but does contain it. Joanna feels desire, as Fauset says: "she was beginning at last to feel the tug of passion at her heart strings" (146). The language describing Joanna's desire is highly conventional, employing terminology such as "tug of passion" and "heart strings." Another language is available in art for the expression of this desire, but Joanna never implements this radical proposition. So she continues to be contained within a patriarchal economy of desire in which she "feel[s] the pull of awakened and unsatisfied passion" (180) without being able to express this passion.

On a discursive level, Joanna never becomes a subject who desires but rather is subjected to desire, and to a language that conventionalizes and ironizes her "passion." Personally, too, Joanna never transcends patriarchal economies of desire that construct women as the objects of men's desires. For example, although she meets women who advocate birth control (234), she herself never seems to consider the possibility of sexual relations outside of marriage — or of an alternative construction of her body that might isolate desire, childbearing, and marriage from each other. Fauset breaks new ground by insisting that Joanna has sexual desires, but finally there is only one safe space for the "expression" of desire — in a marriage to Peter Bye, a marriage that makes the male the desiring subject, the authority, and the female his property, his object of desire.

Fauset's second novel, however, does more than merely articulate feminine desire as a troubling (but finally containable) presence within patriarchal economies of language and desire. *Plum Bun* incorporates feminine desire into the metalinguistic, ethnic art its heroine creates, thereby crafting an alternative economy of desire and language that undermines those of the patriarchy. Therefore, below the overt plot of *Plum Bun* there is a radical message about the disruptive potential of art produced by a subject who is female, ethnic, and desiring.

Hazel Carby argues that although Fauset's works reveal the contradictory conventions of womanhood, they do not transcend the form of the romance (*Reconstructing Womanhood* 168). Yet *Plum Bun* is the only one of Jessie Fauset's four novels that ends with its heroine unmarried. *Plum Bun* does start with the topic of marriage, with the protagonist's (Angela Murray's) dream of marrying a wealthy man. To further this end, Angela leaves her family, passes for white, and has an affair with a white man who abandons her. Angela eventually falls in love with a fellow "passer," Anthony Cross, and after a series of complications, Anthony and Angela declare their true racial identities and are united (yet the novel ends before they marry). The marriage drama, then, is given a good deal of attention by the novel's overt plot. But Angela has always had talent as a painter, and throughout all her romantic travails the growth of her art is the one constant in her life, a theme the novel returns to again and again. Thus *Plum Bun* "passes" for a romance, but its real concern is a more subversive plot depicting the female artist's personal, aesthetic, racial, and sexual maturation.

The novel creates a textual space in which this maturation can occur by continually evoking—but then unmasking and ironizing—what might be called a counterspace and counterimage: the conventions of domesticity and the domestic novel. The nursery rhyme that gives *Plum Bun* its title and structure hints at this:

To Market, to Market,
To Buy a Plum Bun;
Home again, Home again,
Market is done.

Although the rhyme counterpoises and alternates the realm of domesticity (the home) with the realm of commercialism (the market), it still shows the triumph of domesticity over crass materialism by ending with the phrase "Market is done." Fauset's novel, too, ends with a section titled "Market Is Done," but it does not show the safe return to the domestic space. Rather, it ends with its heroine very much in the world of the market, learning her trade as an artist in Paris. The nursery rhyme acts as an ironic contrast to the novel's primary action, an action suggesting that market is never done.

The novel's domestic characters are also portrayed through this ironic, countermodal structure. Mattie Murray, Angela's mother, escapes from her job as a maid by marrying a "prince charming," her employer's chauffeur. Mattie portrays domestic life as a wonderful fairy tale: "When Angela and Virginia were little children and their mother used to read them fairy tales she would add to the ending, 'And so they lived happily ever after, just like father and me'" (33). Yet this use of a fairy tale motif, as McLendon has also noted (29), is quite ironic; Mattie's life of domesticity with her husband Junius is difficult and wearying, and they are poor for many years—a fact her fantasy conveniently ignores. The domestic fairy tale therefore functions as an illusion, a false consciousness. Furthermore, this false consciousness is shown to be extremely debilitating. Mattie is described as a "perfect woman, sweet, industrious, affectionate and illogical," a woman who believes her husband "was God" (33), yet Mattie's adherence to domestic models of subjectivity means she has no identity of her own. When Junius passes away, Mattie follows him swiftly to the grave. Like Thea's mother in Cather's *The Song of the Lark*, who, despite her independent resourcefulness, dies shortly after her husband because she "could not very well get along without Mr. Kronborg" (352), Mattie's subjectivity is totally dependent on her husband's. Immersion in being a "perfect woman" eventually destroys Mattie's own identity; the externally imposed mask, the false consciousness, consumes the real self that might once have existed.

In *Plum Bun*, domesticity and the profile of the True Woman are thus presented primarily as foils to the text's main focus on a new model of feminine identity. This new model figures women as sexual, able to pursue careers with the same vigor as men, and uninterested in marriage for its own sake. Angela's friend Paulette, for instance, is an artist who has numerous affairs and is unashamed of her sexual desires; she believes that a woman has "as much right to feel as a man" (198).[4] She also exhibits a kind of discursive openness that surprises Angela, discussing her affairs with candor and even commenting frankly that "Any woman is better than the best of men" (128). Furthermore, one might hypothesize that Paulette practices some form of birth control, for despite her numerous affairs she does not become pregnant. Fauset also shows African American women who are autonomous, outspoken, and sexual. In one scene, Angela meets a young African American teacher who is "totally without self-consciousness" (115) about her flirtation with a white man. A colleague of Angela's — Miss Powell — is a type of New Woman artist who dreams not of home and domesticity but of winning prestigious prizes to study painting abroad. And indeed, although Angela herself sometimes longs to be "a beloved woman, dependent, fragile, sought for, feminine" (296), she knows her nature is more independent.

In her affair with a white man, Roger Fielding, Angela does temporarily seem to become this dependent woman, but again this profile is evoked as a contrast. Roger is described as the "anchor" for Angela's "frail, insecure bark of life" (195), and we are told that "without him life meant nothing; with him it was everything" (203). Fauset's use of these clichés, however, signals irony, and lest we take Angela's role as dependent mistress too seriously, Fauset undercuts it at every juncture: "For a while his wishes, his pleasure were the end and aim of her existence; *she told herself with a slight tendency toward self-mockery* that this was the explanation of being" (203–4, my emphasis). Angela is self-consciously and mockingly acting a role she will eventually discard. The text even questions the idea that she depends on Roger totally: "*Something quite outside herself, something watchful, proud, remote* from the passion and rapture which flamed within her, *kept her free and independent.* She would not accept money, she would not move to the apartment on Seventy-Second Street" (204, my emphasis). Angela will only play the role of mistress. She will not actually become Roger's kept woman, a plum bun he can buy or sell.

Like many of the women in the novel, Angela is in the process of discovering a more subversive and self-defined identity. When Roger abandons Angela, she does not kill herself or go insane, like a good True Woman would. Rather, she finds a source of fulfillment in her art: "she turned more ardently than ever to her painting; already she was capable of doing outstanding work in portraiture" (235). By the time that Roger returns and proposes to Angela, she is seeking a new identity as an artist and she barely even listens:

> Impatience overwhelmed her. She wished he would go and leave her to her thoughts and to her picture; such a splendid idea had come to her. . . .

"Angèle, you've got to take me back."

" . . . If you've got nothing better to say than that, you might as well get out. . . .
Go away, Roger. I don't want to be bothered with you!" (318–19)

Roger is the wealthy white "prince charming" who can provide Angela with the magical identity of wife, the hero in the domestic drama. But Angela's artistic and racial consciousness has been developing, and she rejects this limiting plot. She also refuses the muting of her voice this plot entails. In the past, Roger has often silenced Angela, but here she asserts her own voice, saying in a very unromantic and undiplomatic manner, "Go away, Roger. I don't want to be bothered with you."

Therefore, Fauset evokes the marriage drama only to swerve radically from it and create another plot that depicts the heroine's growth into linguistic and artistic power. Indeed, each time the marriage drama is evoked, it is subverted by textual coincidences or by Angela's own awakened consciousness. Thus when Angela falls in love with Anthony Cross, she finds him already coincidentally engaged to her sister. And by the time Angela is reunited with another admirer, Matthew Henson, she realizes that "she was not through adventuring, through tasting life" (362). Angela also rejects a less conventional man who seems on the verge of proposing to her — Ralph Ashley — with the following words: "You aren't coming over to ask me to marry you, are you? . . . You'll come as a friend?" (372–73). And finally, Angela is reunited with Anthony Cross, but the novel concludes with the happy couple in Paris, unwed.

Sylvander notes the novel's unconventional ending, commenting that the union with Anthony is "somewhat deceptive, for Angela's resolutions have come previously and on her own, in her own way" (175), but — like Carby — Sylvander still sees the novel as a "romance" (141).[5] Yet the novel ends without a marriage precisely because *Plum Bun*'s marriage plot is a countertext to the novel's primary focus. Angela's mother dreams that her daughters might become "great artists," but her father insists they be given "a good, plain education" (55). The voice of patriarchal authority tries to force African American women to submit to other cultural imperatives than their own artistic drives. Once again, we see the Law of the Father attempting to silence — or at least contain — a feminine voice/presence that might disrupt it. Yet for Angela, art always functions as a voice of her own, "a means of self-expression" (37). Angela's painting is her language, a "way to interpret life" and "write down a history with her brush" (12). *Plum Bun* more fully develops an idea examined in *There Is Confusion*: that women's art may function as an alternative to racist and sexist discourses. Angela's art is a metalinguistic, ethnic discourse that allows her to express her racial consciousness and to speak feminine desire.

The growth of Angela's talent is a textual theme present from the novel's start. Like other artist figures such as Edna Pontellier and Thea Kronborg, Angela is secretive, self-absorbed, and solitary, even at a very young age. She also goes through periods of intense artistic development: "She began to work at her art with growing vigour and interest. She was gaining in assurance; her technique showed an increased mastery; above all she had gained in the power to compose, a certain sympathy, a breadth of comprehension . . . Mr. Paget, the instructor, spoke of her paintings with increased respect" (208). If this passage sounds familiar, it may be because it echoes Chopin's description of Edna in *The Awakening.* Edna's work is said "to grow in force and individuality," and Laidpore, her teacher, tells her that he is "more and more pleased" with it (963). And like Edna, Angela's art begins to provide her with a means of economic support; Angela meets wealthy friends and is well on her way to getting a series of lucrative commissions for portraits (273). Unlike Edna, however, Angela's art also offers psychological support, becoming the "most real force in her life" (332), allowing her to resist Roger's marriage proposal. In Paris, Angela works diligently to perfect her talent: "Her aim, her one ambition, was to become an acknowledged, a significant painter of portraits" (375). At the end of the novel, Angela is struggling to become an artist, not a wife. Fauset, then, rewrites the plot of a novel such as *The Awakening,* the plot of the woman artist who never actually becomes an artist. Fauset's novel shows a woman working toward—and achieving—a realization of her artistic ambitions.

Fauset's text also foregrounds questions of racial and artistic identity faced by an African American, female artist. Fauset suggests that Angela's passing for white enables her financially (allowing her to obtain patronage and win prestigious prizes) but disables her psychologically and artistically (forcing a silencing of self). Angela initially believes "it isn't being colored that makes the difference, it's letting it be known" (78). Jacquelyn McLendon argues that Angela passes to escape her "black" body (9), but this quotation indicates that Angela sees race not as a physical essence but as a discursive one—a product of what is left said or unsaid. When Angela wants to pass, she simply does not tell people about her "brown" father and sister. But race becomes a psychological issue when passing entails denying pieces of her identity. When Roger rails against a group of "coons" who have tried to dine at an expensive restaurant, Angela only sits "silent, lifeless" and "speechless" (133). Angela believes passing is mastering life, but in this scene it seems to involve being mastered by master discourses, such as the discourse of racism in America. Eventually, Angela does speak out about her race and feels a "wave of relief and contentment" (349). Fauset's text therefore retreats from the position that race exists primarily in discourse. When Angela denies her race, she denies not a physical or linguistic fact but a social and cultural history that she is part of, that she must express.

Artistically, too, Angela must learn to articulate her race, to create a voice that is both metalinguistic and ethnic. Angela's success as a painter is fundamentally tied to bringing racial consciousness into her work. But because Angela is "passing," she must continually deny the influence of African American art forms and individuals on her work. Like Joanna, who literally wears a mask in "The Dance of the Nations," Angela too is masked; she is passing for white, and her art is passing for white. For example, when Angela is asked whether the model for one of her portraits is American, she responds by saying "yes she is. She's an old coloured woman who's worked in our family for years and she was born right here in Philadelphia" (70). But her questioner—a racist art student—does not accept this logic: "Oh coloured! Well, of course I suppose you would call her an American though I never think of darkies as Americans" (70). Angela does not contest this statement, for to do so might reveal her racial heritage. In this way, she mutes herself and her art; she lets her painting be construed as a "simple" portrait of a "darkie's" "unhappiness" rather than as a picture of a forceful African American who is also an American. Angela's subtle challenge to ideas about who is an "American" and who is an appropriate subject for "American" art goes unheard.

Yet, as in *There Is Confusion*, the text masks racial identity only to unmask and undermine various binary divisions: white over black, "American" over "ethnic," "high" art over "low" (or popular) culture. As in the first novel, Fauset stages this scene of unmasking in a very public setting, for Angela reveals her racial identity in front of four reporters; as Angela states, "the story will be all over New York by tomorrow morning" (348). When a fellow African American art student—Miss Powell—is denied a scholarship to study in France because of her race, Angela goes to her house to console her. Angela has been awarded this prize, and in the presence of several reporters, she finds herself suddenly declaring: "Miss Powell isn't going to France on the American Committee Fund and I'm not going either. . . . You imply that she's not wanted because she's coloured. Well, I'm coloured too" (346–47). Ironically, the "American Committee Fund" is shown only to belong to "Americans" of a certain color; Angela can only receive it when she is willing to erase her race, to seem "raceless" or "colorless"—that is, white. But Angela's very presence within America undercuts the notion of a pure (colorless, raceless) "American" identity. One reporter's description of this event speaks of "mixed blood" as "the curse of the country," a curse whose "insidiously concealed influence constantly threatens the wells of national race purity" (352). But Angela's acceptance, first, as a "pure American" and her later revelation that she is African American shows that "the wells" of "racial purity" are not—and never were—"pure" in the sense the reporter uses this term. They are "constantly threatened"—constantly undermined—not just by individuals like Angela but by individuals like Miss Powell, who believe they can compete for "American" prizes. Angela's placement within the text and her revelation of her racial identity, then, unmasks the concept that the "American" can be separated off from the racial, the ethnic. Furthermore, her revelation of her racial status overturns binary oppositions between the races in such a way that they cannot be easily reconfigured; the concept of "racial purity" is itself deconstructed.

Angela's art also overturns and subverts racist binary oppositions. Her works often focus on African American characters whom she calls "American," like the maid, Hetty Daniels (66), and her mother (270). In fact Angela's best painting — the one for which she wins the "American" scholarship — is the portrait of Hetty Daniels; as Sylvander argues, this demonstrates the value of an African American art "based partly on Black folk materials" (170). Thus Fauset's text validates the ethnic, but it also uses "the ethnic" to critique the dominant discourse. Through a series of ironic unmaskings, Angela's prize-winning portrait of Hetty Daniels undermines the separation between the "American" and the "ethnic," the "white" and the "black." Angela, an "American" artist (who turns out to be African American), paints a picture of an "American" woman (who turns out to be not really "American"), and wins an "American" scholarship (which turns out to be intended only for white Americans). Yet finally, the scholarship money is given to Angela when it is revealed that the donor is interested "not in Ethnology but in Art" (359). The reporters to whom Angela reveals her racial identity see Angela as "passing" for a (white) American, but in the eyes of the donor, she really is "American," deserving of an "American" scholarship. The category of "the American" is deconstructed, but it is also reconstructed as a more capacious category, one that can accommodate individuals such as Angela, Hetty, and Miss Powell.

The text therefore configures Angela's painting as a discourse that works from within dominant structures to remake their racial and social boundaries; this discourse validates the presence of the ethnic while critiquing the "American"; and finally, it interconnects its metalinguistic placement within discursive paradigms with its challenge as a "minority" discourse. Angela is most effective at unmasking racial codes because she can both conceal, and reveal, racial identities. As a "passer" her physical presence undermines the separation between "white" and "black," but as an artist who creates art that "passes" for white, for "American," yet then turns out to be "black" or "ethnic," her work demonstrates that these categories are constructed as oppositional, when they are in fact imbricated within each other. Whiteness constructs itself by excluding the presence of the ethnic "other," but Fauset's text reveals that this exclusion can be broken down through discourses (such as Angela's paintings) that refuse to separate the ethnic from the "American."

The text also weaves desire into this metalinguistic, ethnic discourse, suggesting that Angela's work gives voice not only to a racial presence excluded by dominant structures but also to a feminine desire that usually remains unspoken. Like Edna Pontellier, who dreams of the voice of the sea, Angela initially dreams of a language that will transcend patriarchal discourse. Dancing with another man,

Angela feels Roger's eyes fixed on her; Fauset tells us that "a long, long look passed between them so fraught it seemed to [Angela], with a secret understanding and sympathy, that her heart shook" (188). Later Roger comments to Angela: "you were thinking of me, I felt it, I knew it... without a word" (189). And Roger promises Angela that this secret discourse, this language beyond the patriarchal, will always be theirs: "If you'd only take happiness with me there we would be with a secret bond, an invisible bond, existing for us alone and no one else in the world the wiser" (189). Yet when Roger and Angela exchange this look, Angela is the object of desire — held by another man, while her own lover fixes her with his gaze. So it should come as no surprise that Roger's promise turns out to be an illusion. When Angela becomes Roger's mistress, she finds herself speaking tritely, and Roger responds in kind: "You knew perfectly well what you were letting yourself in for. Any woman would know it" (231). Fauset's next comment emphasizes that Angela has not found a language outside of patriarchal discourse: "The phrase had the quality of a cosmic echo; perhaps men had been saying it to women since the beginning of time" (231). This is a shopworn discourse that leaves women in the same old linguistic and sexual traps. Roger's "transcendent" discourse only contains Angela's desire — which she would figure as being outside of language — within a patriarchal economy.

Despite this failure, it is important that Fauset's text portrays a heroine who experiences, and is not destroyed by, desire. In this sense *Plum Bun* breaks with nineteenth-century novels such as *Iola Leroy* and *Our Nig*, which responded to the "Jezebel" image of African American women by denying their female characters' sexuality. Furthermore, since Angela's affair with Roger lasts several months and she does not become pregnant, perhaps, like Paulette, Angela practices some form of birth control, isolating her desire not only from marriage but also from reproduction. Yet finally, this sexual desire does not function subversively: the text creates a space for it but also shows how it is continually coopted by patriarchal forces, by patriarchal language. For example, when Fauset describes Angela's desire, the language is once again highly conventional: "He put his arm about her, kissed her; her very bones turned to water... The air was charged with passion" (202). As configured in the patriarchal world, desire remains hegemonic — controlled by men and by a cliché-ridden discourse.

It is only in her art that Angela begins to find an alternative to patriarchal economies of desire, an alternative in which her desire is not conventionalized, objectified, and silenced. This is not a language outside of patriarchy, for there is no such thing, but rather a form of self-expression that undermines the boundaries of patriarchal discourse. Angela's painting of Hetty is an excellent example of such a discourse, for it attempts to articulate what Hetty's spoken discourse denies but her face expresses: her desire. Hetty's favorite spoken topic is "sex morality." Describing her youthful flirtations, she says: "Then young fellars was always 'round me thick ez bees. . . . But I never listened to none of the' talk, jist held out gain 'em and kept my pearl of great price untarnished. I aimed then and I'm continual to aim to be a verjous woman" (66). Hetty harps on clichés (pearl of great price, virtuous woman, and so on) and follows the rhetoric of the domestic saint: women are virtuous, asexual, and morally superior to men. Hetty clearly describes herself as an object of desire (a "pearl of great price") contained within a patriarchal economy. However, Hetty's face denies this conservative discourse as well as her inscription within patriarchal economies of desire: "Her *unslaked yearnings* gleamed suddenly out of her eyes, transforming her usually rather expressionless face into something wild and avid. The dark brown immobile mask of her skin made an excellent foil for the vividness of an emotion which was so apparent, so palpable that it seemed like something superimposed upon the background of her countenance" (66, emphasis added). As McLendon comments, "implicit in this description of Hetty's memory of her youth is the double standard that allows only men to express desire openly" (38); Hetty cannot speak her own yearnings but rather is "spoken by hegemonic discourses that dictate the constructs of female desire" (38). Indeed, hegemonic discourses seem to deprive Hetty of all emotion; when she mouths patriarchal discourse, Hetty's face is "rather expressionless." But sexual desire — her "unslaked yearnings" — transforms her face into something full of expression, full of emotion. Hetty's "vivid," "wild," and "avid" expression is the trace of an excessive, potentially transformative, desire. Angela tries to capture this desire in her painting: "If I could just get that look" (66).

Angela's painting works from within dominant paradigms (the conventional woman with her conventional discourse) to articulate what is unspoken, unconventional, and potentially revolutionary — the excess of feminine sexual desire. Angela's painting tries to speak feminine desire, rather than allowing it to be spoken by racist and phallocentric discourse. Most important, Angela's artwork criticizes what patriarchal discourse ignores — the power of feminine desire to transform the conventional woman into something radically different. Fauset's *Plum Bun* therefore suggests that Angela's art can function as a language that works from within the dominant discursive domain to make what is unspoken (feminine desire) speakable. And through this medium, Angela herself begins to become a desiring subject: a subject who can articulate her own wants and needs. For this painting must certainly be seen as reflecting not only Hetty's desires but Angela's — as reflecting Angela's understanding of how her desire has been repressed (constrained within patriarchal economies of desire) and of how it can be expressed in her art through an alternative language. Finally, Angela's art functions as a space in which she can articulate the denied desires of the female, racial body and critique their erasure in hegemonic discourses.

When Angela first glimpses the Bohemian lifestyle of New York, she comments that she would like to live by her own laws, by her own codes (107). If we take these codes to be signs or signifiers, we can once again observe Angela's desire to find a language outside of patriarchal discourse. But what Angela finds instead is that there is no "outside," no "inside." Various discursive systems are always implicated within each other. Racist and sexist discourses coexist with discourses that are more "feminine" and liberating. Indeed, in both of Fauset's novels, there is no pure realm of feminine self-expression, no pure realm of racial consciousness or desire. There are only metalinguistic, ethnic discourses — such as Joanna's dancing and Angela's painting — that criticize racist and sexist discourses and articulate what they exclude. These articulations exploit the boundaries between different discursive categories so that their binary oppositions are finally undone. Like earlier women writers, Fauset is interested in broadening the notion of what constitutes language and in developing new theories of language. Yet it is not the recovery of a pure feminine speech that Fauset seeks but rather the acknowledgment that within language there are many discourses, and that some of these discourses express what patriarchal society would suppress: the subversive desires of an unruly racial, and feminine, subject.

Rewriting *The Awakening:* The Female Artist in Cather's *The Song of the Lark*

Like *Plum Bun, The Song of the Lark* resists patriarchal language through its portrayal of a metalinguistic, ethnic discourse that recovers denied (feminine, sexual, or racial) voices. But like Fauset, Cather's work does not completely escape dilemmas of feminine subjectivity and discourse enunciated in late-nineteenth-century American women's fiction. For example, earlier works such as Cather's "A Singer's Romance" (1900) and "The Joy of Nelly Deane" (1911) show a splitting of options for the female artist into equally unappealing extremes of either suffocating domesticity or an isolating career — the same binary choice present in texts such as *The Awakening* and "The Yellow Wall-Paper." It is not until *The Song of the Lark* that Cather envisions a female artist who has both a career and a personal life, yet even here Cather's works betray an indebtedness to earlier writers' depictions of this struggle, and in particular to Kate Chopin. *The Song of the Lark* engages in an intertextual dialogue with *The Awakening* and — more generally — the portrayal of women's identity and voice present in late-nineteenth-century American women's fiction. This dialogue reworks a number of the unresolved issues in the prior generations' considerations of feminine subjectivity and language while simultaneously moving toward a new theory of women's voice.

To begin with Cather's intertextual dialogue with Chopin and with other late-nineteenth-century women writers, we must note that there are a number of imagistic parallels between Cather's and Chopin's conception of the female artist. For example, Cather borrows and transforms Chopin's imaging of the female artist as a divided self. Chopin describes Edna's double life: "She had apprehended instinctively the dual life—that outward existence which conforms, the inward life which questions" (893). Thea Kronborg's identity is also divided between an outward existence that conforms to the domestic duties she must perform and an inner, private world: "Thea began to live a double life. During the day, when the hours were full of [household] tasks, she was one of the Kronborg children, but at night she was a different person" (*Song of the Lark* 53). Furthermore, like Edna, Thea has an inner voice that can be heard only in solitude: "The clamor about her drowned the voice within herself" (*Song of the Lark* 52). For both writers, the female artist experiences a dissociation between a private, inner self/voice and a public world that silences this voice.

Yet after evoking this split in the female artist's self/voice, Cather swerves radically in portraying its mediation. In Chopin's novel Edna longs for an identity that resolves the divisions between public and private selves, for "the harmony of an undivided existence" (569). Thea, however, seeks a conversation between the inner self and the outer world, a productive "backward and forward movement of herself" (72). She does not try to erase the division between private and public self, as Edna does, but rather makes this split part of her art. Thea is an artist, as Fred Ottenburg explains, precisely because of this ability to make her inner voice part of her public performance, "There's the voice itself, so beautiful and individual, and then there's something else; the thing in it which responds to every shade of thought and feeling, spontaneously, almost unconsciously. . . . It's almost like another gift—the rarest of all. The voice simply is the mind and is the heart" (365). Thea's teacher, Harsanyi, tells her that "Every artist makes himself born" (160), and Thea's birth as an artist involves doing what Edna could not—expressing this private self within the spheres of public discourse, and breaking down the binary division between women's private selves/voices and their public performances.

Cather also revises some of Chopin's ideas about the connection between women's art and women's language. As argued, Edna seeks in art a discourse that will transcend the problems of patriarchal speech, one located outside the dominant discursive domain that allows women to "know [each other] well" (731). Cather, too, suggests that Thea's art—her singing—might become an alternative language. Thea's mother comments that "Thea can play and sing, she don't need to speak" (18). Thea's singing conveys what her harsh spoken voice does not. Harsanyi notices that while Thea's speaking voice is "hard and full of burrs" her singing voice is "simple and strong," rising and falling "like the little balls which are put to shine in the jet of a fountain" (171). Cather herself believed that women's opera singing was "a notable emotional language, the speech of the soul" ("Three Operas" 657), so the opera singer may be in a perfect position to find a nonhegemonic language.

But what is the nature of this alternative discourse? Like Fauset, Cather depicts not a pure "feminine discourse" outside of patriarchal speech but rather a discourse that traverses the divisions of patriarchal discourse. When Thea sings, her voice overshadows the male voices: "The soprano voice, like a fountain jet, shot up into the light.... How it leaped from among the dusky male voices! How it played *in and about and around and over them*, like a goldfish darting among creek minnows, like a yellow butterfly soaring above a swarm of dark ones" (213, my emphasis). The power of Thea's voice does not exist apart from the performance, apart from the male voices. Rather, its power is achieved through its contrastative presence within the sextet, its ability to leap over and around and between the five other voices. As an analogy for "feminine voice," we can interpret Cather's stance as demonstrating that the feminine voice exercises power not through its refusal of the dominant language but through its interaction with patriarchal and other discourses. For Cather, the "feminine voice" as such exists only through a series of relations between different discourses, through a playful, contrastative presence that demonstrates the limits of dominant discourses.

Furthermore, Cather's conception of "feminine voice" differs from Chopin's in that this voice is empowered not because it is "feminine" but because it is nonhegemonic. Sharon O'Brien has argued that opera provides a unique arena for showing the authority of women's voice, since opera values the female soprano voice over the male baritone or tenor (*Willa Cather* 171). But Cather does not advocate the power of the soprano voice simply because of gender. Rather, the soprano voice has the power to move over and around and above (but not beyond) the male voices, and in so doing, the soprano voice metalinguistically exposes the boundaries of the male voices. Moreover, through contrastative reinterpretations this voice also undermines the masterplots encoded within patriarchal culture. For example, Thea's method of singing *Elsa* implies that this character does not die at opera's end. As Ottenburg says, "She left me with the distinct impression that she was just beginning [to live]" (366). Thea's interpretation creates a woman who is a heroine and a survivor, not a victim. Thea's *Fricka* also involves a revision of patriarchal interpretations of "Rheingold." When sung by Thea, *Fricka* is not a shrew or a jealous spouse but rather a "goddess" signifying "wisdom" (387). Thea's *Fricka* also recovers both the power of the myth and the power of women within the myth: "The *Fricka* of that afternoon was so clear and sunny, so nobly conceived, that she quite redeemed from shabbiness the helplessness and unscrupulousness of the gods. Her reproaches to *Wotan* were the pleadings of a tempered mind, a consistent sense of beauty" (386–87). Thea's performances transform traditional stereotypes of women as "shrews" or "jealous spouses"; instead women become wise, noble, and empowered heroines. Moreover, Thea's unique interpretations play "in and about and around and over" the traditional meanings of patriarchal masterplots, undermining their validity while creating more liberating interpretations of these "traditional" characters.[6]

Thea's art therefore creates alternatives to the "masterplots" offered by patriarchal society, to the hegemony of patriarchal discourse. These alternatives both build on — and move beyond — late-nineteenth-century women writers' consideration of women's voice. Through Thea's characterization, the novel also insists on alternatives to the hegemony of patriarchal stereotypes of feminine subjectivity, alternatives that are situated not outside of culture (as in the novels of Chopin and Gilman) but within it. Thea's mother is a domestic saint who, like Mattie Murray, refuses to live after her husband's death. She also believes it is men's place to speak (115), that women who talk are "tonguey" (116). Yet when the townspeople criticize Thea, her mother defends her. Mrs. Kronborg also keeps the other children away from Thea and insists she be given music lessons. Thea is therefore indebted to her mother, but she must also break with her mother's model of personal and verbal selflessness. This break begins when Thea leaves Moonstone but is completed only when she refuses to return from Dresden to visit her dying mother. Thea has been given a part crucial to her operatic career and, offered a stark choice between duty and ambition, she chooses the path of artistic achievement. She turns away from the vision of feminine identity that demands sacrifice for others. Metaphorically, this can be understood as reflecting Cather's sense that she is indebted to a prior tradition of women's writing, to her literary foremothers, but that she must also break with them in a decisive way.[7]

Cather also breaks from her literary predecessors by investing her character with several attributes that diverge from their characterization of women. Chopin depicts a female artist caught between her desire to be herself and an injunction to "remember the children," but Cather grants her character the right to be self-defined, even self-absorbed, in pursuit of her art. As one character says of Thea, "she is very much interested in herself — as she should be" (250). Thea's attitude toward marriage also differs from that of previous women characters. While a character such as Edna Pontellier falls into marriage almost unthinkingly, Thea (like Joanna Marshall) sees very clearly that it might interfere with her art and repeats several times that she has no intention of marrying (69, 75, 92, 93). Thea does accept Ottenburg's marriage proposal, but she calls marriage "an incident, not an end" (305), a part of her life but not the whole. Of course, Ottenburg is still married, so whether Thea could have managed a marriage and a career as a singer is left unresolved. Thea does eventually marry, but only after her career has been established.

These incidents with Ottenburg, and later incidents with other men, are also included to suggest Thea's difference from previous characters in terms not just of her marital goals but also in her attitude toward sexuality. Like Angela in *Plum*

Bun, Thea has a sexual affair that does not include marriage. Yet her affair with Ottenburg leads not to her death, as in Chopin's *The Awakening,* but rather to her artistic growth. Moreover, Thea's sexual desire for Ottenburg is not censored from the text: "Thea laughed and put her hand on his shoulders. . . . For the first time, she kissed him without constraint or embarrassment" (292). Since this affair does not lead to Thea's pregnancy, it is possible that it involves some form of birth control, something in which Thea's mother did not believe (11); unlike her literary predecessors, then, Thea may separate desire from reproduction and marriage. Frances Kaye argues that "heterosexual passion is not an option for Thea because all possible candidates are unavailable. She does not, in the body of the novel, ever get a chance to try a personal life" (86). Kaye's statement ignores Thea's affair with Ottenburg, of course, but it is also not true that Thea has no "personal life." Cather's comments on this subject are understated, but she does imply that Thea has romantic relationships with at least two other men — Nordquist and Landry. Nordquist and Thea have a tumultuous relationship culminating in a marriage proposal that Thea declines. In Germany, Landry is Thea's constant companion and accompanist, and he apparently returns to New York with her. Cather hints that this is something more than a friendship when Thea calls Landry "Oliver" in such a way that Doctor Archie "looked closely at the red-headed young man for the first time" (372). When Archie and Fred have tea in Thea's apartment, Landry does not leave with the other guests, so perhaps he is not a guest. Cather thus uses Thea's sexuality and her relationships with Ottenburg, Landry, and Nordquist to suggest her divergence from the profile of feminine subjectivity embodied in late-nineteenth-century American women's writing.

But finally, this sexual divergence does not lead to the articulation of an alternative economy of desire; in the text as a whole, Thea's sexual desire is downplayed, rarely spoken, and marginalized. Like Angela, Thea does not find an alternative to patriarchal economies of desire in her personal life. However, like Fauset, Cather suggests that within a patriarchal society and language, there is room for the expression of women's desire in their art. Cather attempts to move beyond the "feminine" language of late nineteenth-century American women's fiction, then, through the formulation of an ethnic discourse that incorporates desire.

This possibility is first formulated in Panther Canyon, where Thea finds an iconography for her art that revises patriarchal theories of creativity. As Susan Gubar argues, in a patriarchal culture the act of creating art is often portrayed as quintessentially masculine: the pen (penis) inscribes the blank (female) page ("'Blank Page'" 295). Even Harsanyi uses this masculine vocabulary: when he first meets Thea he describes her as "a book with nothing written in it" (185). Like Gilman, then, Cather is aware of the link between men and "pens," between the production of art or writing, and phallic constructions of the artist as masculine. However, the canyon where Thea has her artistic awakening is full of sexual imagery that provides an alternative to patriarchal imaging of art. Sharon O'Brien and Ellen Moers note that the gorge is portrayed in feminine terms. More specifically, its contours suggest the sexual spaces of the female body:

> The cañon walls, for the first two hundred feet below the surface, were perpendicular cliffs, striped with even-running strata of rock. From there on to the bottom the sides were less abrupt, were shelving, and lightly fringed with *piñons* and dwarf cedars. The effect was that of a gentler cañon within a wilder one. The dead city lay on the point where the perpendicular outer wall ceased and the V-shaped inner gorge began. There a stratum of rock, softer than those above, had been hollowed out by the action of time until it was like a deep groove running along the sides of the cañon. In this hollow (like a great fold in the rock) the Ancient People had built their houses. (*Song of the Lark* 267)

Thea finds that feminine, sexual enclosures shelter and enable art, for the vulva-like gorge contains the houses of the ancient people, which contain their magnificent art works. The canyon thus becomes a countermetaphor that validates not the attributes of the male body in the production of art but the spaces of the female body.

In Panther Canyon, Thea also finds a theory of art that is specifically feminine and reproductive rather than masculine and destructive. Among the cliff dwellers the women were the artisans, creating the delicate pottery jars that sheathed the essence of life, the water they carried. This allows Thea to reimagine the way art is produced: "what was any art but an effort to make a sheath, a mould in which to imprison for a moment the shining, elusive element which is life itself—life hurrying past us and running away, too strong to stop, too sweet to lose?" (273). Rather than seeing art as an act of destruction, Thea sees art as an act of construction which captures, if but for a moment, the shining elusive quality of life. Cather's imagery is also particularly feminine, evoking pregnancy, the womb, and the birthing process. Thea applies this feminine, gestational imagery to her own art, imagining her throat as a container (womb) for the stream (life): "In singing, one made a vessel of one's throat and nostrils and held it in one's breath, caught the stream in a scale of natural intervals" (273). For Thea, art's source becomes not the destructive, phallic pen but the creative feminine throat/womb.[8]

Cather here borders on, and perhaps endorses, a kind of essentialism that privileges a feminine, bodied concept of art. Yet she finally suggests that while the throat/womb metaphor may function for Thea as an alternative to the phallocentric imagining of art, other artists (such as Harsanyi and Wunsch) still employ their own metaphors (phallic or otherwise) to produce art. In other words, Cather endorses a "feminine" strategy for the imaging of art without suggesting that this is the only viable methodology or subject-position from which to produce or create art. The feminine economy of language and art that exists in Panther Canyon does not preclude the existence of other economies in other spaces within hegemonic culture.

The space of Panther Canyon, however, allows Thea to recover something that Cather envisions as crucial to all art: the body, and the passions of the body. For Cather, art is about making the body speak from within the spaces of the art form. Cather's description of Thea as a young girl implies that the artist must speak a "bodied" voice: "There is no work of art so big and so beautiful that it was not once all contained in some youthful body, like this one which lay on the floor in the moonlight, pulsing with ardor and anticipation" (127). But it is not until her sojourn in Panther Canyon that Thea experiences art's connection to the body; previously, her own body has been denied to her as a source of passion, of art. In Panther Canyon, for the first time, music comes to her in a "sensuous form" (269). She learns how to incorporate this sensuous quality into her art, to use her body as an instrument for the expression of desire. So later, when she sings the romantic duet from *Sieglinde*, the music passes "into her face . . . and into her body as well. . . . And the voice gave out all that was best in it" (407). Her body expresses her art and her desire: "She was conscious that every movement was the right movement, that her body was absolutely the instrument of her idea. . . . She felt like a tree bursting into bloom. And her voice was as flexible as her body" (410). Cather uses feminine and sexual imagery — the tree bursting into bloom — to suggest the embodiment of feminine desire within art, the connection between body, sexuality, and voice. Yet she does not suggest that this is the only form of "bodied" art.

Thea therefore has art but also passion that becomes part of her art. As Judith Fetterley explains, "Cather resolves the opposition, so frequent elsewhere in her work, between women's sensuality and their development, inextricably connecting the artist's passion for her art with the woman's passion for her body and its desires" ("Willa Cather" 228). Thea finds an alternative construction of desire and language that she can incorporate into her art, that she can use to revise the structures of patriarchal discourse and art. This is not to say that Thea experiences an unproblematic life of passion. Her art does sometimes disappoint her, and at times she is bitter. The text also downplays her romantic relationships with Ottenburg, Nordquist, and Landry. Yet a simple glance back to Chopin's Mademoiselle Reisz in *The Awakening* demonstrates how much Cather's portrait of Thea Kronborg achieves. Mademoiselle Reisz's art is disembodied, separate from her wizened physical presence, but Thea's art expresses her body, and her body expresses her art. Thea's singing gives voice to the physical, intellectual, aesthetic, sexual, and emotional sides of her personality. It also creates a space for the desiring, female subject who speaks a "bodied" discourse and is also a creator of art, rather than a male creation.

Fauset's and Cather's Metalinguistic, Ethnic Discourses

In Cather's text the heroine's art functions as a metalinguistic discourse that remakes the boundaries between (male) art and (feminine) body, between (masculine) pen and (feminine) page, between (man as) creator and (woman as) created. But this discourse also remakes some of the ethnic categories surrounding the production of art. While several of Thea's comments show racism toward African Americans (404), she clearly has a respect for the art of ethnic cultures. For example, Thea gains a valuable knowledge from the Native American cliff dwellers about how to create a discourse that speaks the denied knowledge of a feminine, ethnic, and sexual past. In Panther Canyon, Thea finds an earlier tradition of ethnic, female artisans: "On the first day that Thea climbed the water-trail, she began to have intuitions about the women who had worn the path. . . . She found herself trying to walk as they must have walked, with a feeling in her feet and knees and loins which she had never known before. . . . She could feel the weight of an Indian baby hanging to her back as she climbed" (271). The imagery is sexual (a feeling in her "loins"), reproductive (the baby), feminine (she has intuitions about the women, not the men), and ethnic. This vision of the cliff dwellers therefore allows Thea to connect to a heritage of artistic achievement that did not deny the presence of the feminine, the sexual, and the ethnic within the category of "human" art. Viewing pieces of pottery left behind by these Native American women, Thea sees that "these pot-sherds were like fetters that bound one to a long chain of human endeavor" (275). Thea comprehends that she is bound to a tradition of "human endeavor" that includes a variety of individuals of different races and genders, not just the white males authorized by patriarchal tradition. Like Fauset's heroines, who insist on the presence of African American art forms in "American" art, Cather stresses that an ethnic past is part of the present that Thea expresses in her art; as Thea later explains, many of her ideas about art came "out of the rocks, out of the dead people" in Panther Canyon (397). Thea incorporates this concept of a feminine, ethnic tradition into her own art, thereby undoing binary hierarchies.

Of course, as will be discussed, Cather's text creates its own binarisms, but it is important to note its validation of a nonhegemonic art form — the ethnic art of the women cliff dwellers — and its critique of the erasure of this art form from dominant paradigms. This critique of the loss of ethnic art is even clearer in the text's portrayal of Mexican Americans. Thea absorbs a number of ideas about music from Spanish Johnny and from singing with the Mexican community, and she eventually incorporates this knowledge into her operatic performances.[9] Cather's text thus validates a "denied" discourse — the music of the Mexican Americans — but also criticizes the dominant discourse's exclusions. When Thea's sister Anna complains that Thea would rather sing with the Mexicans than with the church choir, Thea responds: "Well, I like to sing over there, and I don't like to over here. I'll sing for them any time they ask me to. They're a talented people" (215).

Anna's response embodies that of the dominant discourse, as she exclaims in disbelief, "Talented!" (215). Anglo American art, or "talent," constructs itself through a derogation of the ethnic as uncivilized, primitive, incapable of producing art. The text displays the dominant discourse's attempt to erase this culture's art, to construct it as "not art," while simultaneously critiquing this erasure and exclusion as "race prejudice" (214) — as a faulty belief system in need of revision. Cather validates not only the art of the Mexicans but also their ability to appreciate art; when Thea sings for them she gains the appreciation of a people who "turned themselves and all they had over to her" (210). Here the novel upsets another binary opposition, suggesting that true appreciation of art rests not with the dominant culture but with those "marginal" individuals it prefers to see as artless, primitive, and uncivilized.

The text situates Thea's art in a boundary space between two communities, two versions of what constitutes art — the "minority" community of the Mexican Americans and Native Americans and the "majority" community of Moonstone and beyond. From its position in this boundary space, Thea's art subverts the separation between these discursive communities, suggesting that art can incorporate, blend, and intermesh elements of several cultures. In the final scene of the novel, for example, Thea sings in New York and is appreciated by traditional sources, such as her teacher Harsanyi, Fred Ottenburg, and the head of a musical publishing house (409). But the audience also contains an individual not validated by the dominant culture to judge art — Spanish Johnny, who sits in the top gallery shouting "Brava! Brava!" (410). Thea's art can be appreciated by both communities of "artists" (the majority and the minority), but it can also criticize the separation between these two communities; finally, Johnny's point of view ends the chapter. Johnny leaves the theater wearing a smile on his face that "embraced all the stream of life that passed him" (411). This smile is described as "the only commensurate answer" to the artist's question of "what was the good of it all?" (411), the question of art's ultimate aim. Johnny's response and his all-embracing vision of the world are finally validated as the only true function of art. Art should attempt to unite communities and individuals by decomposing the boundaries that separate them. Thea's singing works toward a deconstruction of the barriers between various conceptions of art so that they can be reconstructed in a more commodious fashion.

Cather's text therefore demonstrates its heroine's indebtedness to the ethnic cultures of the Mexican Americans and Native Americans; in so doing it creates a metalinguistic, ethnic discourse that undoes some of the binary oppositions that have silenced both the feminine, and the ethnic, in the dominant discourse. Of course, Cather does not put Johnny on stage at the Metropolitan Opera, so it is only through the figuration of Thea's art that binary oppositions are deconstructed; Cather does not extend her challenge to the personal or social level. Similarly, her portrayal of the relationship between Thea's singing and the ethnic art forms of the Native American cliff dwellers reflects a symbolic, rather than an actual, challenge to hegemonic structures. Rather than portraying the art of living Native Americans, Cather recoups a "dead" tradition that her character can be inspired by, that her character can in fact "devour." There is a strong colonialistic impulse, then, in Cather's portrayal of her heroine's utilization of ethnic cultures, an impulse toward taking what is valuable of the "other" and making it one's own, without textually enfranchising this other. Cather's endorsement of an ethnic, metalinguistic discourse needs to be read within this context: it is finally used to enfranchise not the ethnic but the female (white) "Other."

These are the limitations of Cather's theory of voice: it undoes some binary oppositions while maintaining others. The use of an ethnic discourse, then, is perhaps fraught with as many problems as the use of a "feminine" discourse. Finally, some voices are enfranchised at the expense of others. This is also the case with Fauset's use of an ethnic discourse in *Plum Bun* and *There Is Confusion*. Angela Murray can be seen as colonizing the desires of Hetty Daniels, of constructing her own voice and desire at the expense of a less enfranchised character, a maid who remains entrapped within hegemonic discourses. Her art continually constitutes itself through a voicing of the impoverished, the disenfranchised, the marginalized, but she does not take any steps to encourage these individuals to voice their own concerns. Both Fauset and Cather, then, critique some binary oppositions while reinforcing others.

The metalinguistic, ethnic discourse present in texts such as *The Song of the Lark* and *Plum Bun* therefore does not enfranchise all voices equally. It is simply one strategy in women writers' attempt to theorize and move beyond binary structures of a racist and patriarchal society that have figured the speaking subject as male and white, and the silent object as female and ethnic. And yet, as I have suggested, many binary oppositions remain. Is it possible to create a voice that authorizes itself without disenfranchising and silencing an "Other"? In the final section of this book, the concept of a movement "beyond the binary" will be examined as a way of both summarizing and interrogating the development of American women's fiction from 1850 to 1930 that this work has traced.

8

Coda
Beyond the Binary?

In "Choreographies," Jacques Derrida discusses the attempt to move beyond the binary codes of gender and sexuality:

> What if we were to reach, what if we were to approach here . . . the area of a relationship to the other where the code of sexual marks would no longer be discriminating? The relationship would not be a-sexual, far from it, but would be sexual otherwise: beyond the binary difference that governs the decorum of codes, beyond the opposition feminine/masculine, beyond bisexuality as well, beyond homosexuality and heterosexuality which come to the same thing. As I dream of saving the chance that this question offers I would like to believe in the multiplicity of sexually marked voices. (76)

Many late-nineteenth- and early-twentieth-century women writers are interested in the project of moving beyond the binary structures that have constrained their identity and limited their voice, especially those structures that figure the speaking subject as constitutively male and white and the silenced object as female and/or ethnic. A writer such as Frances Harper employs a politics of hybridity to move beyond binarisms, while Freeman, Cooper, Chopin, and Gilman often utilize a feminine voice—a voice of the mother that undermines the Law of the Father—to overturn the structures of patriarchal discourse. In the twentieth century, Cather's and Fauset's metalinguistic voices undermine the boundaries of patriarchal and racist discourses so that categories normally kept separate (such as the "American" and the "ethnic") interpenetrate each other. The ultimate aim of these writers is the creation of a linguistic frontier in which the distinction between masculine and feminine, or enfranchised and disenfranchised, voices is decomposed.

Yet are they successful? When examining late-nineteenth-century writers, in particular, it becomes apparent that it is difficult to undo systems of subjugation through a feminine discourse that actually dominates and silences patriarchal or other hegemonic discourses. Indeed, we might argue that the nonhegemonic voices of women and racial "Others" actually become hegemonic (losing their potential for subversion) when they turn the masculine, white subject into an "Other," an object of language rather than a speaking subject. In a frequently cited formulation, Audre Lorde has stated that "the master's tools will never dismantle the master's house" (99), and we may find ourselves uncomfortable with Freeman's startled and silenced father (in "The Revolt of 'Mother' "), with Gilman's specularized Terry (in *Herland*), with Cooper's language of "dominant tone" (in *A Voice from the South*). We have seen these marginalized, discomposed, silenced subject-positions and discourses before — but they have been produced by female, not male, subjects. Do late-nineteenth-century writers merely invert binarisms? Furthermore, is it ever possible to move beyond the binary, as Derrida suggests, or is this just a utopian dream that cannot be sustained in the "real world," where expressing oneself so often seems to entail silencing another, or an "Other"?

Mid-nineteenth-century writers rarely foreground a movement beyond the binary. These writers challenge the construction of the speaking subject as masculine only indirectly, through a practice of voice that gradually enlarges women's social and verbal sphere of power. Fern's Ruth Hall, for instance, becomes a powerful businesswoman and a respected writer, yet never acknowledges that she might have a need for self-expression or a desire to write as a way of breaking with the domestic ideology. Like many of Alcott's heroines and Wilson's Frado, Ruth remains committed to a historical and domestic voice that does not present a direct indictment of the psycholinguistic theory undergirding patriarchal subjectivity and symbolic language. This is not to say that an awareness of binary structures is absent from mid-nineteenth-century writing. Alcott's "A Whisper in the Dark," for example, focuses on a struggle between a semiotic, disruptive voice of the mother, and a patriarchal, repressive Law of the Father. Yet Alcott presents this binary opposition without undermining it; finally, the voice of the mother must be repressed so that women can take their place within symbolic language and patriarchal systems of subjectivity. Similarly, Wilson's Frado does not succeed in moving beyond those binary structures that confine her. *Our Nig* overturns racial binaries in which a white, female subject-position is achieved through the silencing of an African American female "Other." Wilson inverts this binary but does not, in the body of her text, go beyond it to grant her character a subjectivity that could exist outside of these structures. Wilson herself confounds and dismantles racist systems of signification through a shape-shifting identity, but Frado does not possess this ability to undermine the codes that construct and confine her.

Wilson's utilization of an ethnic discursive tradition — tricksterism — represents a moment in which we can envision how a movement beyond the binary might be achieved. Similarly, Harper's use of hybridization and a discourse of the folk presents a possible avenue out of the impasse of binarisms. Rather than merely inverting hierarchies present in society — such as intellectual over folk worldviews — Harper develops new language systems that commingle and combine discourses, and she creates liminal spaces where identities can be remade. Yet, as I have already noted, the dismantlement of certain oppositions often leads to the construction of new ones. On a theoretical level, it can be argued that Harper grants discursive equality to both the intellectual and the folk. But in the actual language of the text, the folk voices often sound foolish, comic, and unauthentic. We are encouraged, I believe, to respect Aunt Linda's view of the world — but not the way she expresses this view. So Harper may create a new binary opposition in which a nonhegemonic worldview (that of the folk) must be articulated and subsumed by a hegemonic discourse (that of the "intelligentsia") to achieve enfranchisement.

In these texts, then, ethnic discourses offer interesting and radical possibilities of subversion that move beyond the discursive practices of dominant languages, but not a "solution" to the problem of binarism itself. Finally, it seems that binaries can only be escaped in certain liminal moments that hang on the fringes of texts, on the edges of languages. But a liminal space, of courses, is a space-in-between, continually under threat of erasure from the dominant space, the dominant discourse, or the dominant ideology. Late-nineteenth-century writers often call upon this concept of a liminal space where social constructions break down, but they are aware of its tenuous, transitory nature. At the end of "The Revolt of 'Mother,' " of course, Freeman comments that "the landscape *might* have been an ideal one of peace." Cooper calls upon a discourse structured around social interactions of equilibrium, full well realizing how difficult it is to maintain equilibrium, balance, equality between and for all. In her sequel to *Herland*, Gilman tries to suggest that the child produced by the man from "Ourland" (Van) and the woman from Herland (Ellador) will intermesh both cultures and, symbolically speaking, move beyond the binarism of patriarchal discourse versus semiotic, maternal language. But finally, since Herland and "Ourland" are separated geographically from each other, this child will have to live in one world or the other, speaking only one language. Where is the liminal space in which it might be possible to speak some hybrid combination of the language of Herland and the language of Ourland, of matriarchal and patriarchal tongues? Where is the world in which it might be possible to be masculine/feminine or s/he? Gilman signifies the need for this hybrid space without creating it; there is no mechanism presented for the extension of this liminal moment beyond the edge of the text, or beyond the edge of the world in which the characters momentarily reside.

Many of the liminal moments that attempt to move beyond the binary, then, feel transitory and tenuous. It may not be possible to escape binary oppositions altogether. Are they, as one of Charles Johnson's characters phrases it in *Middle Passage*, "a bloody structure of the human mind"? Or does language itself, by its very functioning, instigate binary oppositions? Many late-nineteenth- and early-twentieth-century writers turn to music precisely because it seems to provide a realm where the binary functioning of spoken discourse might be escaped. In spoken language, generally when I begin to speak, you must stop — or attempt to speak over me, to silence me. But in music, "voices" or instruments are combined, commingled; we can "speak" together, in harmony, as it were. For Chopin, Cooper, Gilman, and Harper (in the songs that Iola sings), as well as for Cather in the twentieth century, music seems to offer a way out of the impasse of patriarchal discourse. Yet there are problems, here, too; Chopin's texts finally seem to indicate that we must "talk as women talk," waging our linguistic struggles in the here and now of patriarchal discourse. If I want to make myself heard, I must speak in the language others are using — which is, after all, spoken English, not an operatic performance or a concerto. When my colleagues refuse to hear me, it would be wonderful if I could sing my message or play it on the piano — but I'm afraid I would be granted an involuntary leave for "mental distress." Music offers a theoretical way of thinking beyond the binary, but I question whether this theoretical possibility can be transferred to actual verbal practices. Cooper and Cather, at least, configure musical discourses and metaphors as residing within existing discursive and social matrixes, but for Chopin and Gilman music is outside of them and so cannot function as a direct challenge.

Similarly, the notion of a semiotic (or preoedipal) voice of the mother offers interesting theoretical possibilities of subversion, but, like many of these writers, I question whether it is possible to transfer this subversion to dominant discourses. Chopin and Gilman configure this maternal or semiotic voice as existing outside of patriarchal language; it therefore offers new possibilities of voice without presenting a direct challenge to symbolic language. For Freeman and Cooper, the "voice of the mother" can exist within the patriarchal world; their feminine voices work from within patriarchal discourse to undermine it. In these texts, therefore, the voice of the mother may not in fact be semiotic, pre-symbolic; rather, it may function as a metalanguage, a discourse that undermines patriarchal discourse from within its own paradigms.

The semiotic voice of the mother, then, is finally not a possibility of language that leads to subversion of patriarchal discourse. Yet this possibility of language leads to a questioning of the structures of patriarchal discourse and patriarchal subjectivity. "Silence or capitulation" (to use Josephine Donovan's phrase) seems to be the choice offered to women by symbolic language: be silent or take your place within a system of language that figures you as an absence, a gap, a not-subject. But the semiotic voice of the mother suggests that this system did not always exist, that there was something before. This "language before" cannot, perhaps, be recuperated once we have entered the symbolic, but its very possibility demonstrates that the symbolic order is not absolute. It is no coincidence that a number of these writers explore the concept of a semiotic, maternal language only to reject it and return to subversions that locate themselves within dominant discourses. For these writers, the semiotic voice may not, finally, be a viable strategy, but its very postulation seems to offer a new way of thinking about symbolic language. The notion of a feminine, maternal language theorizes a break in the drama of patriarchal subjectivity that figures the subject as constitutively masculine and white by suggesting that this drama is not absolute and the possibility, however tenuous, that other languages existed before the symbolic order had imposed its closure. Authors such as Chopin and Gilman, then, eventually reject the possibility of a language that resides outside of symbolic discourse in favor of a metalinguistic discourse that transfers this subversive potential to patriarchal language, but their consideration of the semiotic, maternal voice is nonetheless enabling.

Similarly, early-twentieth-century writers such as Fauset and Cather reject the late-nineteenth-century concept of a feminine voice separate from patriarchal discourse in favor of a metalinguistic, ethnic women's language, but their consideration of this verbal strategy is crucial. For example, in Fauset's *Plum Bun* Angela's artwork becomes a radical new form of voice only after she accepts that there is no such thing as a feminine language of desire outside of the "codes," outside of hegemonic discourses. Cather and Fauset employ metalinguistic, ethnic voices, yet even these discourses do not present a "solution" to the problem of binary oppositions. Cather's text colonizes "minority" artisans in order to find a viable voice for its heroine, without textually enfranchising these individuals in their own right. Fauset's light-skinned, upper-middle-class heroines are empowered by African American discourses of the folk and the working class that they speak through their art, yet Fauset never implies that these darker-skinned or working-class individuals will be allowed to speak for themselves. Once again, the movement beyond the binary is not sustained.

Perhaps it is not possible, then, to move beyond the binary, yet the project of attempting to do so unites these diverse writers. Furthermore, theorizing this attempt is enabling. A paradox, then: a tool of the "master"—binary oppositions—becomes enabling to the disempowered. However, because these writers often do not succeed in moving beyond the binary, does this mean that they merely "beat [the master] at his own game" (99), as Lorde might phrase it, without effecting permanent change? Or do these writers accomplish more? Lillian Robinson argues that "It is hard to disagree with Audre Lorde's much-cited dictum that the Master's tools will never dismantle the Master's house. But people have to live in a house, not in a metaphor. Of *course* you use the Master's tools if those are the only ones you can lay your hands on. Perhaps what you can do with them is to take apart that old mansion, using some of its pieces to put up a far better one where there is room for all of us" (34). Binarisms are a tool of the master, and although these writers attempt to move beyond them, they do not succeed entirely. But they take some of the pieces of this way of thinking and refashion them into a new mansion, not "where there is room for all of us" but where there is, perhaps, more room for some of us. These writers, then, do engender a certain degree of liberation. They work to break the binary opposition of speaking, masculine-subject over silent, feminine-object; they find new theories of language in which the experiences and perspectives of female and racial subjects can be articulated.

Finally, the movement beyond the binary, like the semiotic or preoedipal possibility of language, is more important for what it suggests, than for what it achieves. Writers such as Freeman, Cooper, Chopin, Gilman, Harper, Fauset, and Cather are more unruly than their predecessors not because they actually move beyond the binary but because they see a need for such a movement; they see the way binary structures have silenced and erased them. Furthermore, the possibility of a movement beyond the binary presented in these writers' works suggests that binary structures are not absolute. The radical insight postulated by these writers, then, is not that binarisms — or even patriarchal and racist discourses — can be escaped entirely. Rather, their texts suggest it is possible to interrogate various binary structures that have silenced women and "Others," and in so doing open up the language of hegemony, making it permeable, dialogic, and subject to erosion.

Notes

Introduction

1. Of course, other critics have examined American women writers' relationship to language in specific time periods but have not argued for a shift from a historical to a theoretical approach between 1850 and 1930. Works that have influenced my consideration of American women writers' relationship to patriarchal and racist discourses include Susan Gubar and Sandra Gilbert's *The Madwoman in the Attic: The Woman Writer and the Nineteenth-Century Literary Imagination*, Mary Kelley's *Private Woman, Public Stage*, Claudia Tate's *Domestic Allegories of Political Desire*, Elizabeth Ammons's *Conflicting Stories*, Ann duCille's *The Coupling Convention*, Carla Peterson's *Doers of the Word*, and Hazel Carby's *Reconstructing Womanhood*. Furthermore, I am indebted to a number of fine essays on this subject; in particular, I would cite works by Paula Treichler, Patricia Yaeger, Mae Henderson, and Josephine Donovan.

2. Many writers not discussed here are congruent with my argument. Works from the 1850s and 1860s that inscribe women's linguistic power within predominantly historical categories of a domestic discourse include Harriet Beecher Stowe's *Uncle Tom's Cabin* (1852), Harriet Jacobs's *Incidents in the Life of a Slave Girl* (1864), Elizabeth Stoddard's "Lermorne v. Huell" and "The Prescription" (1863–64), and Rebecca Harding Davis's "The Wife's Story" and "Anne" (1863). Works from the 1870s, 1880s, and 1890s that begin to investigate the theoretical underpinnings of women's silence and sometimes show radical feminine or maternal languages include Elizabeth Stuart Phelps's *The Story of Avis* (1877), Sarah Orne Jewett's *The Country of the Pointed Firs* (1896), and Alice Dunbar-Nelson's "The Woman" and "Ellen Fenton" (1895). Early-twentieth-century works that

seem more concerned with a metalinguistic examination of the racial and gendered texts and discourses that confine women than with the possibility of a feminine voice per se include Edith Wharton's *The Age of Innocence* (1920), Ellen Glasgow's *Barren Ground* (1925), Nella Larsen's *Quicksand* (1928) and *Passing* (1929), and Zora Neale Hurston's *Their Eyes Were Watching God* (1937).

3. This shift has remained largely unexamined, even among critics who have discussed the late nineteenth century, most of whom have taken specialized approaches. Josephine Donovan concentrates on New England local color writers, while Anna Elfenbein examines women's writing in the South. In "Tradition and the Female Talent," Elaine Showalter outlines a theory of the evolution of American women's writing from "the empire of the mother" to the New Woman but does not focus on women's voice.

Chapter 2

1. Fern's work has been disparaged in these terms by Fred Lewis Pattee (110–18) and James D. Hart (97). For more recent critics who defend the subversive qualities of *Ruth Hall* see Ann Wood, Joyce Warren, Susan Harris, and Nancy Walker.

2. Nina Baym, Ann Wood, and Mary Kelley equate Fanny Fern with Ruth Hall. Only Harris and Walker avoid collapsing Fern into her protagonist.

3. For other arguments that Jo succumbs to the model of domestic femininity, see Bassil and Fetterley ("Alcott's Civil War"). For alternative points of view see Carolyn Heilbrun and Madelon Bedell.

4. There has been little critical discussion of Alcott's sensational fiction, although Martha Saxton does argue that here "Alcott felt free to experiment with a kind of fiction that was not steeped in the rigid morality of her family" (260); see also Keyser's *Whispers in the Dark*. Much more attention has been paid to *Little Women*. For a summary of these debates see Ann Murphy, who argues that the novel's power derives from its contradictions.

5. *Double Life* 159; parenthetically cited hereafter as DL.

6. *Plots and Counterplots* 148; parenthetically cited hereafter as PC.

7. *Alternative Alcott* 194; parenthetically cited hereafter.

8. For alternative readings of the ending of *Behind a Mask*, see Keyser (*Whispers in the Dark* 49) and Showalter (*Sister's Choice* 50).

9. *Behind A Mask* (116); parenthetically cited hereafter.

10. Gates argues that Wilson "created a novel that partakes of the received structure of American women's fiction, but often inverts the same structure, ironically enough, precisely at its most crucial point" (Introduction, xlvi). For other discussions of Wilson's revisions of the domestic novel and of myths of white femininity, see Angelyn Mitchell (16–17) and Julia Stern (440).

11. I do not mean to argue that Wilson's text is fictional. However, recent research by Barbara White suggests that Wilson deliberately manipulated autobiographical details for aesthetic and political reasons (43, 44). Furthermore, as Priscilla Wald argues, the novel

contains a gap between Frado (as character) and Wilson (as an author writing about the process of authorship) that autobiographical readings often overlook (167–69).

12. Some critics take Wilson's claims about her audience at face value (Carby, *Reconstructing Womanhood* 43), while others question these claims (see Angelyn Mitchell 13 and John Ernest, "Economies of Identity" 425–29). See also Eric Gardner's research concerning Wilson's actual audience (240).

13. "Alida," however, is listed in Hanks and Hodges' *A Dictionary of First Names* as the Hungarian form of Adelaide. The meaning of this name is consistent with my line of argumentation: the Hungarian root "ada" means noble, and "heid" means kind or sort. Adelaide would thus symbolize a noble individual, a name that doubles back to Wilson's other pseudonym: Alfrado, feminine of Alfred, meaning wise or noble counselor.

14. See Hanks and Hodges.

15. Roger Abrahams specifically connects the figure of the Signifying Money with the derogatory term "nigger": " 'monkey' and 'ape' have been used as derogatory words in relation to the Negro, and have achieved a meaning and notoriety not very different from 'nigger' " (144).

Chapter 3

1. Because of Hetty's faltering voice, Glasser believes "A Church Mouse" conveys a "mixed message" (50) about women's voice. On the subject of mixed messages or double plots in Freeman's works, also see Mary Reichardt's *A Web of Relationship* and my essays listed in the bibliography.

2. Important discussions of language in "The Revolt of 'Mother' " have also been provided by Joseph Church, Elizabeth Meese, Elaine Orr, and Patricia Dwyer.

3. Nancy Cott describes these books in *The Bonds of Womanhood* (72).

4. All parenthetical references to Cooper's writing are from *A Voice from the South*.

5. As Todd Vogel argues, Cooper positions herself within discourses of domesticity to "hijack" them (165). For more on Cooper's relationship to the cult of domesticity, see Baker-Fletcher (142), Carby (*Reconstructing Womanhood* 97), and Gaines (137, 142).

6. I have found no critical studies that use feminist methodologies to discuss Cooper's treatment of women's relationship to language.

7. As I argue in chapter 7, Willa Cather also calls upon the power of music and the soprano voice to illustrate that the "feminine" can rise above, but also overturn, patriarchal discourse.

8. Salic Law is defined by *Webster's New World Dictionary* in two ways: 1) a code of laws of Germanic tribes, including the Salian Franks, especially the provision of this code excluding women from inheriting land; 2) the laws excluding women from succeeding to the throne in the French and Spanish monarchies.

9. For an argument that Cooper is not essentialistic, see Carby (*Reconstructing Womanhood* 101). The paradox of Cooper's essentialism is aptly stated by Elizabeth Alexander:

"Cooper wrote out of . . . resistance to a static, monolithic view of what it was to be black, and, specifically, to be a black woman. Attacking racial stereotypes was an important part of Cooper's written agenda, though some of her own arguments about male and female 'nature' were extremely essentialist" (341).

Chapter 4

1. It is important to note here that for Kristeva the semiotic is not associated exclusively with the feminine; in the pre-symbolic realm, in fact, the opposition between feminine and masculine does not exist. For discussion of this subject, see Toril Moi (165).

2. For other critics who focus on Edna's linguistic struggles, see Joseph Urgo, E. Laurie George, and Katherine Kearns. Ivy Schweitzer mentions Edna's search for a semiotic language of instinctual drives but does not develop this point.

3. I believe that the novel begins in 1892 and ends nine months later in 1893. According to Margaret Culley, a hurricane destroyed the resort area of Grand Isle in 1893, so the novel must take place before this date. The novel also refers to the New Orleans Association of the American Folklore Society, a group that was active from 1892 to 1895 (Culley 75). Since the hurricane occurred in 1893 and the society was active from 1892 to 1895, the novel probably starts in 1892. Moreover, when the novel begins Madame Ratignolle is just beginning a pregnancy, and at the end of the novel she delivers a child, so the novel must take place over the course of approximately nine months. We know the novel ends in late February, since Edna comments the day before her death that Léonce will be returning from his business trip very soon, "some time in March" (995). Counting back nine months from February, we can deduce that the novel probably begins in June of 1892, and ends in late February 1893.

4. For other readings of the novel's ending, see Christina Giorcelli (126), Helen Emmitt (321), Patricia Yaeger (216), and Deborah Barker (78–79).

5. Since several critics have already discussed Edna's sexual awakening (see, for example, Seyersted's *Kate Chopin* 134–63, or Sandra Gilbert's "The Second Coming of Aphrodite"), I will not dwell on this subject. I also believe that her sexual awakening is bound up in her awakening to the repressions of symbolic discourse and to the potentially expressive and liberatory aspects of maternal discourses.

6. I have chosen to focus on two later works that concern women who write because Chopin's challenge to patriarchal theories of language is clearest here. Other works written after 1894 that contain strong, unconventional heroines with resistant voices include "An Egyptian Cigarette," "Charlie," "A Respectable Woman," "The Unexpected," and "A Family Affair." No critic has examined resistance to patriarchal discourse in Chopin's short fiction, although a number have argued generally that liberation is a recurrent theme. See, for example, Winfried Fluck and Janet Goodwyn.

7. All year references are to these stories' composition, which Chopin was careful to record. Chopin repeatedly revised "A No-Account Creole" for publication, perhaps soft-

ening the main character. In the end, as Toth notes, "Euphrasie owes her happiness to men's notions of honor" (203).

8. As Chopin explained in a letter to the editor of the *Century*, she made certain changes based upon his criticism: "The marriage is omitted, and the girl's character softened and tempered by her rude experience" (Toth 283). Gilder still would not accept the story.

9. Chopin sometimes associates freedom from social norms with a particular race; for example, Mariequita in *The Awakening* is portrayed as having more sexual liberty than Edna. Of course, many of Chopin's racialized women have no freedom and no voice; see, for example, the quadroon nanny in *The Awakening* who is described as being "patient as a savage" (939). Chopin's complex attitudes toward African Americans and other racialized groups have been discussed by critics such as Anna Elfenbein, Michele Birnbaum, Janet Goodwyn, Elizabeth Ammons (*Conflicting Stories* 74–77), Catherine Lundie, and Lynn Cothern.

10. For more extensive analysis of "La Belle Zoraïde" see Lundie and Cothern.

11. For fuller discussion of "Désirée's Baby," see Peel, Elfenbein, and Lundie.

12. "Mrs. Mobry's Reason" was written in January of 1891 but not published until April of 1893. As Emily Toth notes, it was "Chopin's most rejected story" (198).

13. Chopin wrote "Elizabeth Stock's One Story" in March of 1898, after *The Awakening*. Several editors refused the story, and it was never published during Chopin's lifetime.

14. The narrator's sex is never stated, but s/he does have an aggressive, objective tone that stands in marked contrast to Elizabeth Stock's personal and subjective one, as Barbara Ewell has noted (166). Elaine Showalter believes the narrator is either Elizabeth Stock's nephew or her longtime suitor ("Piecing and Writing" 239–40), but the narrator tells us explicitly that s/he is an outsider to Stonelift.

15. Patricia Klemans and Heather Kirk Thomas have more negative readings of this story; Klemans argues, for example, that Elizabeth "is so bound by self-doubt and self-sacrifice that it is impossible for her to develop her writing talent" (41).

Chapter 5

1. The ending of "The Yellow Wall-Paper" has generated much controversy. For positive readings, see John Bak, Jean Kennard, Catherine Golden, and Sandra Gilbert and Susan Gubar (*Madwoman in the Attic* 82–92). For critics who read the ending as a defeat, see Linda Wagner-Martin, William Veeder, Annette Kolodny, and Jeannette King and Pam Morris. For readings that are neither wholly positive nor negative, see Conrad Shumaker and Paula Treichler.

2. Gilman's views on race were contradictory, as Lanser explains: "Despite her socialist values, her active participation in movements for reform, her strong theoretical commitment to racial harmony, her unconventional support of interracial marriages, and her frequent condemnation of America's racist history, Gilman upheld white Protestant supremacy; belonged for a time to eugenics and nationalist organizations; opposed open

immigration; and inscribed racism, nationalism, and classism into her proposals for social change" (429). These views pervade some of Gilman's later work, such as *Herland* and its sequel, *With Her in Ourland*. Yet Gilman could also assert in "My Ancestors" that all humans are one family (*Forerunner* 4 [Mar. 1913]: 73–75). In the sequel to *Herland*, Gilman also repeatedly chastises America for its negative treatment of African Americans, Mexican Americans, and Native Americans. For other discussions of Gilman's views about immigrants, African Americans, and Jews, see Lane (Introduction xvii; *To Herland* 337) and Carol Farley Kessler (47–48, 76–77).

3. In the last ten years, there have been a number of insightful readings of *Herland*. For critics who feel that Gilman's feminist critique succeeds, see Kessler, Gubar ("She in Herland"), Laura Donaldson, Dorothy Berkson, and Marsha Smith. For critics who believe that the utopia undermines itself, see Kathleen Lant and Thomas Peyser.

4. The men read the geography of Herland as a dismembered feminine body. Herland is surrounded by "a desperate tangle of wood and water and a swampy patch" (3); this imagery suggests that the men see the land as a huge feminine orifice that must be penetrated. They carry guns, and sensing danger, they steal forward with their "weapons [i.e., guns] in hand" (13). When the men hear laughter they stop instantly: "We stood like so many pointers, and then used our glasses, swiftly, carefully" (14). The men try to script a narrative of conquest and colonization onto Herland's "feminine" body but find themselves imprisoned and anesthetized.

5. According to Kathleen Lant, Terry's attempted rape of Alima is the focus of *Herland* and this falsifies Gilman's feminist project by making the novel an archetypal masculine plot. However, I see the novel as focusing on the undermining of phallic power.

6. It should be clear from this paragraph that I do not believe that Ellador is Gilman's "mouthpiece," as Lanser states (430), or even that Gilman presents the Herlanders as perfect.

7. Most critics dismiss Gilman's short fictions as lacking artistic merit because they were written for a purpose. Shumaker states that they are "the kind of purposeful fiction that could not be misunderstood" (82). Shelley Fisher Fishkin calls them "didactic to the core" but also believes they explore "dimensions of human experience that elude logic and reason" (236).

8. "Mrs. Beazley's Deeds," *Forerunner* 7 (1916): 225–32; 225. Parenthetical citations are to this printing. Also available in *The Yellow Wall-Paper and Selected Stories of Charlotte Perkins Gilman*, ed. Denise D. Knight (Newark: University of Delaware Press, 1994).

9. The similarities with Freeman's "The Revolt of 'Mother' " are apparent; Beazley, like Adoniram Penn, squeezes his family into a small house, purchases property simply for the sake of buying more property, threatens the family's continuance through his short-sightedness, and ignores his wife's attempts to speak. Like Adoniram Penn, Beazley takes a trip and returns to find a world turned upside down by a mobilization of feminine force. But whereas Sarah Penn's actions heal the rift in the family, for Maria Beazley no healing is possible. The moral of Gilman's story seems to be that Father cannot—or will not—

understand what Mother is "set on." Gilman admired Freeman's writing, but it is not clear which stories Gilman had read.

Chapter 6

1. See Robert Young's *Colonial Desire* for a more lengthy discussion of nineteenth-century definitions of the word "hybrid." Throughout this chapter, I am indebted to both Young's and Carla Peterson's analysis of hybridity.

2. Both Hazel Carby (73) and Elizabeth Ammons (*Conflicting Stories* 27) argue that *Iola Leroy* melds the domestic sentimental novel with other literary forms, but neither discusses intertextual revisions of "The Quadroons." There has also been little discussion of *Iola Leroy's* challenge to the slave narrative tradition or its revision of *Clotel,* although Elkins (50 and 53, n. 5), Christian (27), and Ernest ("From Mysteries" 516–17, n. 35) mention that Harper's novel has parallels with *Clotel.*

3. Harper herself believed that women's work should not be limited to the domestic sphere. Essays such as "Colored Women of America" (1878) describe women who support their families in nontraditional employments such as managing and cultivating farms, selling cakes, keeping accounts, and running schools (10–15).

4. In discussing Iola's role as part of an ethnic community sphere, I am disagreeing with critics such as Barbara Christian (22), Judith Berzon (100), and Deborah McDowell ("'Changing Same'" 284–85) who have argued that the use of the "mulatta" heroine represents a concession to a white readership. Like Carby I believe that "the figure of the mulatto should be understood and analyzed as a narrative device of mediation" (89), and I see this mediation occurring on multiple levels.

5. A number of critics have disliked *Iola Leroy* for aesthetic reasons; see Sterling Brown, Robert Bone, Christian, Berzon, and McDowell ("'Changing Same'"). Yet another recent group of critics have argued persuasively for the novel's integrity and power in terms of its historic, artistic, and feminist goals; see Foster (Introduction), Carby (*Reconstructing Womanhood*), Ammons, Elkins, Ernest ("From Mysteries"), and Sale.

6. Thomas Jefferson is supposed to be Clotel and Althesa's father; however, according to the novel's actual chronology this could not be the case.

7. See also Fabi's point that the female characters in the novel rely mainly on the passive strategy of "passing" for white, and on silence more than on verbal skills, for some semblance of freedom (642), whereas the male characters use more confrontational and verbal forms of resistance and trickery (640).

8. Blassingame states that "the slaves who escaped were extremely resourceful *men*" (112, my emphasis), yet quotes statistics that show that 11 percent of the escapeés were women (114). Gerda Lerner also provides documentary evidence that slave women purchased their sons and daughters, escaped from slavery, helped others escape, and fought back violently when attacked by their owners (33–65).

Notes

9. For a more lengthy discussion of Jacobs's use of language, see my essay on this topic.

10. In a discussion of Harper's speeches, Maggie Sale makes a similar point, commenting that Harper's representation of a female speaking subject complicates the idea that a discourse of manhood serves black women (706).

11. It should be clear from these examples that I do not believe that Harper places Iola above the folk, as Carby argues (*Reconstructing Womanhood* 77–78), or that the goal of "uplift" is to rescue the race from its own culture, as Christian believes (28, 29). I see the relationship between folk culture and the intellectual community as one of reciprocity.

Chapter 7

1. For more extensive discussion of Cather's review of *The Awakening*, see Carlin (117–19) and O'Brien ("Limits of Passion").

2. Until recently, there has been little positive criticism of Fauset's writing. Barbara Christian (41–43) and Hazel Carby (*Reconstructing Womanhood* 167) attack Fauset's portrayal of a black bourgeois consciousness; Bernard Bell (109) and David Littlejohn (51) dismiss Fauset's novels as sophomoric, trivial, dull, vapid, and narrow. Fauset's writing has recently been defended by Deborah McDowell ("Neglected Dimension"), Jacqueline McLendon, Ann duCille (*Coupling Convention*), and Carolyn Sylvander.

3. Most critics have paid little attention to Fauset's feminist themes, arguing that women's role is a secondary concern. No critics have examined either *There Is Confusion* or *Plum Bun* as female *Künstlerromans*, or discussed their formulation of ethnic discourses that critique dominant conceptions of art.

4. For other discussions of sexuality in *Plum Bun*, see McLendon (37) and Gilbert and Gubar (*No Man's Land* 137).

5. Mary Dearborn states that the novel ends with Angela's return to the black community (121). Wall believes Angela dreams of replicating her mother's life (78), while Gilbert and Gubar argue the ending shows that "if black women sacrifice their ambitions for independence they can resurrect their wounded male doubles and themselves" (*No Man's Land* 144). However, both Sylvander (176) and McLendon (49) argue compellingly that the novel resists closure by having Angela remain in Paris, unwed.

6. Elsa Nettels argues that Cather admired female opera singers of her day precisely because they departed from patriarchal traditions (31). See also Susan Leonardi's comment that "the prima donna, as she reproduces a character (usually a woman created by a man), can improvise — and thus *revise*" (69).

7. Cather's placement within literary tradition has been the subject of much debate. Some critics see *The Song of the Lark* as a standard *Künstlerroman* (Giannone 131), while others see it as a feminine revision of this plot (Rosowski, *Voyage Perilous* 69). More generally, some critics argue, as I do, that in various ways Cather is indebted to the tradition of women's writing and women's art that precedes her. According to Sharon O'Brien, Cather

began her career by identifying maleness with creativity but through her relationship to Sarah Orne Jewett (beginning in 1909) moved toward a female-centered vision of art. Susan Rosowski also provides support for Cather's movement toward a feminine vision of creativity ("Writing Against Silences" and "Willa Cather's Visions and Revisions"). However, some critics maintain that Cather aligns creativity with masculinity (see Nettels 29 and Kaye 71–95).

8. O'Brien argues that Cather eventually developed an alternative to her early association of: sword/penis/pen/male/artist, culminating in the series of associations found in *The Song of the Lark*: vessel/womb/throat/voice/woman/artist (*Willa Cather* 171).

9. As Richard Giannone comments, with the Mexicans Thea "unearths a collective human feeling" that she later incorporates into her own performances (133).

Notes

Bibliography

Primary Texts

Alcott, Louisa May. "Ariel, A Legend of the Lighthouse." 1865. *A Double Life: Newly Discovered Thrillers of Louisa May Alcott*. Ed. Madeleine Stern. Boston: Little, Brown, 1988.

———. *Behind a Mask*. 1866. *Alternative Alcott*. Ed. Elaine Showalter. New Brunswick: Rutgers University Press, 1988.

———. "The Fate of the Forrests." 1865. *A Double Life: Newly Discovered Thrillers of Louisa May Alcott*. Ed. Madeleine Stern. Boston: Little, Brown, 1988.

———. *Little Women*. 1868–69. New York: Modern Library, 1983.

———. "The Marble Woman." 1865. *Plots and Counter Plots: More Unknown Thrillers of Louisa May Alcott*. Ed. Madeleine Stern. New York: William Morrow, 1976.

———. "Pauline's Passion and Punishment." 1864. *Behind a Mask: The Unknown Thrillers of Louisa May Alcott.*Ed. Madeleine Stern. New York: William Morrow, 1975.

———. "A Whisper in the Dark." 1863. *Plots and Counter Plots: More Unknown Thrillers of Louisa May Alcott*. Ed. Madeleine Stern. New York: William Morrow, 1976.

Cather, Willa. Review of *The Awakening*. *Pittsburgh Leader* 17 June 1899: 5. Rpt. in *The World and the Parish: Willa Cather's Articles and Reviews*, vol. 2. Ed. William M. Curtin. Lincoln: University of Nebraska Press, 1970. 697–99.

———. *The Song of the Lark*. 1915. Boston: Houghton Mifflin, 1988.

———. "Three Operas." *Courier* 12 May 1990. Rpt. in *The World and the Parish: Willa Cather's Articles and Reviews*, vol. 2. Ed. William M. Curtin. Lincoln: University of Nebraska Press, 1970. 655–58.

Chopin, Kate. "Aims and Autographs of Authors." *Book News* 17 (July 1899): 612.

———. *The Complete Works of Kate Chopin.* Ed. Per Seyersted. Baton Rouge: Louisiana State University Press, 1969.

Cooper, Anna Julia. "Discussion." *The World's Congress of Representative Women.* Ed. May Wright Sewall. Chicago: Rand, McNally, 1894. 711–15.

———. *A Voice from the South. By a Black Woman of the South.* 1892. New York: Oxford University Press, 1988.

Fauset, Jessie Redmon. *Plum Bun: A Novel without a Moral.* 1928. Boston: Beacon Press, 1990.

———. *There Is Confusion.* 1924. Boston: Northeastern University Press, 1989.

Fern, Fanny [Sara Payson Willis Parton]. *Ruth Hall and Other Writings.* 1855. New Brunswick: Rutgers University Press, 1986.

Freeman, Mary Wilkins. *A New England Nun and Other Stories.* New York: Harper, 1891.

———. *Silence and Other Stories.* New York: Harper, 1898.

———. *The Winning Lady and Others.* New York: Harper, 1909.

Gilman, Charlotte Perkins. "Fighting, Growing, and Making." *Forerunner* 4 (1913): 16.

———. *Herland.* 1915. New York: Pantheon, 1979.

———. "An Honest Woman." *Forerunner* 2 (1911). Rpt. in *The Charlotte Perkins Gilman Reader.* Ed. Ann J. Lane. New York: Pantheon, 1980.

———. "Lost Women." *Forerunner* 3 (1912): 281–84.

———. *The Man-Made World; or, Our Androcentric Culture.* New York: Charlton Co., 1911.

———. "Moore's Fountain Pen." *Forerunner* 1 (1909): 31

———. "Mrs. Beazley's Deeds." 1911. *Forerunner* 7 (1916): 225–32.

———. "Names — Especially Women's." *Forerunner* 2 (1911): 261–63.

———. "Spoken To." *Forerunner* 6 (1915): 29–33.

———. "The Widow's Might." 1911. Rpt. in *The Charlotte Perkins Gilman Reader.* Ed. Ann J. Lane. New York: Pantheon, 1980.

———. "With a Difference (Not Literature)." *Forerunner* 5 (1914): 29–32.

———. "Woman's Achievements since the Franchise." *Current History* 27 (Oct. 1927): 7–14.

———. *The Yellow Wall-Paper and Other Stories.* Ed. Robert Shulman. New York: Oxford University Press, 1995.

Harper, Frances E. W. "Colored Women of America." *Englishwoman's Review* (Jan 15, 1878): 10–15.

———. *Iola Leroy: Or Shadows Uplifted.* 1892. Boston: Beacon Press, 1987.

———. "Woman's Political Future." *The World's Congress of Representative Women.* Ed. May Wright Sewall. Chicago: Rand, McNally, 1894. 433–37.

Wilson, Harriet E. Adams. *Our Nig; or, Sketches from the Life of a Free Black.* 1859. New York: Random House, 1983.

Secondary Sources

Abbott, Harriet. "What the Newest New Woman Is." *Ladies' Home Journal* 20 (Aug. 1920): 154.

Abrahams, Roger D. *Deep Down in the Jungle . . . ; Negro Narrative Folklore from the Streets of Philadelphia.* Chicago: Aldine, 1970.

Adams, John H., Jr. "Rough Sketches: A Study of the Features of the New Negro Woman." *The Voice of the Negro* 1 (Aug. 1904): 323–26.

Alcott, William A. *The Young Wife, Or, Duties of Woman in the Marriage Relation.* Boston: George W. Light, 1837.

Alexander, Elizabeth. " 'We Must Be About Our Father's Business': Anna Julia Cooper and the In-Corporation of the Nineteenth-Century African-American Woman Intellectual." *Signs* 20 (1995): 336–56.

Ammons, Elizabeth. *Conflicting Stories: American Women Writers at the Turn into the Twentieth Century.* New York: Oxford University Press, 1991.

Ardis, Ann L. *New Women, New Novels: Feminism and Early Modernism.* New Brunswick: Rutgers University Press, 1990.

Bak, John. "Escaping the Jaundiced Eye: Foucaldian Panopticism in Charlotte Perkins Gilman's 'The Yellow Wallpaper.' " *Studies in Short Fiction* 31 (1994): 39–46.

Baker-Fletcher, Karen. *A Singing Something: Womanist Reflections on Anna Julia Cooper.* New York: Crossroad, 1994.

Bakhtin, Mikhail. *The Dialogic Imagination: Four Essays.* Ed. Michael Holquist. Trans. Caryl Emerson and Michael Holquist. Austin: University of Texas Press, 1981.

Banta, Martha. *Imaging American Women: Ideas and Ideals in Cultural History.* New York: Columbia University Press, 1987.

Bardes, Barbara, and Suzanne Gossett. *Declarations of Independence: Women and Political Power in Nineteenth-Century American Fiction.* New Brunswick: Rutgers University Press, 1990.

Barker, Deborah E. "The Awakening of Female Artistry." *Kate Chopin Reconsidered: Beyond the Bayou.* Ed. Lynda S. Boren and Sara deSaussure Davis. Baton Rouge: Louisiana State University Press, 1992. 61–79.

Bassil, Veronica. "The Artist at Home: The Domestication of Louisa May Alcott." *Studies in American Fiction* 15 (1987): 187–97.

Bates, Josephine. "Address." *The World's Congress of Representative Women.* Ed. May Wright Sewall. Chicago: Rand, McNally, 1894. 151–53.

Bauer, Dale M. *Feminist Dialogics: A Theory of Failed Community.* Albany: SUNY Press, 1988.

Baym, Nina. *American Women Writers and the Work of History, 1790–1860.* New Brunswick: Rutgers University Press, 1995.

———. *Woman's Fiction: A Guide to Novels by and about Women in America, 1820–70.* 1978. Urbana: University of Illinois Press, 1993.

Beatty, Bess. "Black Perspectives of American Women: The View from Black Newspapers, 1865–1900." *Maryland Historian* 9 (1978): 39–50.

Bedell, Madelon. Introduction. *Little Women.* By Louisa May Alcott. New York: Modern Library, 1983.

Bell, Bernard. *The Afro-American Novel and Its Tradition.* Amherst: University of Massachusetts Press, 1987.

Berkson, Dorothy. "'So We All Became Mothers': Harriet Beecher Stowe, Charlotte Perkins Gilman, and the New World of Women's Culture." *Feminism, Utopia, and Narrative.* Ed. Libby Falk Jones and Sarah Webster Goodwin. Knoxville: University of Tennessee Press, 1990.

Berzon, Judith R. *Neither White Nor Black: The Mulatto Character in American Fiction.* New York: New York University Press, 1978.

Bhabha, Homi. "Signs Taken for Wonders: Questions of Ambivalence and Authority under a Tree Outside Delhi, May 1817." *"Race," Writing, and Difference.* Ed. Henry Louis Gates. Chicago: University of Chicago Press, 1986.

Birnbaum, Michele A. "'Alien Hands': Kate Chopin and the Colonization of Race." *American Literature* 66 (1994): 301–23.

Blassingame, John W. *The Slave Community: Plantation Life in the Antebellum South.* New York: Oxford University Press, 1972.

Bone, Robert. *The Negro Novel in America.* New Haven: Yale University Press, 1965.

Brand, Alice Glarden. "Mary Wilkins Freeman: Misanthropy as Propaganda." *New England Quarterly* 50 (1977): 83–100.

Broughton, Rhoda. "Girls Past and Present." *Ladies Home Journal* 37 (Sept. 1920): 38, 141.

Brown, Hallie Q. "Discussion." *The World's Congress of Representative Women.* Ed. May Wright Sewall. Chicago: Rand, McNally, 1894. 724–29.

Brown, Sterling. *The Negro in American Fiction.* 1937. Port Washington, N.Y.: Kennikat, 1968.

Brown, William Wells. *Clotel, Or, The President's Daughter.* 1853. New York: Carol Publishing Group, 1989.

———. *Clotelle; or, The Colored Heroine: A Tale of the Southern States.* 1867. Miami: Mnemosyne, 1969.

Burnap, George W. *The Sphere and Duties of Woman: A Course of Lectures.* Baltimore: John Murphy, 1847.

Butler, Judith P. *Bodies That Matter: On the Discursive Limits of "Sex."* New York: Routledge: 1993.

———. *Gender Trouble: Feminism and the Subversion of Identity.* New York: Routledge, 1990.

Caird, Mona. "The Duel of the Sexes—A Comment." *Fortnightly Review* 78 (1905): 109–22.

Carby, Hazel. "'On the Threshold of Woman's Era': Lynching, Empire, and Sexuality in Black Feminist Theory." *Critical Inquiry* 12 (1985): 262–77.

————. *Reconstructing Womanhood: The Emergence of the Afro-American Woman Novelist.* New York: Oxford University Press, 1987.

Carlin, Deborah. *Cather, Canon, and the Politics of Reading.* Amherst: University of Massachusetts Press, 1992.

Carpenter, Lynette. "'Did They Never See Anyone Angry Before?': The Sexual Politics of Self-Control in Alcott's 'A Whisper in the Dark.'" *Legacy* 3 (1986): 31–41.

Chapin, E. H. *Duties of Young Women.* Boston: George W. Briggs, 1848.

Child, Lydia Marie. "The Quadroons." 1846. *Fact and Fiction: A Collection of Stories.* New York: C. S. Francis & Co., 1854.

Christian, Barbara. *Black Women Novelists: The Development of a Tradition, 1892–1976.* Westport: Greenwood Press, 1980.

Christy, Howard Chandler. *The American Girl, as Seen and Portrayed by Howard Chandler Christy.* New York: Moffat, Yard and Company, 1906.

Church, Joseph. "Reconstructing Woman's Place in Freeman's 'The Revolt of "Mother."'" *Colby Quarterly* 26 (1990): 195–200.

Cixous, Hélène. "Sorties." *New French Feminisms: An Anthology.* Ed. Elaine Marks and Isabelle de Courtivron. New York: Schocken, 1981. 90–98.

Collins, Joseph. "Woman's Morality in Transition." *Current History* 27 (Oct. 1927): 33–40.

Coppin, Fannie Jackson. "Discussion." *The World's Congress of Representative Women.* Ed. May Wright Sewall. Chicago: Rand, McNally, 1894. 715–17.

Cothern, Lynn. "Speech and Authorship in Kate Chopin's 'La Belle Zoraïde.'" *Louisiana Literature* 11 (1994): 118–25.

Cott, Nancy. *The Bonds of Womanhood: "Woman's Sphere" in New England, 1780–1835.* New Haven: Yale University Press, 1977.

————. *The Grounding of Modern Feminism.* New Haven: Yale University Press, 1987.

Coxe, Margaret. *The Young Lady's Companion, And Token of Affection; In a Series of Letters.* Columbus: Issac N. Whiting, 1839.

Culley, Margaret, ed. *The Awakening.* By Kate Chopin. New York: Norton, 1976.

Cunningham, Gail. *The New Woman and the Victorian Novel.* London: Macmillan Press, 1978.

Cutter, Martha J. "Beyond Stereotypes: Mary Wilkins Freeman's Radical Critique of Nineteenth-Century Cults of Femininity." *Women's Studies* 21 (1992): 383–95

————. "Dismantling 'The Master's House': Critical Literacy in Harriet Jacobs' *Incidents in the Life of A Slave Girl.*" *Callaloo* 19 (1996): 209–25.

————. "Mary E. Wilkins Freeman's Two New England Nuns." *Colby Quarterly* 26 (1990): 213–25.

Dearborn, Mary V. *Pocahontas's Daughters: Gender and Ethnicity in American Culture.* New York: Oxford University Press, 1986.

Delany, Martin Robinson. *The Condition, Elevation, Emigration, and Destiny of the Colored People of the United States.* 1852. New York: Arno Press, 1969.

Derrida, Jacques, and Christie V. McDonald. "Choreographies." *Diacritics: A Review of Contemporary Criticism* 12 (1982): 66–76.

Donaldson, Laura E. "The Eve of De-struction: Charlotte Perkins Gilman and the Feminist Recreation of Paradise." *Women's Studies* 16 (1989): 373–87.

Donovan, Josephine. *New England Local Color Literature: A Women's Tradition.* New York: Ungar, 1983.

———. "Silence or Capitulation: Prepatriarchal 'Mothers' Gardens' in Jewett and Freeman." *Studies in Short Fiction* 23 (1986): 43–48.

Douglass, Frederick. *Narrative of the Life of Frederick Douglass, an American Slave, Written by Himself.* 1845. New York: Penguin, 1968.

Dressler, Mylène. "Edna Under the Sun: Throwing Light on the Subject of *The Awakening.*" *Arizona Quarterly* 48 (1992): 59–75.

duCille, Ann. "Blues Notes on Black Sexuality: Sex and the Texts of Jessie Fauset and Nella Larsen." *Journal of the History of Sexuality* 3 (1993): 418–44.

———. *The Coupling Convention: Sex, Text, and Tradition in Black Women's Fiction.* New York: Oxford University Press, 1993.

Dwyer, Patricia. "Diffusing Boundaries: A Study of Narrative Strategies in Mary Wilkins Freeman's 'The Revolt of "Mother." ' " *Legacy* 10 (1993): 120–27.

Elbert, Monika. "Mary Wilkins Freeman's Devious Women, *Harper's Bazaar,* and the Rhetoric of Advertising." *Essays in Literature* 20 (1993): 251–72.

Elfenbein, Anna Shannon. *Women on the Color Line: Evolving Stereotypes and the Writings of George Washington Cable, Grace King, Kate Chopin.* Charlottesville: University Press of Virginia, 1989.

Elkins, Marilyn. "Reading Beyond the Conventions: A Look at Frances E. W. Harper's *Iola Leroy, or Shadows Uplifted.*" *American Literary Realism* 22 (1990): 44–53.

Emmitt, Helen V. " 'Drowned in a Willing Sea': Freedom and Drowning in Eliot, Chopin, and Drabble." *Tulsa Studies in Women's Literature* 12 (1993): 315–32.

Ernest, John. "Economies of Identity: Harriet E. Wilson's *Our Nig.*" *PMLA* 109 (1994): 424–38.

———. "From Mysteries to Histories: Cultural Pedagogy in Frances E. Harper's *Iola Leroy.*" *American Literature* 64 (1992): 497–518.

Ewell, Barbara C. *Kate Chopin.* New York: Ungar, 1986.

Fabi, M. Giulia. "The 'Unguarded Expressions of the Feelings of the Negroes': Gender, Slave Resistance, and William Wells Brown's Revisions of *Clotel.*" *African American Review* 27 (1993): 639–54.

"Feminism and Jane Smith." *Harper's Monthly Magazine* 155 (1927): 1–10.

Fetterley, Judith. "*Little Women:* Alcott's Civil War." *Feminist Studies* 5 (1979): 369–83.

———. "Impersonating 'Little Women': The Radicalism of Alcott's 'Behind a Mask.' " *Women's Studies* 10 (1983): 1–14.

———. "Willa Cather and the Fiction of Female Development." *Anxious Power: Reading, Writing, and Ambivalence in Narrative by Women.* Ed. Carol J. Singley and Susan Elizabeth Sweeney. Albany: SUNY Press 1993. 221–34.

Fishkin, Shelley Fisher. "'Making a Change': Strategies of Subversion in Gilman's Journalism and Short Fiction." *Critical Essays on Charlotte Perkins Gilman*. Ed. Joanne Karpinski. New York: G. K. Hall, 1992. 234–48.

Fluck, Winfried. "Tentative Transgressions: Kate Chopin's Fiction as a Mode of Symbolic Action." *Studies in American Fiction* 10 (1982): 151–71.

Foreman, P. Gabrielle. "The Spoken and the Silenced in *Incidents in the Life of a Slave Girl* and *Our Nig*." *Callaloo* 13 (1990): 313–24.

Foster, Frances Smith. "Adding Color and Contour to Early American Self-Portraitures: Autobiographical Writings of Afro-American Women." *Conjuring: Black Women, Fiction, and Literary Tradition*. Ed. Marjorie Pryse and Hortense Spillers. Bloomington: Indiana University Press, 1984. 25–38.

———. Introduction. *Iola Leroy*. By Frances Harper. New York: Oxford University Press, 1988. xxvii–xxxix.

———. *Witnessing Slavery: The Development of Ante-Bellum Slave Narratives*. Westport, Conn.: Greenwood, 1979.

Foster, J. Ellen. "Woman as a Political Leader." *The World's Congress of Representative Women*. Ed. May Wright Sewall. Chicago: Rand, McNally, 1894. 439–45.

Freire, Paulo, and Donaldo Macedo. *Literacy: Reading the Word and the World*. South Hadley: Bergin & Garvey, 1987.

Furman, Nelly. "The Politics of Language: Beyond the Gender Principle?" *Making a Difference: Feminist Literary Criticism*. Ed. Gayle Greene and Coppélia Kahn. London: Routledge, 1985. 59–79.

Gaines, Kevin K. *Uplifting the Race: Black Leadership, Politics, and Culture in the Twentieth Century*. Chapel Hill: University of North Carolina Press, 1996.

Gallop, Jane. *The Daughter's Seduction: Feminism and Psychoanalysis*. Ithaca: Cornell University Press, 1982.

Gardner, Eric. "'This Attempt of Their Sister': Harriet Wilson's *Our Nig* from Printer to Readers." *New England Quarterly* 66 (1993): 226–46.

Gates, Henry Louis, Jr. *Figures in Black: Words, Signs, and the "Racial" Self*. New York: Oxford University Press, 1987.

———. Introduction. *Our Nig*. New York: Vintage, 1983.

Gauthier, Xavière. "Is There Such a Thing As Women's Writing?" *New French Feminisms: An Anthology*. Ed. Elaine Marks and Isabelle de Courtivron. New York: Schocken, 1980. 161–64.

George, E. Laurie. "Women's Language in *The Awakening*." *Approaches to Teaching Chopin's The Awakening*. Ed. Bernard Koloski. New York: MLA, 1988. 53–59.

Giannone, Richard. "The Lyric Artist." *Critical Essays on Willa Cather*. Ed. John J. Murphy. Boston: G. K. Hall, 1984.

Gilbert, Sandra M. "The Second Coming of Aphrodite: Kate Chopin's Fantasy of Desire." *Kenyon Review* 5 (1983): 42–66.

Gilbert, Sandra M., and Susan Gubar. *The Madwoman in the Attic: The Woman Writer and the Nineteenth-Century Literary Imagination*. New Haven: Yale University Press, 1979.

———. *No Man's Land: The Place of the Woman Writer in the Twentieth Century, Volume 3: Letters from the Front*. New Haven: Yale University Press, 1994.

———. "Sexual Linguistics: Gender, Language, Sexuality." *The Feminist Reader: Essays in Gender and the Politics of Literary Criticism*. Ed. Catherine Belsey and Jane Moore. New York: Basil Blackwell, 1989. 81–99.

Gilman, Caroline Howard. *Recollections of a Housekeeper, By Mrs. Clarissa Packard*. New York: Harper and Brothers, 1834.

Giorcelli, Christina. "Edna's Wisdom: A Transitional and Numinous Merging." *New Essays on* The Awakening. Ed. Wendy Martin. Cambridge: Cambridge University Press, 1988. 109–48.

Glasser, Leah Blatt. *In a Closet Hidden: The Life and Work of Mary E. Wilkins Freeman*. Amherst: University of Massachusetts Press, 1996.

Golden, Catherine. "The Writing of 'The Yellow Wallpaper': A Double Palimpsest." *Studies in American Fiction* 17 (1989): 193–201.

Goodwyn, Janet. " 'Dah you is, settin' down, lookin' jis' like w'ite folks!': Ethnicity Enacted in Kate Chopin's Short Fiction." *Yearbook of English Studies* 24 (1994): 1–11.

Gubar, Susan. " 'The Blank Page' and the Issues of Female Creativity." *The New Feminist Criticism: Essays on Women, Literature, and Theory*. Ed. Elaine Showalter. New York: Pantheon, 1985. 292–313.

———. "*She* in *Herland*: Feminism as Fantasy." *Charlotte Perkins Gilman: The Woman and Her Work*. Ed. Sheryl L. Meyering. Ann Arbor: UMI Research Press, 1989. 191–202.

Hanks, Patrick, and Flavia Hodges. *A Dictionary of First Names*. Oxford: Oxford University Press, 1990.

Harris, Susan. *Nineteenth-Century American Women's Novels: Interpretive Strategies*. Cambridge: Cambridge University Press, 1990.

Hart, James D. *The Popular Book: A History of America's Literary Taste*. New York: Oxford University Press, 1950.

Hayes, Ellen. "Woman's Dress from the Standpoint of Sociology." *The World's Congress of Representative Women*. Ed. May Wright Sewall. Chicago: Rand, McNally, 1894. 354–62.

Heath, Stephen. "Difference." *Screen* 19 (1978): 51–112.

Heilbrun, Carolyn G. "Louisa May Alcott: The Influence of *Little Women*." *Women, the Arts, and the 1920s in Paris and New York*. Ed. Kenneth Wheeler and Virginia Lee Lussier. New Brunswick: Transaction Books, 1982. 20–26.

Henderson, Mae Gwendolyn. "Speaking in Tongues: Dialogics, Dialectics, and the Black Woman Writer's Literary Tradition." *Feminists Theorize the Political*. Ed. by Judith Butler and Joan W. Scott. New York: Routledge, 1992. 144–66.

Henrotin, Ellen M. "Greeting to the Representative Women of the World." *The World's Congress of Representative Women*. Ed. May Wright Sewall. Chicago: Rand, McNally, 1894. 12.

Higginbotham, Evelyn Brooks. *Righteous Discontent: The Women's Movement in the Black Baptist Church,* 1880–1920. Cambridge: Harvard University Press, 1993.

Hill, Mary A. *Charlotte Perkins Gilman: The Making of a Radical Feminist,* 1860–1896. Philadelphia: Temple University Press, 1980.

Hollingsworth, Leta. "The New Woman in the Making." *Current History* 27 (Oct. 1927): 15–20.

Homans, Margaret. *Bearing the Word: Language and Female Experience in Nineteenth-Century Women's Writing.* Chicago: University of Chicago Press, 1986.

Howard, William Lee. "Effeminate Men and Masculine Women." *New York Medical Journal* 61 (1890): 687.

Howe, Julia Ward. "The Moral Initiative as Related to Woman." *The World's Congress of Representative Women.* Ed. May Wright Sewall. Chicago: Rand, McNally, 1894. 314–21.

Irigaray, Luce. *Speculum of the Other Woman.* Trans. Gillian C. Gill. Ithaca: Cornell University Press, 1985.

Jacobs, Harriet A. *Incidents in the Life of a Slave Girl: Written by Herself.* 1861. Cambridge: Harvard University Press, 1987.

Jacobus, Mary. "The Difference of View." *The Feminist Reader: Essays in Gender and the Politics of Literary Criticism.* Ed. Catherine Belsey and Jane Moore. New York: Basil Blackwell, 1989. 49–62.

Jeune, May. "The Revolt of the Daughters." *Fortnightly Review* 55 (1894): 267–76.

Jones, Ann Rosalind. "Inscribing Femininity: French Theories of the Feminine." *Making a Difference: Feminist Literary Criticism.* Ed. Gayle Greene and Coppélia Kahn. London: Routledge, 1985. 80–112.

Karpinski, Joanne B., ed. *Critical Essays on Charlotte Perkins Gilman.* New York: G. K. Hall, 1992.

Kasmer, Lisa. "Charlotte Perkins Gilman's 'The Yellow Wallpaper': A Symptomatic Reading." *Literature and Psychology* 36 (1990): 1–15.

Kaye, Frances W. *Isolation and Masquerade: Willa Cather's Women.* New York: Peter Lang, 1993.

Kearns, Katherine. "The Nullification of Edna Pontellier." *American Literature* 63 (1991): 62–88.

Kelley, Karol. "Self-Made Man? True Woman? Historical Approaches to the Creation of American Success Models." Diss., Bowling Green State University, 1981.

Kelley, Mary. *Private Woman, Public Stage: Literary Domesticity in Nineteenth-Century America.* New York: Oxford University Press, 1984.

Kennard, Jean. "Convention Coverage or How to Read Your Own Life." *Charlotte Perkins Gilman: The Woman and Her Work.* Ed. Sheryl Meyering. Ann Arbor: UMI Research Press, 1989. 75–94.

Kessler, Carol Farley. *Charlotte Perkins Gilman: Her Progress Toward Utopia with Selected Writings.* New York: Syracuse University Press, 1995.

Keyser, Elizabeth Lennox. "Alcott's Portrait of the Artist as Little Woman." *International Journal of Women's Studies* 5 (1982): 445–59.

————. *Whispers in the Dark: The Fiction of Louisa May Alcott.* Knoxville: University of Tennessee Press, 1993.

King, Jeannette, and Pam Morris. "On Not Reading Between the Lines: Models of Reading in 'The Yellow Wallpaper.'" *Studies in Short Fiction* 26 (1989): 23–32.

Klemans, Patricia A. "The Courageous Soul: Woman as Artist in American Literature." *CEA Critic: An Official Journal of the College English Association* 43 (1981): 39–43.

Kochman, Thomas. "'Rapping' in the Black Ghetto." *Trans-Action* 6.4 (1969): 26–35.

Kolatch, Alfred J. *The Name Dictionary: Modern English and Hebrew Names.* New York: Jonathan David, 1967.

Kolodny, Annette. "A Map for Rereading: Or, Gender and the Interpretation of Literary Texts." *New Literary History* 11 (1980): 451–67.

Kristeva, Julia. *Desire in Language: A Semiotic Approach to Literature and Art.* Ed. Leon S. Roudiez. New York: Columbia University Press, 1980.

————. "Women's Time." *The Kristeva Reader.* Edited Toril Moi. New York: Columbia University Press, 1986.

Lane, Ann J. Introduction. *Herland.* By Charlotte Perkins Gilman. New York: Pantheon, 1979.

————. *To Herland and Beyond: The Life and Work of Charlotte Perkins Gilman.* New York: Pantheon, 1990.

Lanser, Susan. "Feminist Criticism, 'The Yellow Wallpaper,' and the Politics of Color in America." *Feminist Studies* 15 (1989): 415–41.

Lant, Kathleen Margaret. "The Rape of the Text: Charlotte Gilman's Violation of *Herland.*" *Tulsa Studies in Women's Literature* 9 (1990): 291–308.

Larabee, Ann E. "The American Hero and His Mechanical Bride: Gender Myths of the *Titanic* Disaster." *American Studies* 31 (1990): 5–23.

Lemaire, Anika. *Jacques Lacan.* Trans. David Macey. London: Routledge, 1977.

Leonardi, Susan J. "To Have a Voice: The Politics of the Diva." *Perspectives on Contemporary Literature* 13 (1987): 65–72.

Lerner, Gerda A., ed. *Black Women in White America: A Documentary History.* New York: Pantheon, 1972.

Lewes, George Henry. "A Gentle Hint to Writing Women." *Leader* 1 (1850): 189.

Littlejohn, David. *Black on White: A Critical Survey of Writing by American Negroes.* New York: Viking Press, 1966.

Lloyd, David. "Ethnic Cultures, Minority Discourse, and the State." *Colonial Discourse/ Postcolonial Theory.* Ed. Francis Barker, Peter Hulme, and Margaret Iversen. New York: Manchester University Press, 1994. 221–38.

Lorde, Audre. "The Master's Tools Will Never Dismantle the Master's House." *This Bridge Called My Back: Writings by Radical Women of Color.* Ed. Cherríe Moraga and Gloria Anzaldúa. New York: Kitchen Table, 1983. 98–101.

Lowe, John. "Theories of Ethnic Humor: How to Enter, Laughing." *American Quarterly* 38 (1986): 439–60.

Ludovici, Anthony M. "Woman's Encroachment on Man's Domain." *Current History* 27 (Oct. 1927): 21–25.

Lundie, Catherine. "Doubly Dispossessed: Kate Chopin's Women of Color." *Louisiana Literature* 11 (1994): 126–44.

Lynch, Gertrude. "Racial and Ideal Types of Beauty." *Cosmopolitan* 38 (1904): 223–33.

McCoy, Beth. " 'Is This Really What You Wanted Me To Be?': The Daughter's Disintegration in Jessie Redmon Fauset's *There Is Confusion*." *Modern Fiction Studies* 40 (1994): 101–17.

McDowell, Deborah. " 'The Changing Same': Generational Connections and Black Women Novelists." *New Literary History* 18 (1987): 281–302.

———. "The Neglected Dimension of Jessie Redmon Fauset." *Conjuring: Black Women, Fiction, and Literary Tradition*. Ed. Marjorie Pryse and Hortense Spillers. Bloomington: Indiana University Press, 1985.

McIntosh, M. [Maria] J. *Woman in America: Her Work and Her Reward*. New York: D. Appleton & Company, 1850.

McLendon, Jacquelyn. *The Politics of Color in the Fiction of Jessie Fauset and Nella Larsen*. Charlottesville: University Press of Virginia, 1995.

McMenamin, Hugh. "Evils of Woman's Revolt Against the Old Standards." *Current History* 27 (Oct. 1927): 30–32.

Marks, Patricia. *Bicycles, Bangs, and Bloomers: The New Woman in the Popular Press*. Lexington: University Press of Kentucky, 1990.

Meese, Elizabeth. "Signs of Undecidability: Reconsidering the Stories of Mary Wilkins Freeman." *Critical Essays on Mary Wilkins Freeman*. Ed. Shirley Marchalonis. Boston: G. K. Hall, 1991. 157–76.

Meyer, Annie Nathan. "Woman's Place in the Republic of Letters." *The World's Congress of Representative Women*. Ed. May Wright Sewall. Chicago: Rand, McNally, 1894. 140–44.

Meyering, Sheryl, ed. *Charlotte Perkins Gilman: The Woman and Her Work*. Ann Arbor: UMI Research Press, 1989.

Mitchell, Angelyn. "Her Side of His Story: A Feminist Analysis of Two Nineteenth-Century Antebellum Novels — William Wells Brown's *Clotel* and Harriet E. Wilson's *Our Nig*." *American Literary Realism* 24 (1992): 7–21.

Moi, Toril. *Sexual/Textual Politics: Feminist Literary Theory*. London: Methuen, 1985.

Munich, Adrienne. "Notorious Signs, Feminist Criticism, and Literary Tradition." *Making a Difference: Feminist Literary Criticism*. Ed. Gayle Greene and Coppélia Kahn. New York: Routledge, 1985. 238–59.

Murphy, Anne. "The Borders of Ethical, Erotic, and Artistic Possibilities in *Little Women*." *Signs* 15 (1990): 562–85.

Nettels, Elsa. "Tradition and the Woman Artist: James's *The Tragic Muse* and Cather's *The Song of the Lark*." *Willa Cather Pioneer Memorial Newsletter* 36 (1992): 27–31.

O'Brien, Sharon. "The Limits of Passion: Willa Cather's Review of *The Awakening*." *Women and Literature* 3 (1975): 10–20.

———. *Willa Cather: The Emerging Voice*. New York: Oxford University Press, 1987.

Orr, Elaine. "Reading Negotiation and Negotiated Reading: A Practice With/in 'A White Heron' and 'The Revolt of "Mother."' " *CEA Critic* 53.3 (1991): 49–65.

Pattee, Fred Lewis. *The Feminine Fifties*. New York: D. Appleton-Century, 1940.

Patterson, Martha H. "Survival of the Best Fitted: Selling the American New Woman as Gibson Girl, 1895–1905." *ATQ* 9 (1995): 73–87.

Peel, Ellen. "Semiotic Subversion in 'Désirée's Baby.' " *American Literature* 62 (1990): 223–37.

Peterson, Carla L. *"Doers of the Word": African-American Women Speakers and Writers in the North, 1830–1880*. New York: Oxford University Press, 1995.

Peyser, Thomas Galt. "Reproducing Utopia: Charlotte Perkins Gilman and *Herland*." *Studies in American Fiction* 20 (1992): 1–16.

Pinckney, Cotesworth, ed. *The Lady's Token: or Gift of Friendship*. Boston: J. Buffum, 1848.

Reichardt, Mary R. *A Web of Relationship: Women in the Short Stories of Mary Wilkins Freeman*. Jackson: University Press of Mississippi, 1992.

Riegel, Robert. *American Women: A Story of Social Change*. Rutherford, N.J.: Fairleigh Dickinson University Press, 1970.

Riley, Glenda Gates. *Inventing the American Woman: A Perspective on Women's History*. Arlington Heights, Ill.: Harlan Davidson, 1986.

Robinson, Lillian S. "Canon Fathers and Myth Universe." *New Literary History* 19 (1987): 23–35.

Rose, Jacqueline. "Introduction — II." *Feminine Sexuality: Jacques Lacan and the Ecole Freudienne*. By Jacques Lacan. New York: Pantheon, 1982. 27–57.

Rosowski, Susan J. *The Voyage Perilous: Willa Cather's Romanticism*. Lincoln: University of Nebraska Press, 1986.

———. "Willa Cather's Visions and Revisions of Female Lives." *Images of the Self as Female: The Achievement of Women Artists in Re-Envisioning Feminine Identity*. Ed. Kathryn N. Benzel and Lauren Pringle De La Vars. Lewiston, N.Y.: Edwin Mellen Press, 1992.

———. "Writing Against Silences: Female Adolescent Development in the Novels of Willa Cather." *Studies in the Novel* 21 (1989): 60–77.

Sale, Maggie. "Critiques from Within: Antebellum Projects of Resistance." *American Literature* 64 (1992): 695–718.

Saxton, Martha. "The Secret Imaginings of Louisa Alcott." *Critical Essays on Louisa May Alcott*. Ed. Madeleine Stern. Boston: G. K. Hall, 1984.

Schweitzer, Ivy. "Maternal Discourse and the Romance of Self-Possession in Kate Chopin's *The Awakening*." *Boundary Two* 17 (1990): 158–86.

Senf, Carol A. " 'Dracula': Stoker's Response to the New Woman." *Victorian Studies* 26 (1982): 33–49.

Sewall, May Wright, ed. *The World's Congress of Representative Women*. Chicago: Rand, McNally, 1894.

Seyersted, Per. "Kate Chopin." *American Literary Realism* 3 (Spring 1970): 153–59.

———. *Kate Chopin: A Critical Biography*. New York: Octagon, 1980.

———. "Kate Chopin's Wound: Two New Letters." *American Literary Realism* 20 (Fall 1987): 71–75.

Showalter, Elaine. Introduction. *Alternative Alcott*. New Brunswick: Rutgers University Press, 1988.

———. "Piecing and Writing." *The Poetics of Gender*. Ed. Nancy K. Miller. New York: Columbia University Press, 1986. 222–47.

———. *Sister's Choice: Tradition and Change in American Women's Writing*. Oxford: Clarendon, 1991.

Shumaker, Conrad. "Realism, Reform, and the Audience: Charlotte Perkins Gilman's Unreadable Wallpaper." *Arizona Quarterly* 47 (1991): 81–93.

Sigourney, Mrs. L. H. *Letters to Mothers*. New York: Harper & Brothers, 1838.

Smith, Marsha A. "The Disoriented Male Narrator and Societal Conversion: Charlotte Perkins Gilman's Feminist Utopian Vision." *ATQ* 3 (1989): 123–33.

Smith, Valerie. *Self-Discovery and Authority in Afro-American Narrative*. Cambridge: Harvard University Press, 1987.

Smith-Rosenberg, Caroll. *Disorderly Conduct: Visions of Gender in Victorian America*. New York: Oxford University Press, 1985.

Sollors, Werner. *Beyond Ethnicity: Consent and Descent in American Culture*. New York: Oxford University Press, 1986.

Stanton, Elizabeth Cady. "The Civil and Social Evolution of Woman." *The World's Congress of Representative Women*. Ed. May Wright Sewall. Chicago: Rand, McNally, 1894. 327–29.

———. "The Ethics of Suffrage." *The World's Congress of Representative Women*. Ed. May Wright Sewall. Chicago: Rand, McNally, 1894. 483–88.

Stern, Julia. "Excavating Genre in *Our Nig*." *American Literature* 67 (1995): 439–66.

Stuckert, Mary Coleman. "Cooperative Housekeeping." *The World's Congress of Representative Women*. Ed. May Wright Sewall. Chicago: Rand, McNally, 1894. 625–26.

Sylvander, Carolyn Wedin. *Jessie Redmon Fauset: Black American Writer*. Troy, N.Y.: Whitson, 1981.

Tate, Claudia. *Domestic Allegories of Political Desire: The Black Heroine's Text at the Turn of the Century*. New York: Oxford, 1992.

Thayer, William M. *Life at the Fireside*. Boston: Congregational Board of Publication, 1857.

Thomas, Heather Kirk. "Kate Chopin's Scribbling Women and the American Literary Marketplace." *Studies in American Fiction* 23 (1995): 19–34.

Thomas, Mary Martha. *The New Woman in Alabama: Social Reforms and Suffrage, 1890–1920*. Tuscaloosa: University of Alabama Press, 1992.

Ticknor, Caroline. "The Steel-Engraving Lady and the Gibson Girl." *Atlantic Monthly* 88 (1901): 105–8.

Todd, Ellen Wiley. *The "New Woman" Revised: Painting and Gender Politics on Fourteenth Street*. Berkeley and Los Angeles: University of California Press, 1993.

Toth, Emily. *Kate Chopin*. New York: William Morrow, 1990.

Treichler, Paula A. "The Construction of Ambiguity in *The Awakening*: A Linguistic Analysis." *Women and Language in Literature and Society*. Ed. Sally McConnell-Ginet, Ruth Borker, and Nelly Furman. New York: Praeger, 1980. 239–57.

———. "Escaping the Sentence: Diagnosis and Discourse in 'The Yellow Wallpaper.'" *Tulsa Studies in Women's Literature* 3 (1984): 61–77.

———. "The Wall Behind the Yellow Wallpaper: Response to Carol Neely and Karen Ford." *Tulsa Studies in Women's Literature* 4 (1985): 323–30.

Turner, Victor. *The Ritual Process: Structure and Anti-Structure*. Chicago: Aldine, 1969.

Urgo, Joseph R. "A Prologue to Rebellion: *The Awakening* and the Habit of Self-Expression." *Southern Literary Journal* 20 (1987): 22–32.

Veeder, William. "Who Is Jane? The Intricate Feminism of Charlotte Perkins Gilman." *Arizona Quarterly* 44 (1988): 40–79.

Vogel, Todd. "The Master's Tools Revisited: Foundation Work in Anna Julia Cooper." *Criticism and the Color Line: Desegregating American Literary Studies*. Ed. Henry Wonham. New Brunswick: Rutgers University Press, 1996. 158–70.

Wagner-Martin, Linda. "Gilman's 'The Yellow Wallpaper': A Centenary." *Charlotte Perkins Gilman: The Woman and Her Work*. Ed. Sheryl Meyering. Ann Arbor: UMI Research Press, 1989. 51–64.

Wald, Priscilla. *Constituting Americans: Cultural Anxiety and Narrative Form*. Durham: Duke University Press, 1995.

Walker, Nancy. *Fanny Fern*. New York: Twayne, 1993.

Wall, Cheryl A. *Women of the Harlem Renaissance*. Bloomington: Indiana University Press, 1995.

Warren, Joyce W. *Fanny Fern: An Independent Woman*. New Brunswick: Rutgers University Press, 1992.

Washington, Mary Helen. "'The Darkened Eye Restored': Notes Toward a Literary History of Black Women." *Reading Black, Reading Feminist: A Critical Anthology*. Ed. Henry Louis Gates Jr. New York: Meridian, 1990. 30–43.

———. Introduction. *A Voice From the South*. By Anna Julia Cooper. 1892. New York: Oxford University Press, 1988.

Waugh, Patricia. *Feminine Fictions: Revisiting the Postmodern*. New York: Routledge, 1989.

Welter, Barbara. "The Cult of True Womanhood: 1820–1860." *American Quarterly* 18 (1966): 151–74.

White, Barbara A. "'Our Nig' and the She-Devil: New Information about Harriet Wilson and the 'Bellmont' Family." *American Literature* 65 (1993): 19–52.

Whitney, Mrs. A. D. T. *The Other Girls*. Boston: J. R. Osgood and Company, 1873.

Williams, Fannie Barrier. "The Intellectual Progress of the Colored Woman of the United States Since the Emancipation." *The World's Congress of Representative Women.* Ed. May Wright Sewall. Chicago: Rand, McNally, 1894. 696–711.

Wilson, Margaret Gibbons. *The American Woman in Transition: The Urban Influence,* 1870–1920. Westport: Greenwood Press, 1979.

Wittgenstein, Ludwig. *Philosophical Investigations.* Trans. G. E. M. Anscombe. Oxford: Basil Blackwell, 1953.

Wittig, Monique. "The Mark of Gender." *The Poetics of Gender.* Ed. Nancy K. Miller. New York: Columbia University Press, 1986. 63–73.

Wood, Ann D. "The 'Scribbling Women' and Fanny Fern: Why Women Wrote." *American Quarterly* 23 (1971): 3–24.

Yaeger, Patricia. " 'A Language Which Nobody Understood': Emancipatory Strategies in *The Awakening.*" *Novel: A Forum on Fiction* 20 (1987): 197–219.

Young, Robert J. C. *Colonial Desire: Hybridity in Theory, Culture and Race.* New York: Routledge, 1995.

The Young Lady's Book: A Manual of Elegant Recreations, Exercises, and Pursuits. Boston: C. A. Wells, 1830.

The Young Lady's Friend. By a Lady. [Mrs. John Farrar.] Boston: American Stationers' Company, 1836.

Index

Coppin, Fannie Jackson, 9

Covarrubias, Miguel, "Blues Singer," 20, 30

Cott, Nancy, xv, 16

Coxe, Margaret, *The Young Lady's Companion*, 5, 7–8, 9, 50

Cult of domesticity: advocated at the World's Congress, 10; and African American women, 5–6, 12, 56, 57, 78–79, 142–43, 144, 146–48, 150, 151; debate over reality of, 3–4; rhetoric of, 4; synthesis with the New Woman, 11–12, 78, 89, 143, 146–47; and women's discourse, 6–8, 39–40, 41, 42, 44–45, 46, 47–48, 49, 50, 51; and women's identity, 4–6, 35, 49; and women's moral purity, 7, 50, 59; and women's silence, 7–9, 45, 50, 51–52, 59–60

Cunningham, Gail, 19

Current History, 15, 18, 29

Delany, Martin, 57, 62; *The Condition, Elevation, Emigration, and Destiny of the Colored People of the United States*, 57

Derrida, Jacques, 76, 191, 192

Donovan, Josephine, 73, 195

Douglass, Frederick, *Narrative of the Life of an American Slave*, 148, 159

Dresser, Mylène, 89

duCille, Ann, xiv, 5

Egerton, George, 89; *Keynotes*, 15

Elbert, Monika, 70

Elkins, Marilyn, 147

Essentialism, 84, 86, 163, 185

Ewell, Barbara, 107

Fabi, M. Giulia, 151

Fauset, Jessie: boundary making and unmaking, 162–63; and the cult of domesticity, 161, 162, 167, 170, 172; and feminine desire, 165, 170–71, 172–73, 178–79; interrogation of the "Ameri-can," 169, 176–77; interrogation of dominant language, 162, 165–66; metalinguistic ethnic discourse, 161–67, 191, 195; and the New Woman, 16, 20, 161, 172–73; and "passing," 163, 175–76, 177; validation of "denied" speech, 162, 164–65. Works: *Plum Bun*, 161, 163, 164, 165, 166–67, 171–80, 189, 195; *There Is Confusion*, 161, 166, 167–71, 174, 189

Feminine sexuality or desire, 87–88, 93, 99, 135, 170–71, 177–79, 183–86; and African American women, 12, 19–20, 170–71, 178–79; and birth control, 19, 173, 184; and language, 7, 20, 163, 165; and the New Woman, 19–20, 22

Fern, Fanny, 9; compared to character Ruth Hall, 24; writing constraints within the cult of domesticity, 34, 40, 41, 42. Works: *Ruth Hall*, 33, 34–42, 192

Fetterly, Judith, 186

Fleming, Tom, 22, 31

Forerunner, 111–12, 126, 140

Foster, Frances Smith, 57

Foster, J. Ellen, 10

Freeman, Mary Wilkins, 67, 163; concern with language, 67–68, 69, 71, 73, 75–76, 191, 194; and gendered values, 73, 74, 76. Works: "Christmas Jenny," 68; "A Church Mouse," ix, xix, 68; "Evelina's Garden," 68; "Old Woman Magoun," 68; "A Poetess," 68; "The Revolt of 'Mother,'" 67, 68–76, 192, 193; "A Village Singer," 68

Freire, Paulo, 155

Furman, Nelly, 74–75

Gadamer, Hans-Georg, 85

Gaines, Kevin, 84

Gallop, Jane, 43–44, 58

Gates, Henry Louis, Jr., 56, 59, 60, 61, 62, 63–64

Index

Phallus, phallocentricism, 111–12, 116, 117, 119, 121, 122–24, 184
Pinckney, Cotesworth, *The Lady's Token*, 4, 5, 6
Porter, Florence Collins, 10
Progressive Era, 9
Punch, 17–18, 21, 22–23, 27

Race: Anglo-American women writers attitude toward, 67, 116; conjunction with gender, 77, 78, 82, 101
Race, and beauty, 17
Riegel, Robert, xv
Riley, Glenda, 9
Robinson, Lillian, 195–96
Rose, Jaqueline, 165

Semiotic (Kristeva), 55, 89, 91–92, 194
Senf, Carol, 20
Seyersted, Per, 87
Showalter, Elaine, 42
Sigourney, Lydia, *Letters to Mothers*, 4, 5, 7, 9
Slave narratives and novels, 141–42, 148–54
Smith, Valerie, 148
Smith-Rosenberg, Caroll, xv, 9, 14, 16, 18
Sollors, Warner, xvii, 163
Spheres for women: domestic, 4–5, 38, 46, 146; public, 10–11, 78, 146
Stanton, Elizabeth Cady, 9, 11, 14
Stuckert, Mary Coleman, 11
Suffragettes, 22
Sylvander, Carolyn, 169, 174, 177
Symbolic, the; symbolic language, 88, 91–92, 102, 194–95

Tate, Claudia, 146, 147, 167
Thayer, William, *Life at the Fireside*, 7
Thomas, Heather Kirk, 107
Thomas, Mary, 16

Ticknor, Caroline, 22
Todd, Ellen, 15, 16, 22
Toth, Emily, 98, 100
Treichler, Paula, xi, 89, 96, 113, 115
True Woman. *See* Cult of domesticity
Turner, Victor, 19, 143, 162

Voice of the Negro, 17, 26

Wagner-Martin, Linda, 115
Walker, Nancy, 34, 37
Washington, Mary Helen, 79, 151–52
Waugh, Patricia, 120
Wells, Ida B., 10
Welter, Barbara, xv, 4
White, Barbara, 62
Whitney, Mrs. A. D. T., *The Other Girls*, 40
Williams, Fannie Barrier, 9, 12–13
Wilson, Harriet, 9; audience, 62; comparison to her characters, 60; as signifyin(g) trickster, 56, 61–64, 193; writing in the cult of domesticity, 56, 58, 59, 61. Works: *Our Nig*, 35, 56, 58–64, 143, 178, 192–93
Wilson, Margaret, 15
Wittgenstein, Ludwig, 129
Women's art, 101–02, 175; and African American women, 146, 168–69, 171, 174–76; and domesticity, 33, 40–41, 45–46, 47; as escape from patriarchal language, 94, 95–96, 97–98, 168, 181; failure of, 45–47
Women writers, criticism of, 37–39, 46–48, 106
World's Congress of Representative Women, 3, 9–14; racial and ethnic tensions, 10

Yaeger, Patricia, 89, 91, 98
Young Lady's Book, 7
Young Lady's Friend, The, 6, 7
Young, Robert, 142

Index